CHILD THEOLOGY

Child Theology

Diverse Methods and Global Perspectives

Edited by Marcia J. Bunge, PhD

ORBIS BOOKS
Maryknoll, New York 10545

Maryknoll, New York 10545

Founded in 1970, Orbis Books endeavors to publish works that enlighten the mind, nourish the spirit, and challenge the conscience. The publishing arm of the Maryknoll Fathers and Brothers, Orbis seeks to explore the global dimensions of the Christian faith and mission, to invite dialogue with diverse cultures and religious traditions, and to serve the cause of reconciliation and peace. The books published reflect the views of their authors and do not represent the official position of the Maryknoll Society. To learn more about Orbis Books, please visit our website at www.orbisbooks.com.

Copyright © 2021 by Marcia J. Bunge

Published by Orbis Books, Box 302, Maryknoll, NY 10545-0302.

All rights reserved.

The Scripture quotations contained herein are from the New Revised Standard Version: Catholic Edition, Copyright © 1989 and 1993, by the Division of Christian Education of the National Council of the Churches of Christ in the United States of America. Used by permission. All rights reserved.

Chapter 9: Figure 1: Traditional icon of "Extreme Humility." Copyright © Holy Transfiguration Monastery, Brookline, MA, used by permission. All rights reserved. Figure 2: "Nativity of Christ." Copyright © Basil Lefchick, used by permission. All rights reserved. Figure 3: Nativity of Christ (detail). Copyright © Basil Lefchick, used by permission. All rights reserved.

No part of this publication may be reproduced or transmitted in any form or by any means, electronic or mechanical, including photocopying, recording, or any information storage or retrieval system, without prior permission in writing from the publisher.

Queries regarding rights and permissions should be addressed to: Orbis Books, P.O. Box 302, Maryknoll, NY 10545-0302.
Manufactured in the United States of America

Library of Congress Cataloging-in-Publication Data

Names: Bunge, Marcia J. (Marcia JoAnn), 1954– editor.
Title: Child theology : diverse methods and global perspectives / edited by Marcia J. Bunge.
Description: Maryknoll, New York : Orbis Books, [2021] | Includes bibliographical references and index. | Summary: "Theologians rethink and reinterpret theological doctrines and practices regarding the strengths and vulnerabilities of one of the world's most exploited and marginalized groups: children"—Provided by publisher.
Identifiers: LCCN 2021007928 (print) | LCCN 2021007929 (ebook) | ISBN 9781626984318 (trade paperback) | ISBN 9781608338948 (epub)
Subjects: LCSH: Children—Religious aspects—Christianity.
Classification: LCC BT705 .C453 2021 (print) | LCC BT705 (ebook) | DDC 270.83—dc23
LC record available at https://lccn.loc.gov/2021007928
LC ebook record available at https://lccn.loc.gov/2021007929

*With heartfelt gratitude for my parents
and for those who teach us to see the image of God in all people.*

Contents

Acknowledgments	ix
Introduction: Strengthening Theology by Honoring Children Marcia J. Bunge and Megan Eide	xiii
1. Attending to the Cries of Children in Liberation Theologies *Craig L. Nessan (USA)*	1
2. The Power of Engaging Theologies of Creation and Childhood *Michael Welker (Germany)*	21
3. Children in African Theologies of Community and the Human Person *Kenneth Mtata (Zimbabwe)*	33
4. Children's Experiences of Evil in Their Multiple Worlds *Ivone Gebara (Brazil)*	52
5. The God-Child Paradigm and Paradoxes of the Incarnation *Wanda Deifelt (Brazil/USA)*	72
6. Soteriology and Children's Vulnerabilities and Agency *Rohan P. Gideon (India)*	90
7. Children and the Spirit in Luke and Acts *Amos Yong (Malaysia/USA)*	108
8. Placing Ethics and Children at the Heart of Ecclesiology *Agbonkhianmeghe E. Orobator (Kenya/Nigeria)*	129
9. Reclaiming the Virtue of Humility through a Child-Inclusive Lens *Perry T. Hamalis (USA)*	150
10. A Decolonial Approach to Formation and Discipleship *Valerie Michaelson (Canada)*	172
11. Reforming Mission with Child-Attentive Theology *D. J. Konz (Australia)*	190
12. Reimagining Hope *with* and *like* Children *Dirk J. Smit (South Africa)*	206
List of Contributors	231
Index	235

Acknowledgments

This book seeks to strengthen the church's reflection on key topics in theology as well as its commitment to children. All those who inspired and supported this project recognize that children are one of the most imaginative and insightful yet also vulnerable and voiceless groups on our planet. Project contributors also share this common conviction: honoring the dignity and full humanity of children deepens theological reflection, cultivates meaningful relationships, and enlivens faith communities and their work in the world.

Producing this book has been an international and ecumenical endeavor, and I would like to acknowledge the contributions of several individuals and institutions.

I deeply appreciate the wisdom and dedication of the theologians who wrote chapters for the volume. Coming from diverse contexts and theological traditions, they are united by their compassion for children and appreciation of the significance of rigorous theological reflection for Christian faith and life. In addition to being theologians and scholars, they are also respected leaders in their institutions and communities. Thus, as they were working on this book this past year (2020–2021), they were also addressing a host of personal, professional, and political challenges prompted by the global pandemic. Amid suffering and loss, several mentioned how working on the book was a welcome and meaningful task that aligned with their hopes for children and our world.

I also want to express my heartfelt gratitude to two individuals who supported the vision of this project and generously offered their wisdom and skills over the course of bringing it to completion: John Collier and Megan Eide. During the project's various phases, I worked with each of them in a spirit of true collaboration.

Collier is a writer, child advocate, and retired medical researcher and physician who cofounded the Child Theology Movement. He helped me launch this book project by cohosting the international and ecumenical consultation "Child Theology: Perspectives from Global Christianity." With the help of a grant from the Advocacy Office of Compassion International, directed at the time by Carmen (Menchit) Wong, we were able to bring together theologians, child advocates, and church leaders to explore how rethinking Christian beliefs and practices with attention to children might strengthen both theology and child advocacy. In addition to some of the contributors to this volume, participants included other theologians who greatly moved our discussion forward: Corneliu Constantineanu (Romania), Mary Ann Hinsdale (USA), Wonhee Anne Joh (South Korea / USA), and Edesio Sánchez-Cetina (Costa Rica). We were especially grateful that Shiferaw Woldmichael could join us from Ethiopia as a consultant. A lawyer by training, he is an internationally recognized child advocate who directed several efforts for Compassion International and later founded the Child Development Training and Research Center in Addis Ababa, Ethiopia. His eloquence and strategies for promoting child well-being helped all participants better understand Jesus's compassion for children and the "least of these."

The consultation helped us generate guidelines for this book and a list of contributors, and from the time I received full drafts of their chapters until submitting the entire manuscript to the publisher, Megan Eide served as the project's chief editorial assistant. As a scholar and writer, she applied her outstanding critical thinking and communication skills to the detailed work of the editorial process, including proofreading, formatting, checking references, and offering substantive suggestions for various chapters. Furthermore, as a theologian and pastor who is passionate about issues regarding children and the church, she also understood the significance of a book that explores key topics of theology with attention to children. Thus, she engaged her heart and mind as we reviewed chapters, considered the overall shape of the volume, and coauthored the introduction.

All three of us and the volume's contributors are deeply grateful to our publisher, Orbis Books, and to Paul McMahon, the acquisitions editor who oversaw our project. Orbis Books has a long-standing and highly respected record of publishing works that explore global dimensions of faith, invite dialogue across diverse cultures and traditions, and promote peace and justice. These themes deeply resonate with the aims of this book, and we are therefore delighted that this book is published by Orbis. We want to express a special word of thanks to Paul McMahon. He enthusiastically supported the project from the beginning. A kindhearted person and exceptional editor, he patiently and carefully brought the manuscript into its final form.

In addition, I am grateful for the support of Gustavus Adolphus College. This past year the college funded my current student research assistant, Allison E. James, whose positive attitude and excellent research and editorial skills contributed much to the project. Furthermore, at every stage, I was supported by Janine Genelin, the competent and cheerful administrative assistant for faculty members in Old Main. I also want to express my sincere thanks to the Bernhardson family, who generously funded the Rev. Drell and Adeline Bernhardson Distinguished Chair of Lutheran Studies, which supports my teaching, research, and church-related initiatives.

My work has also been nurtured by the child-related activities of several other institutions and individuals around the world. I am deeply indebted to the cofounders of the Child Theology Movement: Keith White, Haddon Wilmer, and John Collier. They introduced me to the idea of Child Theology and placing a child "in the midst" of theological reflection. They also inspired me by their advocacy for and care of children in their midst. Through this movement, I was also introduced to many faith leaders who are advancing child well-being around the world, including representatives of Viva, Compassion International, World Vision, and seminaries in Australia, Africa, and Asia.

Furthermore, I am deeply grateful for the work of many scholars and the collaborative relationships we have built over the years through academic venues focused on children, especially the four-year research project on the history of childhood (*Tiny Voices from the Past*) directed by Reidar Aasgaard at the University of Oslo in Norway, consultations hosted by Gert Breed and Hannelie Yates at North-West University in South Africa, the "Children in the Biblical World" section of the Society of Biblical Literature, and the "Childhood Studies and Religion" unit of the American Academy of Religion. Connections with leaders of several international centers devoted to child well-being have also informed my work for this project, including the Haruv Institute, the Kempe Center for the Prevention and Treatment of Child Abuse and Neglect, the Zero Abuse Project, and the Search Institute.

I dedicate this book to my parents and primary spiritual mentors, Myrene and Richard Bunge, and to those who teach us to see the image of God in all people. My father was a Lutheran pastor, and my mother a teacher and school counselor. They were loving and wise parents as well as powerful and public witnesses to God's love for the world. Through their words and deeds, they embodied biblical mandates to love the neighbor, seek justice, and contribute to the common good. As a young couple, they welcomed Lithuanian refugees into their home, and they carried on this legacy of service throughout their lives. My father passed away when he was fifty-seven, and my mother, now ninety-nine, still offers her ten grandchildren, my siblings, and me a listening ear and strategies for negotiating life's challenges. The example of my parents and other mentors informs what I seek to pass on to my own two children and shaped my passion for this project.

Marcia J. Bunge, PhD
April 2021

Introduction

Strengthening Theology by Honoring Children

Marcia J. Bunge and Megan Eide

Every human being on the planet was or is a child. No one enters the world fully grown; we are all born and develop. Children are part of families, communities, and nations. Although the definition of a child can change across time and place, their presence does not. Based on the commonly used international definition of children as persons below the age of eighteen, they make up nearly 30 percent of human beings on the planet.[1] Whether they comprise 20 or 40 percent of a nation's population, children make a difference in personal, social, and religious life. Even if we have no children of our own, and even if conceptions and treatment of children differ widely among individuals and across cultures, childhood is part of the human experience, and children influence our world.

Although children are all around us, children and childhood have been marginal topics in many academic fields. Recently, however, scholars from a host of disciplines are devoting more attention to children and contributing to the new and burgeoning interdisciplinary field of childhood studies. Like women's studies, racial studies, and other interdisciplinary fields that bring marginalized persons to the forefront by recognizing their full humanity, childhood studies is opening innovative lines of intellectual inquiry and strategies for advocacy by honoring the full humanity and dignity of children. Thus, children are now the focus of study not only in education or psychology but also history, literature, art, sociology, economics, political science, philosophy, ethics, and human rights. Insights from this growing body of research and the actions of young people themselves are creating greater public awareness of children's agency and complexity. Popular books and documentaries on brain development, for example, reveal the complex thinking and moral reasoning of infants and children. Social media also help us see more clearly the courage and leadership capacities of young people in political life.

---

[1] See the United Nations Convention on the Rights of Child (1989) and other human rights documents.

Religious scholars and theologians are also contributing to the growing interdisciplinary field of childhood studies.[2] Current scholarship in several areas is paying greater attention to the agency, role, and status of children in religious communities and public life, past and present. For example, theologians and ethicists are devoting more attention to children's rights and child advocacy.[3] Scholars in various areas of practical theology are providing more engaging forms of faith formation, youth ministry, and intergenerational worship.[4] Biblical scholars and historians are also more attentive to the presence and active participation of children in biblical narratives, historical events, religious rituals, and community life.[5]

Building on scholarship in these and other fields, another growing area of inquiry that focuses directly on children is termed "Theologies of Childhood." The task of such theologies is to articulate informed and robust understandings of children and adult obligations to them. Like other contemporary theologies that have strengthened the commitment to and understanding of groups that are voiceless, marginalized, or oppressed, theologies of childhood focus on one of the world's most voiceless and vulnerable: children and youth. These theologies build on wisdom from the Bible, Christian tradition, human experience, and insights from the sciences and the humanities. Several contemporary theologians have offered sophisticated insights that challenge narrow assumptions about children in both church and society, name injustices against children, and underscore parental and social responsibilities.[6] They have provided multi-

---

[2] For an overview, see Marcia J. Bunge, "The Child, Religion, and the Academy: Developing Robust Theological and Religious Understandings of Children and Childhood," *Journal of Religion* 86, no. 4 (2006): 549–578.

[3] See, for example, Kathleen Marshall and Paul Parvis, *Honouring Children: The Human Rights of the Child in Christian Perspective* (Edinburgh: Saint Andrews Press, 2004); Pamela Couture, *Seeing Children, Seeing God: A Practical Theology of Children and Poverty* (Nashville: Abingdon, 2000); and John Wall, *Ethics in the Light of Childhood* (Washington, DC: Georgetown University Press, 2010).

[4] See, for example, Joyce Ann Mercer, *Welcoming Children: A Practical Theology of Childhood* (St. Louis: Chalice, 2005); Karen-Marie Yust, *Real Kids, Real Faith: Practices for Nurturing Children's Spiritual Lives* (San Francisco: Jossey-Bass, 2009); and Andrew Root, *Faith Formation in a Secular Age* (Grand Rapids: Baker Academic, 2017).

[5] For biblical and historical studies, see, for example: Roy Zuck, *Precious in His Sight: Childhood and Children in the Bible* (Grand Rapids: Baker Books, 1996); Julie Faith Parker and Sharon Betsworth, eds., *The T & T Clark Handbook of Children in the Bible and the Biblical World* (London: Bloomsbury / T & T Clark, 2019); Marcia J. Bunge, ed., *The Child in Christian Thought* (Grand Rapids: Eerdmans, 2001); and Marcia J. Bunge, Beverly Roberts Gaventa, and Terence Fretheim, eds., *The Child in the Bible* (Grand Rapids: Eerdmans, 2008).

[6] See, for example, Karl Rahner, "Ideas for a Theology of Childhood," in *Theo-

faceted understandings of children that highlight their moral and spiritual capacities, needs and strengths, and vulnerabilities and agency. Consequently, these theologies inspire and empower more respectful treatment of children in homes, congregations, and societies.

Theological Challenge

Regardless of the strides made in religious studies and theology, including theologies of childhood, children still play a marginal role in many key areas of theological reflection. Although theologies of childhood and other child-related fields certainly draw necessary attention to the dignity, needs, and strengths of children, the role and significance of children are almost invisible in many areas of systematic, constructive, or contextual theology. This pattern is evident throughout the history of Christian thought: the rocky road of moving from acknowledging marginalized persons as human beings, fully and equally made in the image of God, to rethinking and reframing major theological themes in the light of these persons. Feminist theology primarily began, for example, with a focus on women's agency, equality, and gender justice. Thus, numerous studies were published about women's equality and the role of women in the Bible and the history of Christianity. However, feminist theologians soon challenged the church to rethink its notions not only of women and gender relations but also of other central beliefs and doctrines, such as the language of God, the nature of the church, and sin.

Similarly, although theologians are contributing significantly to many areas related directly to children, they have devoted less attention to how honoring children might reframe and readjust our thinking about other major themes in theology. We can certainly applaud the many recent studies directly focused

---

logical Investigations VIII, trans. David Bourke (London: Darton, Longman and Todd, 1971), 33–50; Dawn DeVries, "Toward a Theology of Childhood," *Interpretation* 55, no. 2: 161–173; David H. Jensen, *Graced Vulnerability: A Theology of Childhood* (Cleveland: Pilgrim Press, 2005); Jerome W. Berryman, *Children and the Theologians: Clearing the Way for Grace* (New York: Morehouse, 2009); Deusdedit R. K. Nkurunziza, "African Theology of Childhood in Relation to Child Labour," *African Ecclesial Review* 46, no. 2 (2004): 121–138; Marcia J. Bunge, "Beyond Children as Agents or Victims: Reexamining Children's Paradoxical Strengths and Vulnerabilities with Resources from Christian Theologies of Childhood and Child Theologies," in *The Given Child: The Religions' Contribution to Children's Citizenship*, ed. Trygve Wyller and Usha S. Nayar (Göttingen: Vandenhoeck and Ruprecht, 2007), 27–50; Bonnie Miller-McLemore, *Let the Children Come: Re-Imaginging Childhood from a Christian Perspective* (2003; repr. Minneapolis: Fortress Press, 2019); and Jan Grobbelaar and Gert Breed, eds., *Theologies of Childhood and the Children of Africa* (Durbanville, South Africa: Aosis Publishing, 2016).

on children as persons in biblical studies, the history of Christianity, ministry, faith formation, advocacy, human rights, and theologies of childhood. Yet how deeply have Christian theologians truly reflected on how honoring children—recognizing them as persons—might change the way Christians think about other major theological topics or "loci," such as sin, salvation, the doctrine of creation, and the concept of God? In other words, how does respect for children help us reexamine or rethink Christian thought and practice for the sake of the whole church and its work in the world?

The Primary Aim

This volume takes up this challenging question and aims to strengthen theological reflection across the church by rethinking, reinterpreting, and reevaluating fundamental Christian beliefs and practices with attention to children. Building on a wide range of sources, chapters offer new insights into selected and central theological themes, such as creation, the human person, Christology, sin, salvation, mission, and hope. While the volume primarily aims to transform theological reflection for the whole body of Christ and its work in the world, contributors also seek to strengthen the church's understanding of and global commitments to children.

Theologians worldwide use various terms and phrases to designate the specific task of rethinking theology in the light of children and childhood. The title of this book, *Child Theology*, is a term first used by Keith White, Haddon Willmer, and John Collier, who together cultivated international awareness of this task.[7] They were inspired by and built their initial work on a close reading of Matthew 18. Here Jesus places a "child in the midst" of his disciples in response to a question about who is the greatest in the kingdom of heaven and says to them, "Truly I tell you, unless you change and become like children, you will never enter the kingdom of heaven. Whoever becomes humble like this child is the greatest in the kingdom of heaven. Whoever welcomes one such child in my name welcomes me" (18:1–5).

---

[7] The term "Child Theology" was first used by Keith White in 2002. White, Willmer, and Collier organized the first consultation of the Child Theology Movement (CTM) in Penang in 2002. They have since hosted consultations in other parts of the world and contributed various publications to this new research domain, including Keith J. White and Haddon Willmer, *An Introduction to Child Theology* (London: Child Theology Movement, 2006); John Collier, ed., *Toddling to the Kingdom: Child Theology at Work in the Church* (London: Child Theology Movement, 2009); and Haddon Willmer and Keith J. White, *Entry Point: Towards Child Theology with Matthew 18* (London: WTL Publications, 2013). For more information about CTM, reports of consultations, and resources, see childtheologymovement.org.

Although they developed a specific approach, these pathfinders as well as the contributors to this volume all recognize that theologians worldwide who pursue the distinct task of reexamining central beliefs and practices through a child-attentive lens take different approaches, incorporate diverse sources, and designate their work using various terms. Our contributors and others describe this work, for example, as "child-attentive theology," "theology using the 'lens' of child/children as a category of analysis," or "theology in solidarity with children." They generally avoid terms such as "child-centered" or "child-centric" theology, since, as D. J. Konz and others argue, theology focuses on God and God's relation to the whole world.[8] Furthermore, they are careful not to confuse this task with other important and related but distinct tasks, such as child advocacy, religious education, children's spirituality, theologies for children, children's own theologies, or theologies of childhood.

Theologians pursuing this specific area of theological inquiry share some similarities with feminist, womanist, Black, Dalit, and liberation theologians. Like these and other contemporary forms of theological reflection, child-attentive theologies recognize the dignity and full humanity of a group of people who are often voiceless, marginalized, or exploited—children, in this case. Child theology attends to children's challenges and contributions, honors their vulnerabilities and strengths, and emphasizes adult duties and responsibilities to children. Thus, Child Theology contributes and is intimately related to theologies of childhood. However, by taking the next step of rethinking and reinterpreting theological doctrines and practices in the light of children and childhood, Child Theology offers new insights into central themes of the Christian faith, thereby sometimes tweaking and other times causing seismic shifts in our understanding of many theological doctrines, practices, and methodologies.[9]

---

[8] D. J. Konz, "Child Theology and Its Theological Method, Past and Future," *ANVIL: Journal of Theology and Mission* 35, no. 1 (2019): 21–27. Konz prefers the term "child-attentive" to some of the methodological adjectives used in biblical studies (including "childist," "child-centered," and "child-centric" readings of Scripture) because "the term doesn't centre the child in the same way, and in doing so risks displacing God as the primary object of theology" (26).

[9] In the area of philosophical ethics, John Walls emphasizes a similar move by calling for a new "childism": an effort that not only pays greater attention to children but responds "more self-critically to children's particular experiences by transforming fundamental structures of understanding and practice for all." See John Wall, "Childism: The Challenge of Childhood to Ethics and the Humanities" in *The Children's Table: Childhood Studies and the Humanities*, ed. Anna Mae Duane (Athens: University of Georgia Press, 2013), 68.

Diverse Methods and Global Perspectives

This volume uniquely brings together theologians from various parts of the world who engage a wide range of sources and methods. Contributors live in diverse cultural contexts and self-identify with different theological traditions, including Orthodox, Roman Catholic, and various forms of Protestantism, such as Lutheran, Reformed, Episcopalian, Evangelical, and Pentecostal. Like other contemporary Christian theologians, they build on common sources of theological reflection, including scripture, wisdom from the Christian tradition, insights from various disciplines across the academy, and the experiences of individuals and communities.

However, as an ecumenical and international group seeking to deepen theological reflection that takes children into account, they build on diverse sources that are based in their particular theological traditions and speak to questions and experiences in their specific social and cultural contexts. Furthermore, just as all theologians who have attended to various marginalized or exploited persons have discovered, contributors find that focusing on children opens their eyes to both new and neglected sources. They have mined, for example, insights from neglected biblical and theological sources, research in the humanities and the sciences on childhood, experiences of children, and memories of their own childhoods. By incorporating these and other resources, contributors strengthen theological reflection across a range of topics. Taken as a whole, the volume also reminds readers of the gifts of world Christianity, which, as Lalsangkima Pachuau states, is owned "by people of diverse cultures and societies from every region and every continent, and portrayed in the multiplicity of church traditions, cultural expressions of faith-practices, and doctrinal voices."[10]

The following examples demonstrate some of the diverse and often untapped resources that contributors incorporate, arranged under the four major sources of theological reflection that inform the work of all contributors.

The Bible

Contributors build primarily on biblical sources related directly to the topic of their chapter yet also incorporate a number of significant child-related passages. Several chapters integrate biblical mandates to care for the poor, seek justice, and love the neighbor; stories of named and unnamed children; and accounts of Jesus's childhood and interactions with children. Contributors reflect care-

---

[10] Lalsangkima Pachuau, *World Christianity: A Historical and Theological Introduction* (Nashville: Abingdon Press, 2018), 3.

fully, for example, on well-known Gospel accounts of Jesus welcoming, blessing, and healing children. Others refer to particular children, such as those Jesus healed or the boy with five barley loaves and two fish in the story of Jesus feeding the five thousand (John 9:6). Others draw attention to passages that include children but are rarely considered "child-related" biblical texts. For example, in his chapter on hope, South African and Reformed theologian Dirk J. Smit draws attention to a verse in Hebrews that focuses on faith and that states how the parents of Moses "saw that the child was beautiful" (11:23). This passage prompts Smit to reflect on how prominent South African theologians reimagined hope and courageously fought for justice during apartheid by engaging with and being inspired by children. Pentecostal theologian Amos Yong, in his exploration of the Holy Spirit, focuses primarily on Luke and Acts, and by attending carefully to just a few passages regarding children, he not only expands our view of the Spirit but also strengthens our understanding of children as Spirit-filled.

However, reflecting on central theological themes with attention to children does not mandate that biblical sources are limited to passages that directly refer to children. In revisiting biblical sources relevant to their chosen topic, contributors discover new dimensions and implications of the sources simply by remembering that references to human beings, in general, or to specific groups of people, such as tribes, communities, or slaves, are also references to children. For example, Reformed theologian Michael Welker enriches his reflections on the first chapter of Genesis and several creation topics—such as the image of God and the realm of life shared by plants, animals, and human beings—not only through dialogue with the natural sciences but also by honoring the full humanity, vulnerabilities, and contributions of children.

Whether reflecting on biblical texts that refer directly or indirectly to children, contributors strengthen theological reflection about both their chapter's primary topic and children. As these theologians and many biblical scholars find, the Bible provides a rich and multifaceted view of children that challenges narrow conceptions of them in church and society. Children are made in God's image and fully human, yet are also developing beings in need of instruction and guidance. They are vulnerable orphans and neighbors, yet also social agents with gifts and strengths that contribute to our world. They are members of the community who are nurtured by adults, yet also serve as models for adults.[11]

---

[11] Bunge frequently builds on such paradoxes in her theological reflections on children. See "Beyond Children as Agents or Victims" (cited above); "Conceptions of and Commitments to Children: Biblical Wisdom for Families, Congregations, and the Worldwide Church," in *Faith Forward: Launching a Revolution through Ministry with Children, Youth, and Families*, vol. 3, ed. David M. Csinos (Lake Country, BC: Wood Lake, 2018),

Christian Tradition

Contributors also draw from a range of Christian theological texts and spiritual practices and build on important sources from their denominational affiliation, theological training, or cultural context. Eastern Orthodox theologian Perry Hamalis offers insights into humility from ancient Christian sources, such as Chrysostom, Saints Anthony the Great and Dorotheos of Gaza, as well as Orthodox liturgies, iconography, and contemporary virtue ethics. Australian systematic theologian and Barth scholar D. J. Konz articulates a healthy and compassionate practice of mission that respects children and adults living in pluralistic settings by critically incorporating a variety of popular theologies of Christian mission as well as insights from the dogmatics of Reformed theologian Karl Barth. In her chapter, Wanda Deifelt, a Lutheran and feminist theologian, provides wisdom from feminist theologians, South American and Black liberation theologians, Martin Luther, and contemporary Lutheran theologians to articulate the meaning and depth of the paradoxes of God's incarnation as an infant.

Other Disciplines

Contributors also build on creative and insightful research pursued in disciplines outside biblical studies and theology. The chapter authors incorporate ideas from disciplines commonly used by theologians, such as philosophy and ethics. They also integrate research on children and childhood, especially from the social sciences and law, where scholars are exploring insightful questions about child development and children's social status, rights, and responsibilities. Social scientists and child advocates devoted to child well-being are also increasingly interested in the many positive roles of religion, religious communities, and spirituality in the resilience of both adults and children.[12] Overall,

---

94–112; and "The Vocation of the Child: Theological Perspectives on the Particular and Paradoxical Roles and Responsibilities of Children," in *The Vocation of the Child*, ed. Patrick McKinley Brennan (Grand Rapids: Eerdmans, 2008), 31–52.

[12] See, for example, David Hay and Rebecca Nye, *The Spirit of the Child* (London: Fount, 1998), and numerous studies by the Search Institute (search-institute.org), including E. C. Roehlkepartain, P. E. King, L. M. Wagener, and P. L. Benson, eds., *The Handbook of Spiritual Development in Childhood and Adolescence* (Thousand Oaks, CA: Sage, 2006), and K.-M. Yust, A. N. Johnson, S. E. Sasso, and E. C. Roehlkepartain, eds., *Nurturing Child and Adolescent Spirituality: Perspectives from the World's Religious Traditions* (Lanham, MD: Rowman and Littlefield, 2006); and the work of the National Study of Youth and Religion (youthandreligion.nd.edu), including the study by Christian Smith with Melinda Lundquist Denton titled *Soul Searching: The Religious and Spiritual Lives of American Teenagers* (Oxford: Oxford University Press, 2005).

by harnessing the strengths and contributions of a wide range of disciplines, the chapter authors enrich our theological understanding of children and offer pertinent ways in which we can honor their dignity and full humanity.

Like others informed by various forms of liberation theology, many contributors also incorporate research from sociology, political science, and economics, as well as the voices of the oppressed to address the injustices they face. However, contributors greatly expand their sources to understand and address the unique forms of suffering and challenges that children face by building on research in the areas of child development, child maltreatment, and children's rights. Several contributors also refer to the groundbreaking Adverse Childhood Experiences (ACE) study and the Search Institute's Developmental Assets Framework. Although it is more difficult to hear the voices of children than adults, much of this contemporary research includes interviews and testimonies of children themselves.

For example, Craig L. Nessan sees his work as contributing to what some are calling "child liberation theology" and to discussions of theological method more broadly by building on social-scientific studies of child abuse and neglect, the dangers of corporal punishment, and effective approaches to child protection and well-being. Rohan P. Gideon notices, even among Dalit theologians in India, the lack of attention to the harsh realities and exploitation of children. As he seeks to expand Christian understandings of salvation, Gideon utilizes research on child labor and children's rights and recognizes the intersectionality of children's multiple identities. He also calls for creating more spaces for listening to their unique stories, experiences of discrimination, and hopes. Finally, Kenneth Mtata exposes adult-centered and hierarchical notions of personhood in church and society. He finds that despite their attention to community and the marginalized, even Black, womanist, and liberation theologies in Africa are often child-blind. Mtata paves the way toward a stronger, more child-inclusive theological anthropology by using resources from philosophy, linguistics, and cultural anthropology as well as theology.

Experience

Another significant source for all contributors is the experience of individuals and communities, including the experience of children. "Experience" in the case of children involves learning about the many issues facing children, families, and communities past and present through sources such as social-scientific studies, testimonies, and stories. Attending to these experiences also involves listening to children's own perspectives or adult memories of childhood.

Contributors incorporate children's experiences and perspectives in various ways. For example, Brazilian theologian Ivone Gebara examines sin and evil not only by building on feminist theology and the ideas of the French philosopher Paul Ricoeur but also by reflecting on her conversations and daily interactions with children and their families. She also taps into her childhood memories of reading *Alice in Wonderland* to understand and address children's fascination and interactions with the virtual world. In his chapter on the church, Jesuit theologian Agbonkhianmeghe E. Orobator draws on Roman Catholic theology, the work of African theologians across denominations, and materials from the United Nations on children's rights and well-being. However, he also mines African proverbs, stories, and novels by Camara Laye, Uwem Akpan, and Chinua Achebe as resources for understanding attitudes toward children and their experiences. Valerie Michaelson, a health science researcher and Anglican theologian, draws on decolonial studies to rethink faith formation, discipline, and discipleship. She also incorporates social-scientific qualitative and quantitative research on the corporal punishment of children and its detriments as well as testimonies by Indigenous peoples about their experiences of abuse and neglect in Canada's residential schools.

As they tap into such sources, contributors recognize the challenges and risks associated with seeking to learn about children's experiences. In particular, they acknowledge the difficulty in finding and hearing the "child's voice" not only in literature, social-scientific studies, and adult memories of childhood but also in conversations directly with children. Children are vulnerable and often want to please parents and other adults. Furthermore, adult preconceptions about children's experiences are bound to influence how adults "hear" children. Even the questions posed to children about their experiences and ideas shape their responses. Cautiously trying to include children as full participants in particular research projects or discussions with adults can easily cross inappropriate emotional or intellectual boundaries, thereby even calling into question how "appropriate boundaries" are defined and defended.

Although no approach can solve these and other difficulties of incorporating the voices of children as serious sources for theological reflection, the contributors and other theologians recognize the significance of striving to do so. Furthermore contributors understand their work as a starting point for constructing child theologies that incorporate more sources and spaces for children's ideas, stories, and experiences. To learn more about children's experiences, scholars and theologians are cautiously beginning to mine other sources, such as children's artwork, graffiti, stories, newspapers, essays, letters, and diaries. They are also learning more about the experience of children past and present by studying material culture, architecture, and medical and legal records.[13] Although imperfect, such attempts are important; they help draw

---

[13] See some of the creative ways that those studying the history of childhood are

attention to children as creative moral agents with questions, concerns, experiences, and ideas of their own. Incorporating the "child's voice" in theology and other disciplines also checks adult preconceptions about children and sparks new questions for investigation.

Lessons for Theological Studies and the Church

Once we acknowledge children's full humanity and cultivate more multidimensional and biblically informed conceptions of their many strengths and vulnerabilities, we strengthen theological reflection in many ways. Recognizing the full humanity of children helps us reexamine Christian doctrines and practices by raising questions related to human experience across the life span, shedding new light on familiar theological and biblical sources, and opening the door to additional resources. By drawing more intentionally on childhood studies, we discover new dimensions of our common humanity and our relationship to God and the world. Learning about children's unique challenges and contributions also deepens our understanding of human suffering, alerts us to often hidden injustices facing the most vulnerable, and reminds us of the creativity and potential of all human beings, regardless of age. Consequently, Child Theology can benefit how the church across denominations and cultures reflects on a range of important Christian beliefs and practices.

While robust child theologies strengthen theological reflection on key doctrines and practices, they also benefit the whole church by challenging narrow conceptions of children and strengthening our commitments to them. As we enrich theological reflection by honoring children, we also deepen our conceptions of them. Thus, although they are distinct tasks, child theologies and theologies of childhood closely inform and influence one another. In this way and others, the chapters of this volume provide many additional lessons for the whole church.

For example, the contributors expose several narrow assumptions about children that inhibit us from honoring their full humanity—regarding them as persons who are made in the image of God and who deserve to be treated with dignity and respect. They demonstrate how adult-centered our perceptions and priorities can sometimes be. Whether in our homes, churches, or larger societies, we often value the ideas, contributions, and presence of adults above those

---

seeking to understand children's experiences, including publications that came out of the research project "Tiny Voices from the Past: New Perspectives on Childhood in Early Europe" directed by Reidar Aasgaard at the University of Oslo, such as Christian Laes and Ville Vuolanto, eds., *Children and Everyday Life in the Roman and Late Antique World* (London: Routledge, 2017).

of children and youth. Just as we, at times, judge the value of people according to class, race, or gender, we often value people according to age. We also carry thin and flat views of children, whether as cute or strong-willed, innocent or sinful, sources of pleasure or economic burdens, wise or ignorant. For various reasons, we often fail to recognize children as thinking beings with their own agency, growing moral capacities, and spiritual questions and experiences. We also neglect to see how children and youth, like adults, have complex identities and are often deeply affected by multiple injustices related to their socioeconomic status, religion, education, sexuality, gender, ethnic background, nation, or race.

Given these and other narrow views, children often fall through the cracks in both church and society. Children worldwide face malnutrition, lack of adequate education and health care, abuse, neglect, anxiety, and depression. Furthermore, many Christian communities are failing to take seriously the spiritual questions and leadership capacities of children and young people. Instead, congregations of all persuasions are sometimes stuck in common and nonstimulating ruts of religious education. In the North American context, for example, some churches take benign approaches to Sunday school, filled with throwaway crafts and lackadaisical lessons; others take domineering approaches with little room for young people's questions. Consequently, as research shows, many young people who grew up in the church feel they do not belong and hold major misconceptions of Christianity. Many are leaving the church and becoming part of the growing number of "nones"—those who do not affiliate with any religious community and mostly identify as "nothing in particular"— even though many are interested in spiritual questions and long for a sense of worthiness, community, and belonging.[14]

Child theology can strengthen the church's efforts in child advocacy and faith formation by reminding us of the full humanity of children and their significance in all areas of Christian faith and life. If our church leaders and faith communities consistently honored and emphasized the full humanity of children, then we would unleash many creative energies in our homes and congregations for experiencing the abundant life in Christ more fully and for serving others more generously. Research about faith communities and our own experience tells us that children and youth are key to cultivating thriving congregations that pass on the faith and contribute to their communities.[15]

---

[14] For statistics and resources on the nones and religion, see the Pew Research Center (pewforum.org).

[15] As one study says, "growing young" energizes an entire congregation. See Kara Powell, Jake Mulder, and Brad Griffin, *Growing Young: 6 Essential Strategies to Help Young People Discover and Love Your Church* (Grand Rapids: Baker Books, 2016), 23.

When we recognize children and youth as equal members of the body of Christ, we more readily welcome, respect, and care for them. We find that we not only teach, guide, and empower them but also learn from and are energized, inspired, and delighted by them. In our homes and congregations, we are more eager to share stories, cultivate meaningful conversations about faith and doubt, and pray and worship together. We also become more aware of the suffering and injustices facing children, including abuse and corporal punishment, and work collaboratively and more intentionally to protect and foster the well-being of all children.[16] These and other meaningful interactions—made possible simply by honoring children's full humanity—enrich families, communities, and the lives of children and adults.

Conclusion

Child theologies can challenge and empower theologians and church leaders to honor children, incorporate child-related concerns in all areas of theological education, and advance child well-being in religious and public life. Many more approaches to the task of Child Theology—as defined and carried out in this volume—can be discovered in some of the neglected work of past theologians, and contemporary theologians in many parts of the world continue to offer new approaches. Hopefully, this volume inspires more theologians and church leaders across denominations and theological traditions to embrace the significance of Child Theology for Christian faith and life and challenge all of us, whatever our cultural contexts or places of responsibility, to honor children's dignity and full humanity.

---

[16] For strong theological and social-scientific grounds for rejecting the physical punishment of all children and fostering healthy approaches to discipline across church and society, see Valerie E. Michaelson and Joan E. Durrant, eds., *Decolonizing Discipline: Children, Corporal Punishment, Christian Theologies, and Reconciliation* (Winnipeg: University of Manitoba Press, 2020); for theological grounds, see chapters in that volume by Marcia J. Bunge, "The Significance of Robust Theologies of Childhood for Honouring Children's Full Humanity and Rejecting Corporal Punishment" and "Rethinking Christian Theologies of Discipline and Discipleship," 108–122, 152–160, respectively.

1

Attending to the Cries of Children in Liberation Theologies

Craig L. Nessan

One of the fundamental questions facing all theologies involves the understanding and articulation of method. Although theologians build on common sources, such as the Bible and the Christian tradition, they incorporate a range of additional sources and formulate distinctive approaches to theological reflection.

For example, many forms of contemporary apologetic theology that seek to answer questions posed by nonbelievers use the "method of correlation," which was first articulated by Paul Tillich:

> In using the method of correlation, systematic theology proceeds in the following way: it makes an analysis of the human situation out of which the existential questions arise, and it demonstrates that the symbols used in the Christian message are the answers to these questions.[1]

According to Tillich, theologians analyze the human situation by examining human cultural materials (e.g., from literature, the arts, or popular culture) to identify significant questions for theology to address. David Tracy has been prominent in refining the method of correlation in contemporary theology.[2]

One of the most significant developments in contemporary theology that employs a distinctive and powerful method of correlation is liberation theology. However, for various forms of liberation theology, the point of departure does

---

[1] See Paul Tillich, *Systematic Theology: Reason and Revelation / Being and God*, vol. 1 (Chicago: University of Chicago Press, 1951), 59–66.

[2] David Tracy, *The Analogical Imagination: Christian Theology and the Culture of Pluralism* (New York: Crossroad, 1981). See also David Tracy, *Fragments: The Existential Situation of Our Time: Selected Essays*, vol. 1 (Chicago: University of Chicago Press, 2020), 243–244, 247–250.

not involve questions posed by the "non-believer" but rather the situation of the "non-person." In the words of Gustavo Gutiérrez, "The challenge does not come to us primarily from the non-believer, but from the *non-person*, that is to say from [the one] who is not recognized as such by the existing social order: the poor, the exploited, one who is systematically deprived of being a person, one who scarcely knows that he or she is a person."[3]

Taking the nonperson as a point of departure, liberation theologies operate with a method that is normed by praxis, a complex interaction involving biblical and theological reflection about concrete life experiences that is oriented toward social change. This method generally consists of five elements: identification with particular forms of oppression and suffering, prophetic critique of that condition, social analysis of the causes of oppression and suffering, biblical and theological engagement to address that suffering and overcome that oppression, and advocacy of structural change toward a greater approximation of justice.

Building on this method, liberation theologies have paid attention to various nonpersons and forms of systemic suffering and thereby contributed significantly to contemporary global theology. Over recent years, major expressions of liberation theology have developed from particular vantage points of oppression, suffering, and nonpersonhood—Latin American liberation theology, Black liberation theologies, feminist theologies, womanist theologies, Latinx and *mujerista* theologies, Native American liberation theologies, LGBTQIA+ liberation theologies, Dalit theologies, and ecojustice theologies.

It is noteworthy, however, that most forms of liberation theology have underrepresented or entirely omitted attention to children, even though millions of children worldwide lack basic needs, suffer maltreatment or exploitation, and are "systematically deprived of being a person." As early as the 1970s, some theologians did begin shaping what they called "child liberation theology." One of the earliest references to child liberation theology is by Janet Pais, who focuses on the suffering and oppression of abused children.[4] Her work addresses the powerlessness of children and unique aspects of their oppression. For Pais, "Children are inherently disadvantaged. They form the one group whose liberation can never change this. As long as a child is a child, she or he will never have access to power or resources equal to adults."[5] In her

---

[3] Gustavo Gutiérrez, "Faith as Freedom: Solidarity with the Alienated and Confidence in the Future," *Horizons* 2 (Spring 1975): 43.

[4] For a constructive introduction to child liberation theology and the work of Janet Pais, see Rohan Nelson, "Suffer the Children: A Review Article," *Currents in Theology and Mission* 48, no. 1 (2021): 59–63.

[5] Janet Pais, *Suffer the Children: A Theology of Liberation by a Victim of Child Abuse* (Mahwah, NJ: Paulist Press, 1971), 17.

pathbreaking book, *Suffer the Children: A Theology of Liberation by a Victim of Child Abuse*, Pais claims,

> Children do not have the education or the resources necessary to speak for themselves or, having spoken, to effect any change. In fact, their plight is worse than a lack of education or resources. An outstanding feature of their oppression is that their feelings and perceptions of reality are often denied; abused children are often denied the ability to know what is happening to them or that it could possibly be any other way.[6]

Furthermore, Pais describes the powerlessness and limited range of "actions" available to abused children: "Conforming to adult wishes, running away, dropping out, suicide, substance abuse, behavior problems, and mental illness, tend not to liberate children, but rather to make their oppression worse."[7]

Despite the early work of Pais and other occasional efforts, child liberation theology has not yet found its rightful place as a central, if not primary, vantage point for addressing the suffering and oppression of children in all of their forms—including child abuse and the multiple dimensions of child neglect—to disclose and denounce the systems of injustice that contribute to children's suffering. As theologian Ryan Stollar recently argued, "The liberation of children must extend to and embrace every single child everywhere," and "a truly liberating Child Theology must therefore take seriously all the intersecting oppressions that impact children of various genders, races, cultures, classes, and so forth."[8]

As a way forward, Stollar poses a series of critical and challenging questions that liberation theology must seek to answer, including:

> How have our theological concepts been grounded in *adultism*—the viewing of theological concepts from the vantage point of adults rather than the vantage point of children? . . .
>
> In the same way that faith communities ought to fight against classism, racism, sexism, homophobia, and transphobia in these other spheres, how can faith communities work together to dismantle systematic prejudice and discrimination against children not only within, but also without, the church? . . .
>
> How do we elevate the voices of children themselves?[9]

---

6 Pais, *Suffer the Children*, 16.

7 Pais, *Suffer the Children*, 17.

8 Ryan Stollar, "Towards a Child Liberation Theology," *Patheos*, April 7, 2016, http://www.patheos.com/blogs/unfundamentalistparenting/2016/04/towards-a-child-liberation-theology/.

9 Stollar, "Towards a Child Liberation Theology."

Given these questions and the urgent needs of children around the world, liberation theologians need to be more consistent in engaging children as persons and taking into account their suffering and oppression. The needs of children cry out for advocacy, insofar as the experiences of childhood mark and mar their very identity and existence for life. As the church, operating as the body of Christ, seeks to address the root causes of social disease and disorder, its praxis must prioritize those issues that affect the lives of children.

Liberation theology, and indeed every form of theology, has not been without blind spots. For example, liberation theologians focusing on economic injustice were hesitant to forge coalitions with Black liberation theologians and feminist theologians from the global North.[10] However, liberation theologies have demonstrated increasing capacity to expand their horizons to incorporate insights from newly emergent forms of contextual theology around the globe; some forms of liberation theology are already expanding their concern to children.

Acknowledging my own complicity in failing to address the experiences of children theologically in my earlier work, this chapter reclaims and advances the nascent beginnings of a child liberation theology by highlighting a few important methodological insights from my own context. The chapter is divided into three major parts that reflect the elements of method in liberation theologies: forms of suffering experienced by children, promising biblical and theological resources, and strategies for structural change in church and society. I conclude by drawing methodological implications for strengthening approaches to child liberation theologies in particular as well as liberation theologies in general. Each expression of liberation theology cannot afford to dismiss those forms of suffering that often begin in childhood and the vast and varied systemic structures of injustice that affect people of all ages.

While this chapter draws attention to children among liberation theologians, there are also implications for theologians using a range of other theological methods. It is imperative that theologians, whatever their context or method, take the personhood of children seriously. Across the church, children must be recognized as those who have been systematically deprived of being a person—those who are scarcely acknowledged as persons. Since children's suffering remains a largely hidden or invisible experience in theology, the experiences of children need to be a manifest theme articulated explicitly across theological traditions and methodologies.

---

[10] Cf. the exchanges between Latin American, Black, and feminist theologians in Sergio Torres and John Eagleson, eds., *Theology in the Americas* (Maryknoll, NY: Orbis Books, 1976).

Forms of Suffering Experienced by Children

Children experience particular forms of suffering, and recognizing their unique experiences must be the methodological starting point of child liberation theology. One of the primary sources that helps the whole church better understand both the well-being and suffering of children comes from the social sciences. Research is growing in all areas of the social sciences regarding children's intellectual, emotional, physical, and spiritual development. Many of these socialscientific studies include solid qualitative data and interviews with children. Such studies are being carried out by the academy, medical centers, child protection agencies, human rights organizations, and the World Health Organization.

One example of how the social sciences can inform theology, for example, is through the insightful distinctions being made regarding four specific forms of child abuse and neglect and their causes: material deprivation, neglect, corporal punishment and physical abuse, and sexual abuse. Each of these four forms of suffering holds children in bondage and has extensive consequences for their well-being not only in childhood but throughout their entire lives.[11]

Freedom from Material Deprivation

Children remain the most vulnerable victims of widespread poverty globally and domestically. Among the factors that affect children directly are malnutrition, the unavailability of clean water, inadequate sanitation and poor hygiene, the lack of medical care, disease (especially childhood diseases preventable through immunization), infant mortality, and environmental degradation. The disparity of global wealth has established an infrastructure that serves economic elites at the expense of children and their families, especially women. Other forms of liberation theology, especially those originating in Latin America, have analyzed the devastating effects of poverty.[12] Here we focus only on how these devastating effects of poverty impact children.

Bread for the World statistics are compelling:

> Every year, 2.6 million children die as a result of hunger-related causes. In the U.S., nearly 16 million children—one in five—live in households that struggle to put food on the table. Even short-term episodes

---

[11] Portions of this section of the chapter are taken from Craig Nessan, "Child Liberation Theology," *Currents in Theology and Mission* 45 (July 2018): 6–13, and are used with permission.

[12] Cf. Craig L. Nessan, *The Vitality of Liberation Theology* (Eugene, OR: Wipf and Stock, 2012), 1–13.

of hunger can cause lasting damage to a child's development. Hunger puts children at risk of a range of cognitive, behavioral, emotional, and physical problems.[13]

Because children are entirely dependent upon adults for their well-being, they suffer high risks from hunger. Moreover, their rapidly growing bodies are exceptionally vulnerable to the lasting effects caused by hunger.

Noted journalist and activist Roger Thurow documents through case studies from four diverse settings across the world—Uganda, India, Guatemala, and the United States (Chicago)—how the first one thousand days of life are crucial for child development. The failure to provide adequate nutrition for children and pregnant mothers results in the stunted development of one in five children—a total of about 170 million children worldwide.

> A child who is severely stunted is sentenced to a life of underachievement: diminished performance in school, lower productivity and wages in the workplace, more health problems throughout life, and a greater propensity for chronic illnesses such as diabetes and heart disease as an adult. And that life sentence is most often rendered by the time a child is two. For stunting is largely the result of a debilitating mix of poor nutrition, unclean environment, and lack of caregiver stimulation during the 1,000 days.[14]

While the diagnosis for treating the problem of child development in the first one thousand days might seem obvious, the challenges in equipping women to act on best practices in prenatal and early childhood care are enormous. In the settings Thurow examines, he finds that even in those contexts where concerted efforts have been made to educate people about nutritious diet (including vitamin supplements), immunizations, hygiene, sanitation, and child development, the obstacles to implementation are formidable.

The availability of and especially the cost of purchasing fruits, vegetables, sources of protein, and vitamin supplements to provide the micronutrients necessary for healthy development are beyond the means of poor people. The accessibility to, adequacy of, and cost of prenatal care, including what is needed for home hygiene and sanitation measures, make recommended practices unavailable to poor people. These realities, coupled with the actual

---

[13] This and the following quote are from Bread for the World, "Who Experiences Hunger," accessed November 4, 2020, http://www.bread.org/who-experiences-hunger.

[14] Roger Thurow, *The First 1,000 Days: A Crucial Time for Mothers and Children—And the World* (New York: Public Affairs, 2016), 2.

birthing conditions for many poor mothers, make the first day "the most perilous day of life." Each year, one million babies die within twenty-four hours of their birth.[15]

The living conditions of poor people also greatly increase the risks to children in their first two years. Gender discrimination against girls in many societies places them at greater risk for stunting and infant mortality. While breastfeeding provides babies with the best possible nutrients, incentives from corporations to substitute expensive formula (often promoted through birthing hospitals) and the demands of daily life dissuade many mothers from following the best instruction. The World Bank finds that "child mortality is about fifteen times greater in lower-income countries than in the global north, and maternal mortality is nearly thirty times higher. Almost all of those deaths are preventable."[16]

Thurow draws this stunning conclusion:

> If we want to shape the future, to truly improve the world, we have 1,000 days to do it, mother by mother, child by child. For what happens in those 1,000 days through pregnancy to the second birthday determines to a large extent the course of a child's life—his or her ability to grow, learn, work, succeed—and, by extension, the long-term health, stability, and prosperity of the society in which that child lives.[17]

Generally, the great limiting factors of providing what is necessary for basic nutrition and medical care during those crucial thousand days around the world are poverty and related systemic socioeconomic injustices.

Freedom from Neglect

Although "abuse" and "neglect" are often used interchangeably in informal conversation, social scientists and child advocates formally distinguish child neglect from physical or sexual child abuse: "Unlike physical and sexual abuse, neglect is usually typified by an ongoing pattern of inadequate care and is readily observed by individuals in close contact with the child."[18] Neglect is characterized not only by overtly harmful acts but also by the omission of needful care. The Centers for Disease Control and Prevention (CDC) includes the following types of maltreatment in its definition: physical neglect, emotional neglect,

---

[15] Thurow, *First 1,000 Days*, 125.
[16] Thurow, *First 1,000 Days*, 102, citing World Bank: "Repositioning Nutrition as Central to Development: A Strategy for Large Scale Action" (2006).
[17] Thurow, *First 1,000 Days*, 7.
[18] "Child Neglect," *Psychology Today*, accessed November 4, 2020, https://www.psychologytoday.com/conditions/child-neglect.

medical and dental neglect, educational neglect, inadequate supervision, and exposure to violent environments.[19]

The causes of child neglect are manifold. Although most poor families provide devoted attention to the care of their children despite economic hardship, parents who suffer from economic scarcity may give priority to procuring food and other items needed for physical survival at the expense of caring adequately for children. Other causes of neglect can also relate to the incapacity of parents and caregivers to maintain a level of care for their own lives. The disorder in their own existence leaves dependent children in precarious circumstances. Studies indicate, for example, that children whose parents abuse alcohol or drugs are far more likely (three times or more) to neglect their children than those who do not abuse substances. Likewise, those parents or caregivers who suffer from certain forms of untreated mental illness are less likely to be able to care adequately for their children.

Another prevailing problem contributing to child neglect is the inadequate preparation of parents for the tasks of caring for and raising children. The default position for many parents is what they learned about child raising from their own parents, who may or may not themselves have been skilled in parenting. Where deficient and neglectful parenting is passed on from generation to generation, intervention may be necessary to interrupt the cycle.

Freedom from Corporal Punishment and Physical Abuse

Contrary to the massive research and evidence that demonstrates the harmful and lasting physical, emotional, and spiritual consequences of corporal punishment, parents and caregivers continue to use physical punishment at alarming rates. Increasingly in countries around the world, statutes are being put in place to criminalize corporal punishment.[20] Many adults assume that corporal punishment is a normal means of child discipline. Without regard for the harmful effects, spanking and other forms of physical punishment have been passed down from one generation to the next.

The medical risks of corporal punishment are immediate and long term. Corporal punishment is painful and can include the tendency to be excessive: "In the U.S., 28% of children are hit so hard that they receive injuries."[21]

---

[19] "Adverse Childhood Experiences (ACEs)," Centers for Disease Control and Prevention, accessed November 4, 2020, https://www.cdc.gov/vitalsigns/aces/index.html.

[20] Victor I. Vieth, "Augustine, Luther, and Solomon: Providing Pastoral Guidance to Parents on the Corporal Punishment of Children," *Currents in Theology and Mission* 44, no. 3 (2017): 31, http://currentsjournal.org/index.php/currents/article/view/78.

[21] Vieth, "Augustine, Luther, and Solomon," 32.

Research indicates that "parents who are out of control emotionally, or who are using objects, are at greater risk to engage in abusive behaviors including kicking, beating, burning, shaking, or hitting a child in places other than the buttocks."[22] It is not only the risk of injury that should dissuade parents and caregivers from corporal punishment but also other long-term health risks. "Even in the absence of more severe child maltreatment, researchers have found that harsh physical discipline (pushing, shoving, grabbing, slapping, and hitting) is associated with higher risks of cardiovascular disease, arthritis, obesity, history of family dysfunction, and mental disorders."[23] Victor Vieth, director of education and research at the Zero Abuse Project, states, "This is one reason the American Academy of Pediatrics discourages parents from venturing down the path of hitting children as a means of discipline."[24]

The mental health and behavioral risks are also substantial. Research shows "no evidence that spanking is associated with improved child behavior and rather found spanking to be associated with increased risk of 13 detrimental outcomes."[25] While this should not be interpreted to mean that corporal punishment is determinative of negative outcomes, the research does demonstrate that corporal punishment is "a risk factor and notes that the more a child is hit and the harsher the discipline, the greater the risk factors for poorer mental health, including depression, anxiety, anger management, and inability to sustain healthy relationships."[26]

The spiritual risks of corporal punishment also need serious consideration. When religion is used to justify child abuse or religious communities ignore the signs of child maltreatment, children are left with unsettling spiritual questions; thirty-four major studies, involving more than nineteen thousand abused children, demonstrate that large numbers of children "are spiritually damaged from maltreatment."[27]

---

[22] Vieth, "Augustine, Luther, and Solomon," 32, citing Adam J. Zolotov et al., "Speak Softly—and Forget the Stick: Corporal Punishment and Child Abuse," *American Journal of Preventative Medicine* 35 (2008): 364–365.

[23] Vieth, "Augustine, Luther, and Solomon," 32, citing Tracie O. Afifi et al., "Harsh Physical Punishment in Childhood and Adult Physical Health," *Pediatrics* 132 (2013): 333–338.

[24] Vieth, "Augustine, Luther, and Solomon," 32, citing Committee on Psychosocial Aspects of Child and Family Health, "Guidance for Effective Discipline," *Pediatrics* 723 (1998): 101.

[25] Vieth, "Augustine, Luther, and Solomon," 33, citing Elizabeth T. Gershoff and Andrew Grogran-Kaylor, "Spanking and Child Outcomes: Old Controversies and New Meta-Analysis," *Journal of Family Psychology* 30, no. 4 (2016): 465.

[26] Vieth, "Augustine, Luther, and Solomon," 33.

[27] Vieth, "Augustine, Luther, and Solomon," 33, citing Donald F. Walker et al., "Changes in Personal Religion/Spirituality during and after Childhood Abuse: A Review and Synthesis," *Psychological Trauma: Theory, Research, Practice and Policy* 1, no. 2 (2009): 130.

The ongoing use of corporal punishment by parents and caregivers comes not only from lack of education but is also promoted by influential religious leaders. Many Christian churches continue to advocate for corporal punishment as necessary for child-rearing, perpetuating the cycles leading to child abuse. Many of these sources cite biblical passages, especially from the book of Proverbs, to justify their arguments. Vieth holds that the research about the relation of corporal punishment to child abuse and the concomitant interpretation of Scripture warrant the opposite conclusion:

> Whether holding extreme or moderate views on corporal punishment, Protestant proponents of the practice contend, or at least suggest, there is a biblical basis for their beliefs. Many respected biblical authorities beg to differ. According to these scholars the Bible does not require parents to discipline their children by hitting them. Some of these scholars argue that the Bible actually discourages corporal punishment; a handful of them even make the argument the Bible does not authorize the physical discipline of children.[28]

For these and other reasons, the church needs many more voices and resources to put an end to Christians' practice of corporal punishment of children.[29]

Freedom from Sexual Abuse

Child sexual abuse is the silent destroyer of the sacred lives of persons and families in our society. "The ACE [Adverse Childhood Experiences] study estimated that approximately 1 in 4 women and 1 in 6 men were sexually abused before the age of eighteen."[30] These statistics indicate the massive number of lives affected by child sexual abuse. As noted by Tchividjian and Berkovits, these "staggering estimates underscore the pervasiveness of child sexual abuse and make it likely that every reader of this [article] knows someone who has been, or is currently, the victim of sexual abuse."[31]

---

[28] Vieth, "Augustine, Luther, and Solomon," 29.

[29] See Samuel Martin, *Thy Rod and Thy Staff, They Comfort Me: The Book of Hebrews and the Corporal Punishment of Children in the Christian Context,* Book II (Jerusalem: New Foundation for Biblical Research, 2019).

[30] Basyle Tchividjian and Shira M. Berkovits, *The Child Safeguarding Policy Guide for Churches and Ministries* (Greensboro, NC: New Growth Press, 2017), 11. See also Centers for Disease Prevention and Control, "Adverse Childhood Experiences: Vital Signs," https://www.cdc.gov/vitalsigns/aces/.

[31] Tchividjian and Berkovits, *Child Safeguarding Policy Guide,* 11.

How is the extent of this scourge possible? Perpetrators intentionally act under a veil of secrecy to hide their grooming and exploitation by imposing secrecy through intimidation and threats against their victims, who as children are limited in their ability to disclose what has happened to them. The prevailing sense of societal shame that accompanies child sexual abuse also condemns many victims to silence about what they have suffered. The unwillingness of others to believe the accounts of victims about their sexual abuse further prolongs and magnifies the suffering. According to Tchividjian and Berkovits, "Denial of abuse is one of the primary impediments toward its prevention. Child sexual abuse is not a new phenomenon; it cuts across socioeconomic status, geographic location, race, and religion."[32]

Sexual abuse includes contact behavior (all forms of inappropriate and exploitative touching) and noncontact behavior (for example, spoken or written sexual communication, voyeurism, viewing pornography, exhibitionism, or exposing a child's naked body). Various terms are used to describe these dynamics, including "child molestation," "rape," and "abuse."[33]

Biblical and Theological Resources

In addition to understanding the suffering of children through the social sciences, child liberation theology must incorporate biblical and theological resources in accordance with other forms of liberation theology to affirm the dignity of all people. Here we highlight one foundational source, the image of God, as well as promising directions from Pais and Stoller, among others, that focus on the incarnation and God as Child.

The Image of God

The biblical and theological authority for supporting the dignity of all persons, including children, is the conviction that all human beings are created in the "image of God" (Gen 1:27). In wonder at God's creation of humankind, the psalmist builds on this theme: "Yet you have made them a little lower than God, and crowned them with glory and honor" (Ps 8:5). In the New Testament there is also clear affirmation of the status of human beings made in God's image (see 1 Cor 15:49).

As Stoller claims, child liberation theology affirms that all children bear the image of God:

---

[32] Tchividjian and Berkovits, *Child Safeguarding Policy Guide*, 11.
[33] See Tchividjian and Berkovits, *Child Safeguarding Policy Guide*, 10–11.

> Child liberation theology . . . begins not just with one child or one group of children but all children. Not only the white children, not only the children of Western Civilization, but *all* children. Children of all colors, sizes, abilities, genders, and sexualities. Children of the U.S. and children of China, children of Guatemala and East Timor and Papua New Guinea and South Africa. Children who grew up in suburbs segregated by classism and racism and children who grew up homeless in third-world streets. Children who have everything and children who have nothing. Children from the Warring States Period and children from the Middle Ages and children of the postmodern now.[34]

The extent of God's affirmation that all people are made in the image of God is disclosed in Jesus Christ. Jesus Christ is the image of God in the flesh: "He is the image of the invisible God, the firstborn of all creation" (Col 1:15). Moreover, the work of Jesus Christ is interpreted as restoring the image of God to fullness after the fall into sin (see 2 Cor 4:4). The church as the body of Christ takes on the character of Jesus Christ by participating in his work of reclaiming God's image in us, especially as we enter into solidarity with the suffering of others (see 2 Cor 5:10–16).

The biblical affirmation of human dignity resonates with the Universal Declaration of Human Rights (UDHR) and the United Nations Convention on the Rights of the Child (CRC).[35] These documents outline rights that befit human beings of all nationalities, religions, ethnicities, languages, genders, ages, disabilities, sexual orientations, and classes. Regardless of how well the international community has been able to address violations of human rights in particular instances, the concept of human rights has established unprecedented standards for human decency and expectations for right conduct, including the inherent rights of children.

The Incarnation and God as Child

Another central conviction of a child liberation theology is that "God is Child."[36] Just as other liberation theologians affirm the normativity of specific forms of suffering as definitive for the character of God, child liberation theology centers attention on the revelation of God incarnate in the person of the Child Jesus. As Pais states,

---

[34] Stoller, "Towards a Child Liberation Theology."
[35] For both documents, see the United Nations website (www.un.org).
[36] Pais, *Suffer the Children*, 14–16.

Christian faith is centered on the belief that God became human flesh in the person of the Christ child. Jesus is the Word made flesh, God the Son (or Child) incarnate. Jesus tells us that when we receive a child in his name we receive him, and not him, but the one who sent him. In other words, when we receive a child in Christ's name, we receive Christ. We receive God's creative Word in the flesh, we receive God the Child incarnate.[37]

Jesus rebuked the disciples for not allowing the children to come to him: "But when Jesus saw this, he was indignant and said to them, 'Let the little children come to me; do not stop them; for it is to such as these that the kingdom of God belongs'" (Mark 10:14). Moreover, by extending a radical welcome to children, Jesus was breaking the moral standards of his time, as well as ours, by relating to them with full personhood: "'Truly I tell you, whoever does not receive the kingdom of God as a little child will never enter it,'" Jesus said, and "he took them up in his arms, laid his hands on them, and blessed them" (Mark 10:15–16).

Jesus, who was a child and experienced all the vicissitudes of childhood, makes the child a sacrament of the kingdom of God. Only by honoring, respecting, and becoming children can we ourselves know what it is to participate in the kingdom: "If we are to take seriously Jesus' words and receive each child in his name as Christ, then we must not have any attitude toward any child that would cause us to relate to that child differently from the way we would relate to the Christ child. We all share responsibility for the fate of all children."[38] Jesus not only welcomes children but also makes the status of the child normative for all those who would access God's kingdom.

Building upon a range of ancient and contemporary sources, Stollar has contributed a series of articles expanding on key theological themes, including the incarnation. In "Jesus as Child," he reflects on the centrality of the incarnation for Christology, the Christian faith, and our treatment of children. Jesus entered fully into the human condition to experience every aspect of what it means to be a vulnerable child. God became a "marginalized, fully human child." He was a "powerless, fully human god-child born into a violently anti-child world." He was born, "went through and experienced" every stage of child development, grew in wisdom (as Luke 2:52 reminds us), and became an adult. Stollar concludes by stating, "By becoming a marginalized, fully human child, God ushered in a topsy-turvy Kingdom where the last are first and the first are last and children are at the center of what it means to pursue God."[39]

---

[37] Pais, *Suffer the Children*, 23.
[38] Pais, *Suffer the Children*, 24.
[39] Ryan Stollar, "Jesus as Child," *Patheos* (blog), June 14, 2017, http://www.patheos.com/blogs/unfundamentalistparenting/2017/06/jesus-as-child/.

Additional Theological and Biblical Resources

While not framed in terms of child liberation theology, many other biblical and theological resources can serve this effort.[40] For example, Judith M. Gundry focuses on biblical understandings of the kingdom, writing, "Mark's Gospel illustrates how, in the light of the dawning of God's kingdom in Jesus, children's traditional social and religious inferiority can no longer justify their marginalization, but instead requires their emulation and devoted service by adult members of Jesus' 'family' of disciples."[41] Vieth has centered the Christian response to child abuse by attending to the life and words of Jesus.[42] He provides a detailed analysis of child abuse in the New Testament era and makes a compelling case that Jesus was an advocate for protecting children from harm. Here, Christology becomes a foundation for grounding the church's proper response to child maltreatment.

Expressing themes belonging to the central concerns of child liberation theology, Walter Brueggemann states, "The implications for public policy concern the safety, dignity, respect, and economic wherewithal for every child, whose value is attested by the protection and care of society."[43] The work of Jerome W. Berryman, originator of the "Godly play" movement, is also a significant resource. Berryman has documented the reflections of theologians about children across Christian history from New Testament times to the present.[44] He seeks to move beyond ambivalence, ambiguity, and indifference to claim children in Christian theology as a "means of grace." In relation to its foundational ritual actions, he demonstrates how "the sacramental quality of children is a part of the life of the church" that needs to be affirmed and appropriated as such.[45]

---

[40] See, for example, Marcia J. Bunge, *The Child in the Bible* (Grand Rapids: Eerdmans, 2008), and Marcia J. Bunge, *The Child in Christian Thought* (Grand Rapids: Eerdmans, 2001).

[41] Judith M. Gundry, "Children in the Gospel of Mark, with Special Attention to Jesus' Blessing of the Children (Mark 10:13–16) and the Purpose of Mark," in Bunge, *Child in the Bible*, 176.

[42] Victor I. Vieth, *On This Rock: A Call to Center the Christian Response to Child Abuse on the Life and Words of Jesus* (Eugene, OR: Wipf and Stock, 2018).

[43] Walter Brueggemann, "Vulnerable Children, Divine Passion, and Human Obligation," in Bunge, *Child in the Bible*, 422.

[44] See Jerome W. Berryman, *Children and the Theologians: Clearing the Way for Grace* (Harrisburg, PA: Morehouse, 2009).

[45] Berryman, *Children and the Theologians*, 244.

Strategies for Structural Change

For social-scientific, biblical, theological, and other reasons, the church must give high priority to the material, emotional, social, educational, and spiritual needs of children in its advocacy and educational efforts. The retrieval of and commitment to child liberation theology can inspire the church to make the following core commitments: freedom from material deprivation, freedom from neglect, freedom from corporal punishment and physical abuse, and freedom from sexual abuse. Through these core commitments, the church can contribute to the liberation of children and the life-giving relationships that belong to the shalom of God.

Liberating children from material deprivation, neglect, corporal punishment and physical abuse, and sexual abuse requires the work of both social service and social advocacy. Social service involves efforts organized by institutions, including the church, to provide direct relief and aid for addressing the immediate needs of children. Social advocacy involves efforts by the public, including church members, to change societal structures, promote economic policies, and enact legislation that is consistent with God's purpose of bringing forth the kingdom on behalf of children.[46]

The roots of these problems are multiple and complex. Therefore, the church must carry out multiple strategies in advocating for structural changes not only in society but in the church itself. In my own context, I have sought to promote structural change by focusing on three areas: education and child protection policies in churches, theological education in seminaries, and public advocacy. Hopefully, by offering these examples from my own context, readers are inspired to promote structural change in their contexts.

Education and Child Protection Policies in Churches

One dimension of structural change begins with churches—pastors, deacons, and other leaders interpreting the Bible and Christian teaching from the perspective of children, especially those who are suffering from any form of maltreatment and bondage. Child liberation theology takes seriously the research and social analysis that demonstrates conclusively the significant and lasting harm done to children through these forms of oppression.

---

[46] Cf. Craig L. Nessan, "Luther's Two Strategies and Political Advocacy: Law, Righteousness, Reason, Will, and Works in Their Civil Use," in *Lutheran Theology and Secular Law: The Work of the Modern State*, ed. Marie A. Failinger and Ronald W. Duty (New York: Routledge, 2018), 63–74.

Educational efforts among church members and the public need to be accompanied by a clear ethical stance guiding advocacy on behalf of vulnerable children. While many social messages and social statements of Christian denominations make references to the needs of children, these teachings have rarely been devoted explicitly to social teaching and advocacy about the specific needs of children.[47]

For example, it is imperative that the church unequivocally reject the corporal punishment of children and teach against this practice. Religious leaders, pastors, and churches must educate members and the public that the Bible does not warrant corporal punishment[48] and that contemporary research demonstrates convincingly the harmful physical, mental, behavioral, and spiritual damage done by corporal punishment. Moreover, a consistent ethic of nonviolence by Christians would clearly insist on refraining from all forms of corporal punishment. The lasting harm and damage done to children through Christian advocacy of corporal punishment, which fundamentally contradicts what God has revealed about children in Jesus Christ, means that a child liberation theology must advocate for an end to corporal punishment.

Conventional teachings about original sin and the commandment to "honor" your parents are also among those teachings in need of serious reconstruction. The fall into original sin is not about the inherent sinfulness of children based on the transmission of sin through the sexual process of conception, but rather original sin involves the harmful treatment of children passed on from one generation to the next through the transmission of shame, repression, and injury caused by parents and caretakers, who themselves were likely recipients of the same treatment as children. The commandment that instructs children to "honor your father and mother" needs to be predicated on the moral imperative that parents are to honor their child in the same way they would honor the Child Jesus (cf. Mark 9:36–37). In his explanation of the Fourth Commandment, Martin Luther contends that parents are obligated to care for and protect the children entrusted to them.[49]

Furthermore, because churches are greatly affected by the prevalence of child sexual abuse, both by what occurs in the lives of their members and

---

[47] See the list of social messages and social statements of the Evangelical Lutheran Church in America, accessed November 4, 2020, https://elca.org/Faith/Faith-and-Society.

[48] William J. Webb, *Corporal Punishment in the Bible: A Redemptive-Movement Hermeneutic for Troubling Texts* (Downers Grove, IL: InterVarsity Press, 2011).

[49] According to Luther, "Everyone acts as if God gave us children for our pleasure and amusement.... We really must spare no effort, time, and expense in teaching and educating our children to serve God and the world." Cited by Timothy J. Wengert, *Martin Luther's Catechisms: Forming the Faith* (Minneapolis: Augsburg, 2009), 56.

through activities organized by congregations, new vigilance is urgently needed through education and comprehensive child protection policies. This commitment can and should be expressed widely and incorporated into church mission statements and policies.

Excellent and practical resources for introducing, developing, and implementing child protection policies have been developed and published for congregational use. One example is *The Child Safeguarding Policy Guide for Churches and Ministries* published by Godly Response to Abuse in the Christian Environment (GRACE). This comprehensive resource provides educational foundations (defining abuse, indicators, impact, and descriptions of people who sexually abuse children); descriptions of protective practices (screening, safe behaviors, and routine protective measures); needful responses to violations of child abuse policy (limited access agreements, reporting, and independent reviews); guidance on how to support survivors; and instruction for implementing child protection policy (training, dissemination, evaluating, and updating).

The manual contains step-by-step worksheets to guide congregations in developing comprehensive and effective child protection policies. GRACE also offers child safeguarding certification to accompany congregations through every stage in the process. Given the prevalence of child sexual abuse in our society and the susceptibility of churches in providing access to vulnerable children, we need to transform the climate of secrecy by creating new standards of expectation through the development of child protection policies and their implementation throughout the church.

My own denomination, the Evangelical Lutheran Church in America, has put child protection policies in place. The social statement *Human Sexuality: Gift and Trust* affirms the importance of protecting children from sexual abuse and exploitation in all settings. The statement also adopted this policy for preventing and responding to abuse in congregations:

> This church calls for the adoption of preventive measures, including educational programs, appropriate policies, and screening of individuals who care for, supervise, or work with children within this church. It expects that all church leaders will report all instances of suspected child abuse.[50]

---

[50] Evangelical Lutheran Church in America, Social Statement on *Human Sexuality: Gift and Trust*; see page 25 of the statement in the section on "Protecting Children and Youth in and for Trusting Relationships," accessed November 4, 2020, https://elca.org/Faith/Faith-and-Society/Social-Statements/Human-Sexuality.

The adoption and implementation of such child protection policies remain urgent priorities for all religious congregations.

Theological Education in Seminaries

In addition to crafting clear and substantive policies for families and congregations, the church needs to embrace in theological education the ethical challenges of child neglect and abuse. While seminary curricula address many themes in Scripture, church history, theology, and the pastoral arts, the incidence of child abuse and corporal punishment among Christians warrants focused attention. Because many adult church members themselves experienced physical and sexual abuse as children, providing focused education on these topics to future pastors prepares them for ministering more effectively in relation to people's deep experiences of suffering and trauma. Giving attention to child protection and child abuse in pastoral care and ethics courses, as well as referencing these themes in other courses, can contribute to the transformation of the church as a safe and welcoming place for children.

One example of education at my institution, Wartburg Theological Seminary, is the elective course "When Faith Hurts: Recognizing and Responding to the Spiritual Impact of Child Abuse," taught by Victor Vieth. This subject is in the early stages of being introduced into the curriculum at other theological schools. The theme of child abuse and child protection also has been introduced into my required ethics course. Students in the last course engaged in research and writing a rationale for a proposed social state-ment on "Child Abuse and the Church: Prevention, Pastoral Care, and Healing."[51] This work aimed to draw greater attention to this theme in the ELCA and can serve as a resource for other denominations.

Public Advocacy

By public advocacy we mean efforts on the part of the church to change societal structures, promote just policies, and enact legislation to protect children from harm and promote the welfare of children as a social good. Many denominations have organized advocacy efforts at the national and state levels to educate church members about urgent issues and provide guidance on how to contact elected representatives about legislation currently under deliberation. Church members can reference these materials through webpages or email alerts to participate efficiently and effectively in the democratic process toward the common good of children.

---

[51] Craig L. Nessan, ed., "Rationale for a Social Statement on Child Abuse and Child Protection." Currents in Theology and Mission 48 (April 2021): 43–56.

Strategies to address injustices against children, both in the church and broader society, include measures such as the following:

- Advocating for structural change to ensure that the needs of children for nutritious food, clean water, medical care, hygiene, and education are the highest economic and political priority.
- Supporting measures to guarantee that the first thousand days of life meet the nutritional and health care needs of every child.
- Advocating for adequate support services to assist parents and families in meeting the basic physical, medical, mental, emotional, social, and educational needs of children.
- Promoting educational efforts for parents and caretakers about responsible and effective child-rearing practices.
- Advocating to end corporal punishment based on research that demonstrates how it contributes to the physical abuse of children.
- Educating church members and the public that the Bible does not warrant corporal punishment, and that research demonstrates the harmful physical, mental, behavioral, and spiritual damage done by corporal punishment.
- Advocating to end all forms of commercial sexual exploitation and human trafficking, specifically of children.
- Exercising leadership through the development and implementation of certified child protection policies by every congregation to guard against the sexual abuse of children.

Conclusion and Implications

Liberation theologies have developed a powerful method for raising up the voices of suffering people as the focal point of theology.[52] Bonhoeffer wrote that "the view from below" has become "a more useful key, a more fruitful principle than personal happiness for exploring the world in contemplation and action."[53] Whereas liberation theologies have attended to many marginalized groups and brought their experiences explicitly into theological reflection, until recently, children have remained a group whose cries and experiences of suffering have been underrepresented or even absent. The challenge to the method of liberation theologies is to correct this deficit by now incorporating the suffering of children as the basis for social analysis, biblical-theological reflection, and engaging in praxis for social change.

---

[52] See Nessan, *Vitality of Liberation Theology*.
[53] Dietrich Bonhoeffer, "After Ten Years," in *The Bonhoeffer Reader*, ed. Clifford J. Green and Michael P. DeJonge (Minneapolis: Fortress, 2013), 775.

This method of theological engagement has contributed to the transformation of the entire range of theological disciplines, including biblical studies, systematic theology, and ethics. Under the influence of liberation theologies, theology has been notably transformed from an academic exercise in a university context to a discipline that engages the urgent issues facing marginalized people and an endangered creation.

If all theologians attended to the experiences and suffering of children, how would this transform the practice of theology in its various disciplines? It would mean, above all, seeing children as persons and recognizing that the forms of suffering that children experience are not the same as those of adults. We would expand the range of sources employed in theological study, giving attention to the process of human development, socioeconomic issues affecting children, resources from childhood studies (including history and literature), and other sources that allow the voices and ideas of children to be heard. We would view all the urgent issues facing our society—including environmental crises, systemic racism, gender justice, poverty, and education—from the perspective of their impact on children, and develop strategies for deepening and expanding public advocacy efforts that focus on the issues facing children.

This chapter argues that the experiences of children have been either absent from or underrepresented in the work of liberation theologians and offers directions for renewed focus on children across diverse theological disciplines. Any form of theological method has the capacity and opportunity to recognize children as persons, take seriously their experiences, and hear their cries of suffering as well as their stories, ideas, and hopes. Only by drawing attention to the unique, varied, and complex experiences of children within the very method of theology will they no longer remain ciphers or nonpersons within the work of theology. "Let us put our minds together and see what life we can make for our children" (Sitting Bull).

2

THE POWER OF ENGAGING THEOLOGIES OF CREATION AND CHILDHOOD

Michael Welker

Christians worldwide believe that God "created the heavens and the earth" (Gen 1:1), and theologies of creation explore the meaning of this confession of faith. In doing so, theologies of creation address fundamental questions about the nature of God, human beings, and the world. Given the major role science plays in our understanding of the world today, many contemporary theologies of creation also directly address relationships between biblical understandings of creation and various scientific explanations, such as of the human genome, evolution, and climate change.

As a Reformed theologian who has a long history of interdisciplinary engagement with philosophy and the sciences, I have sought to provide an alternative to theologies of creation that dismiss scientific discoveries or theologically conceptualize "creation" by means of simplistic conceptual dichotomies. Theologians are easily tempted to build on dichotomies in exploring the meaning of creation because the distinction between creator and creature is fundamental to Christian theology. Since Christians believe that God is the creator of the universe, the creator/creature dichotomy tends to govern creation theology from the outset. Shaped by the nondichotomous thinking of complex modern systematic thinkers like Alfred North Whitehead, G. W. F. Hegel, and Niklas Luhmann, but most of all by careful attention to the complexities of the biblical witnesses, my work emphasizes that the biblical distinction between creator and creature cannot be reduced to familiar dichotomies such as "cause/effect," "determiner/determined," or "former/formed." By attending carefully to the biblical witness, my work on creation highlights multiple and dynamic structures and relationships in our world that speak to our lived experience and resonate with scientific findings.[1] Devoted to the dialogue between theology

---

[1] For my theological work on creation and relationships between theology and science,

and the sciences, I have worked with church leaders and religious educators who understand that simplistic misconceptions of creation are inadequate not only for adults but also children.

Regardless of the range of resources being developed by theologians and church leaders for thinking and teaching about creation in meaningful and biblically informed ways, simplistic notions of creation that our work has sought to dismantle are still being passed on to children in homes and congregations. For example, when our twin daughters were two years old, "paradise" became a big topic in bedside conversations. Paradise was fascinating. The angels were there, God was there, Great-Grandmother was there. Our children imagined it as a wonderful place, full of joy, harmony, and love. The notion of paradise prompted their speculations and questions, and it gave rise to much awe and wonder. One night, however, the little girls asked my wife, "What are we going to eat in paradise?" The answer came: "In paradise we are not going to eat and drink. We will praise God for ever and ever." Our children expressed a deep sigh of disappointment, followed by the remark, "Well, we are still little kids [Na, wir sind ja noch klein]." And paradise vanished from our conversation. When we told this story to a very kind and experienced pastor, my wife and I received the following lesson: "You should have said: 'I do not know what we are going to eat and drink in paradise. But I'm sure it will be much better than what we have here.'" Were we to pass down the simplistic notion of God and heaven—always bigger and better?

Simplistic "theology" was also passed down to me in my early childhood. My siblings and I liked to sing the religious song: "Do you know how many stars there are in the deep blue sky above? . . . God alone has counted them all so that not one is missed from their enormous number" [Original German: Weisst du, wieviel Sternlein stehen an dem blauen Himmelszelt? . . . Gott der Herr hat sie gezählet, dass ihm auch nicht eines fehlet an der ganzen großen Zahl].[2] And so the song went on from stars to clouds, gnats, fish, and children. God has counted them all. God knows their number. The All-Counting, Almighty God! Early in my childhood this song sounded comforting. But already in my preelectronic and pre–social media childhood this trust in the all-counting and in analogous ways all-knowing and almighty God became shaken whenever

---

see, for example, *The Spirit in Creation and New Creation: Science and Theology in Western and Orthodox Realms,* ed. Michael Welker (Grand Rapids: Eerdmans, 2012); Michael Welker, *Creation and Reality* (Minneapolis: Fortress Press, 1999); and *The End of the World and the Ends of God: Science and Theology on Eschatology,* ed. Michael Welker and John Polkinghorne (Harrisburg, PA: Trinity Press International, 2000).

[2] This song, with lyrics written by the German pastor and poet Wilhem Hey in 1837 and set to a melody based on a folk song, has been included in German Protestant hymnals through today. See Nr. 511 in the *Evangelisches Gesangbuch.*

our pets died or beloved grandparents became terminally ill. Today, children are still struggling to bring together the message of the almighty, all-knowing, and all-determining God with the everyday news of a fragile, finite, suffering, and violence-ridden world. Children are handed fairy-tale and Disney visions of God and creation that everyday realities constantly tear apart.

Against this background, those who seek to articulate theologies of creation framed in the light of a strong theological understanding of children face a double challenge. On the one hand, theologies of creation need to attend more explicitly to children and young people when discussing human nature or communities. Acknowledging that children are part of God's creation with their unique needs and strengths will enrich many aspects of theologies of creation. Just as feminist theologies deepened many areas of theological reflection by drawing attention to gender biases and discrimination, child-attentive theologies will strengthen theological reflection by exposing age-based and adult-centered biases. On the other hand, creation topics framed in the light of a strong theology of childhood have to engage classic texts and topical theological insights and ask: In what ways have creation topics been presented and taught to children, and in what ways should they be taught in the future? Where did religious education materials and pedagogies create a false and misleading trust in creation, in nature, in life, in the world, and in the creator? Where did they give a paltry picture of God's creativity and loving care, presenting God flatly and one-dimensionally and thereby generating among young people a deep suspicion against "the blind watchmaker"[3] and eventually against the church itself?

In addition to these two challenges, theologies of both creation and childhood have to recognize children's honesty, their ability and willingness to engage religious ideas and highly speculative thoughts, and their experiential realism. Children are complex human beings, as research in a growing number of fields related to child well-being indicates, including studies of brain development and emotional intelligence.[4] Systematic theologians and religious educators both need to challenge simplistic views of children and their spiritual and religious experience. Respect, realism, and honesty are crucial in theological discussions with children as well as adults, and any approach to the religious education of children must deal responsibly with the enormous potentials for creative imagination in young minds and with the vulnerability of young hearts.

---

[3] Richard Dawkins, *The Blind Watchmaker: Why the Evidence of Evolution Reveals a Universe without Design* (New York: W. W. Norton, 1996).

[4] Cf. John Gottman, *Raising an Emotionally Intelligent Child* (New York: Simon and Schuster, 1998); Daniel Siegel, *The Developing Mind*, 2nd ed. (New York: Guilford Press, 2012).

Keeping in mind the complexity of children, the primary aim of this chapter is to contribute to theologies of both creation and childhood by reviewing four central creation topics that I have addressed in my previous work and raising these two questions: First, how might attention to children enrich and expand our understanding of these topics? Second, in what way might adults present these central biblical and doctrinal creation topics to children in order to stimulate their religious imaginations, on the one hand, and to protect their sense of honesty and realism, on the other? In this chapter I introduce each of the four creation topics along with commonly raised questions, and I draw implications of each topic, first, for theologies of creation and then for religious formation. Although many more implications from these four creation topics can be drawn, the primary aim is to indicate how attention to children can strengthen theologies of creation and how robust theologies of creation can honor children's questions, spark their religious imagination, and strengthen child-adult relations. Being honest with children and having the readiness to correct a cheap triumphant theism early in their lives will have positive repercussions not only for children but also for parents, teachers, and the church. Hopefully, these brief reflections inspire systematic theologians and religious educators to draw further implications as they reflect on and teach a host of additional creation topics and encourage the church to resist the temptation to perpetuate narrow dichotomies between God and creation as well as adults and children.

Creation in Seven Days?

In its first chapter, the Bible states that God created the world in seven days. Contemporary science states that the world (the cosmos) is 13.8 billion years old. Is the Bible naïve?—offering stories "just for kids"? It is a most important dimension in theologies of childhood and child advocacy to get rid of any condescending "just for kids" perspective in religious education.[5] The creation account (Gen 1) does not offer a fairy tale. It presents serious insights. It expresses a much more differentiated perception of reality than grasped by those who see this account as the expression of a naïve and outdated worldview. This becomes obvious as soon as we concern ourselves with some of the apparent inconsistencies or even contradictions of the text.

On one hand, Genesis states, "Then God said, 'Let there be light'; and there was light. And God saw that the light was good; and God separated the light from the darkness. God called the light Day, and the darkness God called Night. And there was evening and there was morning, the first day" (Gen

---

[5] Marcia J. Bunge, ed., *The Child in Christian Thought* (Grand Rapids: Eerdmans, 2001), 25–28.

1:3–5). On the other hand, nine verses later, Genesis describes the creation of the sun, moon, and stars that are to separate day and night: "And God said, 'Let there be lights in the dome of the sky to separate the day from the night; and let them be for signs and for seasons and for days and for years.'" (Gen 1:14ff).

If we approach these statements without sensitivity to this text's particular perception of the world, then it seems to be propounding contradictory nonsense. How could God create light without creating the sun, moon, and stars? Why is the separation of day from night carried out twice? Is this separation carried out directly by God, or are the sun, moon, and stars to separate day from night? Such questions, which with apparent cleverness hold themselves aloof from this supposedly naïve text that cannot clearly work out its ideas, do not perceive the differentiated view of reality that is developed here.

The light of God—the light in which God creates, rests, and is alive and effective—is not simply identical with the light in which human beings and other creatures live. The Bible differentiates the "days of the Lord" and the days on earth, below the sky. And it knows that the "days of the Lord" are immense spans of time: "For a thousand years in [God's] sight are like yesterday when it is past, or like a watch in the night" (Ps 90:4). In these long spans of time, the Bible depicts first the creation of cosmological, then biological, then cultural, and finally religious processes at work. It describes a great architecture of creation, an insight that is valid also in today's scientific perspective.[6] Only when domains of life are interwoven do they become "creation" in the strict sense.

Implications

As theologians reflect on domains of life and the great architecture of creation, they should recognize more carefully the role of children in the dynamic development of the human species, communities, cultures, and religious traditions. This means articulating theologies of creation that respect children as persons, recognize their needs, and honor their gifts and contributions to creation's vast architecture and various domains.

In addition, if we want to nurture children's spiritual lives as we teach them about creation, then it is crucial to help them understand the relativity of time—long days, short days, patience, impatience, hope, human and divine perspectives—and biblical thinking in different time systems. In learning about Genesis 1, children should engage the texts imaginatively. Unimaginative readings aimed strictly at religious learnings flatten the complexities and narrative

---

[6] Welker, *Creation and Reality*, chapter 1; Michael Welker, *The Theology and Science Dialogue: What Can Theology Contribute?* (Neukirchen-Vluyn: Neukirchener Verlag, 2012), 23–30.

richness of Genesis 1 and neglect children's agency in their spiritual development. Furthermore, flat and "factual" lessons taught to children about Genesis 1 set children up for unnecessary quandaries as they wrestle one day with the relationship between faith and science. Thus, as we teach children about creation, we must invite their questions and insights, engaging them in developmentally appropriate ways.

Does God Do Everything in Creation?

No! God does not do everything in creation. The creature's own activity is not simply a consequence and result of a creation that is already completed. Rather the creature's activity is embedded in the process of creation and participates in that process (cf. Gen 1:11ff.). God gives enormous power to all creatures, not only human beings. Anxiety about the creature's own power being too great is apparently foreign to the classical creation texts of the biblical traditions, and this anxiety tends to entrench itself behind the theistic model of absolute causation and absolute dependence. God is the "all-determining reality," the "cause of everything." This primitive model of God's so-called omnipotence is poisonous. It provokes the question: Why does God allow finitude, suffering, and death in creation?

Instead of dreams about the "perfect watchmaker," we encounter in the classical creation texts a rich description of that which is creaturely engaged in the activity of separating, ruling, producing, developing, and reproducing itself. Yes, God separates the cosmic powers; but that which is creaturely—the firmament of the heavens, the gathering water and the stars—also assumes functions of separation (Gen 1:6, 9, 18). Yes, God rules; but that which is creaturely—the stars—also rules by the establishment of rhythm, differentiation, and the gift of measure and order (Gen 1:14ff.). Yes, God brings forth; but creatures also bring forth creatures: animals of all species and plants in an abundance of species (Gen 1:12, also 1:11, 20, 24). That which is creaturely develops and reproduces itself, as is recorded explicitly and in detail with regard to plants, animals, and human beings. The Bible describes creation, as itself active, separating, ruling, and imparting rhythm, as itself producing and giving life.

From a biblical perspective, creation and evolution are not incompatible. Indeed, the biblical view of creation cannot abstract from its evolutionary activity. It is most important to notice that the participatory activity of that which is creaturely is not only reserved for human beings.

Furthermore, the creation narratives of the Bible speak of God's *reactive experiencing and acting* as he responds to the presence of that which is created. They describe God intervening in that which is already created. Seven times the first creation account says, "And God saw that what had been created was good" (Gen 1:4a, 10b, 12b, 18b, 21b, 25b, 31a). Three times it emphasizes God's activity of naming (Gen 1:5a, 8a, 10a). Twice God intervenes in that which is already created in order to separate it (Gen 1:4b, 7b). God saw, God evaluated, God named, God separated, God brought to the human being, God allowed to be named, and God reacted to the needy situation of loneliness and helplessness of the human being who is not yet differentiated into man and woman (Gen 2). According to the classical creation texts, all these activities and re-activities are part of the complex "creation" event. All these reactive activities, which relate to that which is already "produced," are requisite in order to bring the process of the creation of heaven and earth to a close.

Implications

Insights into the creative and participatory activity of all of God's creatures can strengthen theologies of creation and help the church appreciate more fully that human beings have creative powers, not only as adults but also as children. After all, from the start, infants are thinking, sorting out, and creatively interacting with the world. Insights from both the Bible and new, groundbreaking social-scientific research on brain development and child development can help us all more deeply appreciate the growing capacities and contributions of children and young people.

Furthermore, we must honor children's growing spiritual and intellectual capacities when we talk to children about God's powers and relation to the world. Biblical insights into God's reactive experiencing and acting specifically remind us that an abstract theism of a God who does "everything" is not biblically sound, and this notion should not be passed along as "good enough" for either children or adults. The church has a responsibility to critique this metaphysical ideology at every level of religious education and spiritual formation.

Do the Creatures Become God?

If God gives such a great power to the creatures, if God reacts to the activity of the creatures, then is there not the danger of confusing "both sides": the divine and human, the infinite and the finite? The basic problem here is the idea of there being only "two sides." Most religious and metaphysical thinking regards "God and man," "God and the world," and "creator and creation" in a one-to-one figure. In this figure, any co-creativity threatens the power of the Divine. The biblical creation account, however, presents multiple dimensions and structures. God relates creatively to different co-creative creatures and to different creaturely realms of powerful and even evolutionary activity. It is remarkable how the biblical creation account seems interested in a compatibility of its insights with general observations on the course of natural history. In contrast to some other ancient oriental creation accounts, the biblical account honors creaturely powers while eliminating any deification of sun, moon, and stars, of the heavens and the earth. It counteracts the divinization of the powers of heaven and earth as well as the eerie monsters from the deep. The stars and the "great sea monsters," the *taninim*, are not gods on high or anti-gods from the deep. They are creatures with great powers yet not divine. To make this point, Genesis explicitly emphasizes that "God created the great sea monsters" (1:21) or, as Luther translates, "the big Whales."

Implications

The biblical appreciation of creaturely powers as well as the distinction between creature and creator can help us think more dynamically and deeply about human relations, including child-adult relationships. If we think of all human beings, children and adults alike, as fellow co-creators, then people of all ages might relate to one another more respectfully, nimbly, and creatively.

Furthermore, a robust theology of creation that both cultivates a sense for creaturely powers and honors people of all ages as co-creators could, in turn, foster more meaningful and intergenerational theological conversations within families and congregations.

How Is Creation "Good"?

On the basis of these observations, the creation account clearly speaks of the world in which we live. Creation is not paradise. Creation is not glorious. God calls it "good"—which means "life furthering." But it is not an extension of the Divine. It is radically different from God. Honest talk about creation has to acknowledge the ambivalence of nature and life. All life lives at the expense of other life! The regulation of conflicts between the human beings and the animals and the "call to dominion" expresses this clearly:

> Then God said, "Let us make humankind in our image, according to our likeness, so that they have dominion over the fish of the sea, and over the birds of the air, and over the cattle, and over all the wild animals of the earth, and over every creeping thing that creeps upon the earth." . . . God said to them, "Be fruitful and multiply, and fill the earth and subdue it; and have dominion over the fish of the sea and

over the birds of the air and over every living thing that moves upon the earth." God said, "See, I have given you every plant yielding seed that is upon the face of all the earth, and every tree with seed in its fruit; you shall have them for food." (Gen 1:26, 28, 29a)

Both verbs used here in the biblical text—*rdh* (trample under, subjugate) and *kbs* (subjugate)—belong "in the context of violent subjugation and domination." Both words for domination are otherwise applied to slaves or to a conquered land.[7] How is this compatible with human beings' ordination to be the *imago Dei*? What light do these human beings reflect back upon the God whose likeness they are?

Genesis 1:30, a verse that normally receives little attention in the context of the question we are posing, offers a key that is at first glance wholly unremarkable. Genesis 1:29 reads, "God said: 'See, I have given you every plant yielding seed that is upon the face of all the earth, and every tree with seed in its fruit; you shall have them for food.'" Then follows verse 30: "'And to every beast of the earth, and to every bird of the air, and to everything that creeps on the earth, everything that has the breath of life, I have given every green plant for food.' And it was so."

Both human beings and animals are to take their nourishment from the plants that sprout on the surface of the whole earth. Human beings and animals thus have a common realm of life and nourishment. One can already envision problems, tensions, and colliding interests. How will conflicts of interest between human beings and animals be regulated? How should human beings behave toward animals when, in the latter's interests in nourishment, they drive the human beings away from plants yielding seed? How should animals behave toward human beings, when human beings use the plants yielding seed for their own nourishment? It is at this point that the situation necessitates the so-called mandate of dominion.

The mandate of dominion serves to impart a differentiated order to the "world of nourishment" shared by human beings and animals. This order is established through a hierarchy of power. On the one hand, human beings and animals are neighbors and live together in a common sphere. On the other hand, it is clear and unequivocal that animals—analogous to slaves and subjugated peoples—are living beings secondary and subordinate to humankind. There is no question of allowing one's neighbor to starve in favor of one's house pet. Human beings have primacy over animals. In no case may an animal be given higher status than a human being. That is radically excluded. At the same

---

[7] C. Westermann, *Genesis 1–11: A Commentary*, trans. J. Scullion (Minneapolis: Augsburg, 1984), 161, cf. 147ff., 158–159.

time, there is a *community* of nourishment and of interests between human beings and animals. Just as the admittedly lesser rights of slaves are secured in the Old Testament bodies of law, and just as the subjugation of foreign peoples can extend to taking them into service but not to exterminating them, so the relation of human beings to animals is a relation of tolerance and of preservation in human beings' own interest.

Of course, biblically based and theologically sound Christian theology today does not support slavery nor subjugating persons because, as the biblical witness states, all human beings are made in the "image of God." Furthermore, as the Bible commands and as Jesus's own teachings and example confirm, we are called to "love your neighbor as yourself," and the foreigner, the stranger, and the marginalized are all our "neighbors."

However, the mandate of dominion provides for an unquestionably one-sided and hierarchical relation between human beings and animals. We should not cultivate romantic images about this relation. At the same time, this unquestionably hierarchical relation must not involve brutal or indifferent extermination. Instead, it is positively determined in a twofold manner. *First*, it is God's will that human beings stand in a community of solidarity not only with each other but also with other creatures. *Second*, as "God's image," human beings stand in a specific relation over against animals. They are made "royal deputies of God the Creator."[8]

As such royal deputies, human beings have to exercise justice and mercy among their fellow creatures. They thus are to extend God's righteousness and care regardless of their designated domination over other creatures. The fact that they are supposed to have "dominion" over the animals also means that they must exercise responsibility toward animals. As rulers over animals, human beings must grant animals a relative level of "rights." The "call to dominion" singles out both conflicts and tensions in creation and a divine care that involves the creativity of human beings.

The call to dominion and the image of God go hand in hand. God privileges and ennobles human creatures to care for the earth and their fellow creatures. Care, love, and responsibility are expected from human creatures. This call opens up enormous realms of ethical reasoning for all people. Many ethical issues come to mind that need addressing: from issues of very individual and personal behavior to threats of global ecological self-endangerment and gigantic political responsibilities.

---

[8] Erich Zenger, *Gottes Bogen in den Wolken: Untersuchungen zu Komposition und Theologie der priesterschriftlichen Urgeschichte*, 2nd ed., Stuttgarter Bibelstudien 112 (Stuttgart: Verlag Katholisches Bibelwerk, 1987), 90.

Implications

As the church seeks to address ethical and environmental issues, it is crucial to discuss concrete challenges and actions in the framework of a robust theology of creation that emphasizes respect for the powers of creation as well as its frailty and its self-endangerment (sickness, death, and sin) among all generations. A theology of creation framed in the light of a strong theology of childhood also needs to recognize more fully that all human beings, including children, are made in God's image and called to care for the earth. By honoring children's full humanity, the church might more intentionally support and empower children as well as more readily recognize the creative and effective initiatives for environmental justice and human rights that young people worldwide are already leading.

Furthermore, any theological discussion of creation with young people cannot avoid recognizing the realities young people themselves see around them, including the tensions, ambivalences, inner power struggles, and brutalities involved in creation as well as urgent social and environmental injustices. As we honor young people's realism, concerns, and activism, we can, at the same time, nurture the church's commitment to care, love, and responsibility by emphasizing God's "good" and "life-furthering" creation, the biblical meaning of dominion, the "common realm of life and nourishment" shared by human beings and animals, and our "community of solidarity." We cannot start early enough with these messages.

Conclusion

A theology of creation is not a theology with simple answers to complex questions. A theology of creation has to help children and adults honestly explore ethical tensions and conflicts. It has to deal with the deep truth that children and adults both experience life in the tension between frailty, helplessness, despair, a sense of power, encouragement, and hope. The complexity of creation topics challenges us to enter again and again into the community of new learning. To navigate honestly and responsibly both cognitively and ethically in this tense field is crucial for this intergenerational community of learning.

The farewell to simplistic notions of the Divine and of creation is crucial for children and adults. We have to see that God did not create a paradise but a world that is very different from God and God's heavenly existence. This creation is called "good" in the biblical creation account: a creation in which fragile and finite beings are endowed with powers and capacities. God does not spare us from this life. God is also not omnipotent. But God reveals us his power to create new and good things even out of suffering, need, and death.

Furthermore, a robust theology of creation deepens our awareness of the enormous breadth and depth of human persons, including children. On the one hand, we are frail and poor and helpless, "dust from dust" (cf. Gen 3:19). On the other hand, God has made us "little lower than God" (Ps 8:5). Here we see the seeds and grounds of human dignity and human glory. The enormous tensions in creation and in human personhood and existence raise a sense of awe and wonder as well as deep gratitude and hope.

As we continue to explore issues related to theologies of creation and childhood, we must expand and build on other domains and subfields in theology. We cannot separate these topics from other areas of theological reflection. Theologies of creation and childhood can, for example, build on and enrich the area of theological anthropology.[9] Doing so will help us to overcome reductionist perspectives on the human being and to investigate the fascinating polyphony of human existence: flesh, body, heart, soul, conscience, reason, and spirit. Keeping in mind the full humanity of people of all ages, we can also appreciate more fully the enormous array of human gifts and powers as well as limits and vulnerabilities across stages of human development. Theological anthropology will also be strengthened by paying attention to God's dealing with this existence in the power of God's Spirit and God's reign, in the guidance through the life, work, and reign of Jesus Christ. In these and other ways, various domains and subfields can continue to enrich one another.[10]

---

[9] For more on theological anthropology, see Michael Welker, "Flesh–Body–Heart–Soul–Spirit: Paul's Anthropology as Interdisciplinary Bridge-Theory," in *The Depth of the Human Person: A Multidisciplinary Approach,* ed. M. Welker (Grand Rapids: Eerdmans, 2014); and Michael Welker, *In God's Image: An Anthropology of the Spirit* (Grand Rapids: Eerdmans, 2021).

[10] With gratitude to Marcia J. Bunge, Megan Eide, and John F. Hoffmeyer for their careful review of and positive suggestions for the chapter. Marcia Bunge has also written and added most of the passages on "Implications" in this chapter.

3

CHILDREN IN AFRICAN THEOLOGIES OF COMMUNITY AND THE HUMAN PERSON

Kenneth Mtata

Understandings of humanity and the human person have shaped Christian theology in many ways. This is indeed also true of African theology. As Zimbabwean theologian Gwinyai Muzorewa observed, "How African humanity has traditionally perceived itself is of primary importance to a developing African theology."[1]

Over the past century, African theologians have offered various insightful perspectives on the human person in the context of changing cultural and political realities. For example, in reaction to colonialism and missionary domination, early twentieth-century African theologians formulated conceptions of the person that seriously considered African traditions and cultures. In the context of racial segregation in apartheid South Africa, Black theologians highlighted blackness as a God-given source of pride in opposition to the pejorative perspectives of the racists. African feminist and womanist theologians expanded African constructions of the human person by showing how all the previous constructions worked with an assumption of a male African person. African theology's advancement was therefore closely tied to advances in the expansion of its anthropology.

Although varied, these and other African theologies integrally connect understandings of the individual to community and articulate what have been called "communitarian notions of personhood." Such notions emphasize that the human person can only be understood and defined in relation to others. African communitarian understandings of the human person were prompted in part by critiques of Western anthropologies that defined the self as rational

---

[1] Gwinyai H. Muzorewa, *The Origins and Development of African Theology* (Maryknoll, NY: Orbis Books, 1985), 16; cf. John S. Mbiti, *Introduction to African Religion* (New York: Praeger, 1975), 77–81.

and autonomous and by the spread of the African concept of *ubuntu* ("I am because we are"). This concept existed in cultures of southern Africa, shaped early African theologians, and was later made popular by Nelson Mandela and Desmond Tutu. These diverse and robust African theologies have addressed important dimensions of community and the human person that have helped to inform not only African theologies but also other contextual theologies worldwide.

Despite these theological advances, a weakness in various understandings of the African person is the exclusion and marginalization of the child. Such an omission has not only impoverished African theology but is also surprising if one considers that Africa is today the youngest continent, with more than 60 percent of the population being below twenty-five years of age.[2] This is also surprising if one looks at the vulnerability of the African child from challenges of health services and education.

This chapter seeks to pave the way toward a stronger, more child-inclusive African theological anthropology by providing a critical review of selected African theologies of personhood over the past century (section 1), showing how and why they have each excluded children (section 2), and articulating elements of a theological anthropology that takes children into account as full human beings (section 3). The chapter argues that although African theologians have rightly emphasized the significance of community for understanding the human person, their uncritical reception of the African communitarian model of anthropology has resulted in hierarchical and adult-centered theologies that tend to minimize children's full humanity and their vital role in communities. We can observe that even African theologies that have attended to racial and gender equality have remained adult-centered, thereby also neglecting to regard children as persons. A sound theological understanding of the human person can build on and incorporate the wisdom of previous African theologies with their attention to community, culture, race, gender, and embodiment, yet still account more fully for children by emphasizing a highly relational concept of the human person that honors the full humanity of children and expands our understanding of children's agency and roles in our communities. This child-attentive theological anthropology offers many implications for our preferential treatment of children and for theology more broadly, including how we view God's grace and build peaceful communities. Although the chapter focuses on African theologies of the human person, it can serve as a model for attending to children's full humanity in theologies in other contexts around the world.

---

[2] See "Africa's First Challenge: The Youth Bulge Stuck in 'Waithood,'" Mo Ibrahim, July 19, 2019, https://mo.ibrahim.foundation/news.

Personhood in African Theology

The following overview of major trajectories in African theology acknowledges the contributions of African theologians to conceptions of the human person while, at the same time, pointing out the specific ways in which they have neglected and marginalized children. Although a number of theologians have already provided detailed overviews of African theology,[3] we focus specifically on anthropological assumptions that inform the work of African theologians at different epochs.[4] While these periods overlap, they help provide a framework for analysis.[5]

Early African Theologies

African theology grew in identifiable stages, and each stage was in some way a response to the changes in the sociopolitical and economic environment in which the theologians operated. In its early stages, African theology sought to respond to the colonial reality of cultural domination by emphasizing the value of African culture. It also had to contend with the missionary presence that often had an ambivalent relationship with the colony. Theological views of African personhood were intimately shaped by the struggle toward African cultural integrity. Muzorewa locates the formalization of this early phase of African theology with the "inauguration of the All Africa Conference of Churches (AACC)" in Kampala in 1963, although the preparatory work had begun in Ibadan in 1958.[6] The project was part of the general Zeitgeist of pan-Africanism presided over by African "elites," most of whom had been educated in missionary schools and overseas universities.[7] For these pioneers, theological reflection contributed to both the "rediscovery" and "recovery" of the "authentic African

---

[3] For a culture-oriented approach to African theology, see K. A. Dickson, *Theology in Africa* (Maryknoll, NY: Orbis Books, 1984); E. M. Katongole, ed., *African Theology Today* (Scranton, PA: University of Scranton Press, 2002); Tinyiko Maluleke, "Half a Century of African Christian Theologies: Elements of the Emerging Agenda for the Twenty-First Century," *Journal of Theology for Southern Africa* 99 (1997): 4–23; John Parratt, ed., *A Reader in African Christian Theology* (London: SPCK, 1987). For a general overview of African theology bibliographies, please see Josiah U. Young III, *African Theology: A Critical Analysis and Annotated Bibliography*, no. 26, *Bibliographies and Indexes in Religious Studies* (Westport, CT: Greenwood, 1993).

[4] The categorization used here is critically borrowed from Young, *African Theology*.

[5] As Maluleke notes, although it is difficult to categorize the various stages of African theology, for purposes of analysis, one can outline acceptable generalizations. See "Half a Century of African Christian Theologies," 6.

[6] Muzorewa, *Origins and Development of African Theology*, 57.

[7] Young, *African Theology*, 13.

man [sic]" from the one corrupted by Western (colonial and missionary) domination. By integrating African cultural-religious ideas, practices, and institutions into theological reflection, African theologians aimed at liberating African theology from its Western philosophical clothing, which, until then, had informed Christian education and ecclesiological organizations.

The mind-set of this early generation of African theologians resonated with that of the predominant pan-African political ideology propagated by political leaders. Politicians like Kwame Nkrumah (1909–1972), Julius Nyerere (1922–1999), and others—most of whom were Christian due to their education and upbringing—were also in search of the authentic self. While African communitarianism was the philosophical starting point for some of these politicians, they had to find a balance in appropriating some contextualized forms of Marxism. In the same vein, these early African theologians sought the cultural harmonization of biblical and African traditions. For theologians like Edward Blyden (1832–1912), Bolaji Idowu (1913–1993), and Kwesi Dickson (1929–2005), the emancipation of the "African personality" would lead to the restoration of African cultural pride. The loss of African pride was blamed on the derogatory image of the "savage" propounded by colonial and (sometimes) missionary narratives.[8] Driven by this "cultural nationalism," this generation of African scholars was more focused on religio-cultural analysis, with little, if any, social analysis.[9]

John Mbiti (1931–2019) emerged as one of the leading representatives of this early generation of African theologians, in part because he clearly articulated the significance of doing theology in Africa.[10] Mbiti was very clear in describing the characteristics of this authentic African cultural personhood to inform African theology:

> In traditional life, the individual does not and cannot exist alone except corporately. He owes his existence to other people, including those of past generations and his contemporaries. He is simply part of the whole. The community must therefore make, create or produce the individual; for the individual depends on the corporate group.... Whatever happens to the individual happens to the whole group, and whatever happens to the whole group happens to the individual. The individual can only say: "I am, because we are; and since we are, therefore I am." This is a cardinal point in the understanding of the African view of man.[11]

---

[8] Young, *African Theology*, 15–16.
[9] Young, *African Theology*, 13–21.
[10] Young, *African Theology*, 17.
[11] John S. Mbiti, *African Religions and Philosophy* (London: Heinemann, 1990), 108–109.

Insights from Black, Liberation, and Womanist Theologies

Although Mbiti and his generation of African theologians did much to affirm this African cultural identity, by the 1960s some theologians began to challenge the anthropological assumptions of their predecessors. This new perspective questioned the presentation of the African person as only "cultural." This was true of Black African theologians especially, for example, from apartheid South Africa, where race had been used as a weapon against Black people. Consequently, these theologians saw race as the appropriate lens through which they could understand the African person. African liberation theologians informed by Marxist economic perspectives also raised concerns of economic marginalization that transcended culture. For African feminist scholars, it was women's exclusion and oppression, sometimes legitimated by African patriarchal culture, that informed their theological perspectives.[12] But all this critique was characterized by a level of adultism that failed to see the exclusion of the African child. In the next section I argue that an uncritical appropriation of the communitarian person was one reason childhood did not inform African theological anthropology.

Communitarian Concepts of Personhood and the Marginalization of Children

These newly emerging African theologies each contributed to holistic understandings of the human person as someone gendered, economically and socially located, and with racial and cultural identities. One major anthropological assumption of these theologies was the emphasis of the communitarian or relational dimension of the person. However, the critiques of the early generation of African theologians did not offer an extended appreciation of the human person that included children.

One explanation for this absence of childhood in African theological anthropology can be traced to the nature and foundations of communitarian assumptions. Tracing the genealogy of the idea of African communitarianism surprisingly reveals two Western roots. The first was the reaction by Western missionaries and anthropologists to the industrialization developments taking place back home where high individualism and destruction of community were occurring. This individualism was connected to the philosophical statement of the French thinker René Descartes, "Cogito, ergo sum" (I think, therefore I

---

[12] Maluleke, "Half a Century of African Christian Theologies," 20; Muzorewa, *Origins and Development of African Theology*, 57. For themes in the works of one leading feminist, Mercy Amba Oduyoye, see Young, *African Theology*, 25, and the annotated bibliography (entries 452–459), 181–184.

am), which stood in stark contrast to the *ubuntu* philosophy of "I am because we are." The second was an attempt to contextualize Marxist ideas in the African context. Marxist perspectives on the collective ownership of the means of production found its authentication in African communitarian practices and necessitated the establishment of the appropriation language—hence "Ubuntu" and other similar categories.

Although this communitarian concept of the person powerfully raised awareness of human interdependence, African theologians did not fully acknowledge its hierarchical dimensions. While they clearly critiqued hierarchies of race, economic, and gender privilege, they could not see the adultism inherent in their critique. African theologies of personhood excluded or marginalized children because the communitarian notion was adult-centered and assumed that full personhood is attained. Clarifying the logic and examining some streams of thought that influenced communitarian constructions of the human person can create space for articulating more comprehensive anthropologies that attend to children and childhood.

Influences on the Communitarian Concept

As stated earlier, although Africans of the time of the missionaries largely lived in clan-based communities, they took this communitarian notion for granted. They did not reflect on it as their identity or use it to oppose individualism. Regarding identity, the influence of the Western missionaries and anthropologists is unmistakable.[13] Africans' contact with Western missionaries and colonizers heightened the politics of identity of both groups, although Westerners had more capital to impose their meaning of identity as superior and therefore to be adopted. While the early missionaries denigrated African cultures as backward and to be eradicated, a later generation of missionaries-cum-anthropologists, who were disapproving of the social implications of industrialization in Europe, started to see African culture as the last pristine cultural frontier to be preserved, and hence were more sympathetic to their understanding of African culture. Among the many anthropological descriptions of the African person, the one that stood out and that had a lasting influence was the designation of the African as communitarian—an idea that deeply shaped African theology as early as the 1950s.

Since many African theologians then and still today incorporate this communitarian construal of the African self, one widespread assumption is that this notion of the self was developed purely by Africans who were asserting their

---

[13] On the relationship between missionaries and anthropologists, see F. A. Salamone, "Anthropologists and Missionaries: Competition or Reciprocity?," *Human Organization* 36, no. 4 (1977): 407–412.

own identity. However, this is only part of the story. In reality, African theologians were in conversation with this second generation of missionaries who had "begun" to see something positive about African culture, in contrast to their predecessors, who had connived with colonialists to forge a derogatory narrative about African culture and personhood.

These later missionary/anthropologists had not necessarily rediscovered authentic African culture but rather shaped their understanding of it in response to their alienation from Western thought and culture. Missionaries of this generation were either born in Africa or had left Europe during the period of rapid industrialization and accompanying socioeconomic challenges. At the same time, the Western construal of the person as an individual, autonomous, and rational being had become generally accepted. For these missionaries, industrialization and individualistic notions of the identity posed negative social and religious consequences. For them, traditional and communitarian Africa represented the invaluable vestiges of their past selves.[14] Informed by cultural conservatism as well as Pietism's emphasis on service to the broader community, they became impressed with African culture and wanted it to inform their own theologies and perspectives on personhood. Their construal of the African person as communal was therefore primarily a critique of highly individualistic Western constructions of the self. In other words, they defined the other in terms of the self, a process called "othering" (such as in the work of Edward Said) or "worlding" (such as in the work of Gayatri Chakravorty Spivak).

Among the Western missionary/anthropologists of this communitarian view was Belgian Franciscan missionary Placide Tempels (1906–1977), whose influential book *Bantu Philosophy* (1959) became the textbook for most early African theologians, such as Mbiti and Alexis Kagame. In fact, Kagame (1912–1981), an African philosopher inspired by Tempels, claimed that if Tempels had not written this book, he would not have written his doctoral thesis on the same subject![15] Tempels claimed that while Westerners hold a "static" conception of being, Africans have a "dynamic" conception.[16] As scholars have noted, Tempels posited a "radical conceptual difference between Africans and non-Africans on the essential nature of beings and entities in general and human beings in particular."[17] Apart from some methodological concerns that Kagame

---

[14] Robert James Thornton, "Narrative Ethnography in Africa, 1850–1920: The Creation and Capture of an Appropriate Domain for Anthropology," *Man* 18, no. 3 (1983): 502–520. There are many other Western missionaries not included here for concerns of space who contributed to the communitarian view.

[15] Liboire Kagabo, "Alexis Kagame (1912–1981): Life and Thought," in *A Companion to African Philosophy*, ed. Kwasi Wiredu (Oxford: Blackwell, 2004), 233.

[16] Placide Tempels, *Bantu Philosophy* (Paris: Présence Africaine, 1959).

[17] Didier N. Kaphagawani, "African Conceptions of Personhood and Intellectual

had with Tempels, he accepted the communitarian notion of personhood proffered by Tempels as descriptive of the African people.[18]

Geoffrey Parrinder (1910–2005), a British Methodist in Benin, was another missionary attracted to communitarian personhood. In his *African Traditional Religion* (1968), Parrinder pointed to African personhood as demonstrating "no sharp dividing-line between sacred and secular such as is usually assumed in Europe."[19] According to Parrinder, the "material and spiritual are intertwined, the former as a vehicle of the latter."[20] Desmond Tutu (b. 1931), a student of Parrinder, also utilized the communitarian understanding of the African person in his quest for a theology of reconciliation. Tutu did not believe that Black South African Christians would forgive their oppressors based on their faith alone but rather also on their assumptions of the African person characterized by *ubuntu*.[21] For Tutu, *ubuntu* was intrinsically and ontologically a characteristic of African personhood, whose manifestation was seen in the forgiveness Black South Africans offered to white South Africans for their crimes under the regime of apartheid.[22] Mbiti also saw in Parrinder's description of the African person an "excellent and accurate presentation of the main items in African religions."[23]

Several other influential Western missionaries promoted the communal notion of the self. For example, John Taylor (1914–2001), an Anglican priest who worked in Uganda, expressed his admiration for African concepts of personhood and "cosmos oneness" and stated that in primal religions, "not only is there less separation between subject and object, between self and not-self, but fundamentally all things share the same nature and the same interaction one upon the other."[24] Taylor saw this cosmology permeating the "consciousness of African thinkers and writers even after long acquaintance with the Western world."[25] Another Westerner who shaped notions of the African communal self was German theologian Theo Sundermeier (b. 1935), who spent many years in Namibia and

---

Identities," in *The African Philosophy Reader*, ed. P. H. Coetzee and A. P. J. Roux (London: Routledge, 1998), 170.

[18] Kagabo, "Alexis Kagame," 238.

[19] E. G. Parrinder, *African Traditional Religion* (London: SPCK, 1968), 27.

[20] Parrinder, *African Traditional Religion*, 27.

[21] Lyn S. Graybill, *Truth and Reconciliation in South Africa: Miracle or Model?* (Boulder, CO: Lynne Rienner Publishers, 2002), 32.

[22] This view has been rejected by some African theologians, especially Tinyiko Maluleke.

[23] Mbiti, *African Religions and Philosophy*, 12.

[24] John V. Taylor, *The Primal Vision: Christian Presence amid African Religion* (London: SCM Press, 1963), 64.

[25] Taylor, *Primal Vision*, 64.

taught at Umphumulo Lutheran Seminary (South Africa).[26] He claims that "for the Westerner, life means individuality," as contrasted to the African life, which is "communal."[27] Sundermeier sees this communitarian ethos developing from various African myths of origin that understand communities as originating from the same source. For example, Zulu myths understand all Zulu people as emerging from a single "reed" or *Uhlanga* and thereby belonging to an "*Uhlanga* collective."[28]

Many African philosophers and theologians embraced the communitarian notion of personhood as it allowed them to claim distinction from Western notions of the person. They presented the African notions of being human in a positive light while they denigrated Western constructions of personhood influenced by rationality, individuality, and equality. For some, collectivism is so ingrained in African thought that "individualism and self-seeking [are] ruled out."[29] Mbiti, for example, believed Taylor's works, especially *The Primal Vision*, penetrated and set important trends in African thought.[30] It is not surprising that, in describing African personhood, Mbiti could offer that the African should say, "I am, because *we* are; and since *we are, therefore I am*,"[31] as opposed to the Cartesian position, "I think, therefore I am" (*Cogito ergo sum*). If personhood is conferred by the community, personhood could be conferred upon achieving something in the community, hence the exclusion of the child.

Patriarchal Hierarchies and Personhood as Attained or Achieved

In its African construction, being a full human being was qualified by those "attributes, capacities, and signs" of what it means to be "properly" considered a social person in a particular society.[32] As Gilbert H. Herdt observes, in many patriarchal societies, only males are considered to have the capacity to "attain complete personhood."[33] This notion of the ultimate sign of personhood being the

---

[26] For Sundermeier, Umphumulo was, at the time, the primary think tank of Black and African theology. See Theo Sundermeier, "My Pilgrimage in Mission," *International Bulletin of Missionary Research* 31, no. 4 (2007): 200–204.

[27] Theo Sundermeier, *The Individual and Community in African Traditional Religions* (Hamburg: LIT Verlag, 1998), 17.

[28] Sundermeier, *Individual and Community,* 17–18.

[29] Jomo Kenyatta, *Facing Mount Kenya* (1965), cited in Kwame Gyekye, "Person and Community in African Thought," in *Philosophy from Africa: A Text with Readings*, ed. Pieter Hendrik Coetzee and A. P. J. Roux, 2nd ed. (Oxford: Oxford University Press, 2002), 298.

[30] Mbiti, *African Religions and Philosophy*, 10–12.

[31] Mbiti, *African Religions and Philosophy*, 108–109. Emphasis mine.

[32] Gilbert H. Herdt, *Rituals of Manhood: Male Initiation in Papua New Guinea* (Berkeley: University of California Press, 1982), 103.

[33] Herdt, *Rituals of Manhood*, 103.

attainment of ancestor-hood by men alone is an example of what social anthropologist Arlette Ottino and others have called "hierarchical personhood."[34] Here, personhood is "acquired along an evolution undertaken over an entire lifetime, of which ancestor-hood represents the culmination," meaning that personhood is "not attained at birth but through the fulfilment of a number of requirements which include procreation in marriage and reproduction through the procreation of one's own children."[35] In addition to procreation, full personhood is attained by discharging one's duties to her or his immediate family and to "the senior generations and the deceased forebears."[36] As Ottino notes, the "progression of the individual to the state of personhood is a common feature of hierarchically ordered societies, in which identity cannot be separated from the attributes attached to the position and the functions of the person within society, at successive stages in life."[37]

The hierarchical conception that persists in many African societies today seems to be more descriptive of a notion of African personhood informed by the dominant forces of culture than missionary-colonial influences. In this hierarchy, the primary tribal male ancestor is placed at the top, followed by other significant older males, and then women. At the bottom of the pyramid are children. As observed by Geneva Smitherman, a scholar of African American language, this hierarchy of existence permeates the structuring of the entire "universe," constituted as it is by the hierarchy of "nature, with God at the head of the hierarchy, followed by lesser deities, the 'living dead' (ancestral spirits), people, animals, places."[38] Other scholars have examined carefully, which Smitherman does not, the hierarchy of the people among themselves, pointing out that "personhood does not follow automatically simply because one is born of human seed. Rather, personhood must be earned."[39]

---

[34] Ottino is not basing his work on Africa; nevertheless, his contribution informed by "traditional" societies is useful here. See, for example, Arlette Ottino, *The Universe within: A Balinese Village through Its Ritual Practices* (Paris: Karthala, 2000), 274.

[35] Ottino, *The Universe within*, 274.

[36] Ottino, *The Universe within*, 275.

[37] Ottino, *The Universe within*, 275.

[38] Geneva Smitherman, *Talkin and Testifyin: The Language of Black America* (Detroit: Wayne State University Press, 1986), 75. See also Jeffrey E. Anderson, *Conjure in African American Society* (Baton Rouge: Louisiana State University Press, 2005), 144–145. Godfrey Mwakikagile claims that there was no hierarchical structure among the Kikuyu. Space does not allow further engagement with this position based as it is on Mwakikagile's overly positive presentation of African culture against the disturbances brought by colonial rule. See Godfrey Mwakikagile, *Africa and the West* (New York: Nova, 2000).

[39] N. Mkhize, "Psychology: An African Perspective," in *Self, Community and Psychology*, ed. K. Ratele, N. Duncan, D. Hook, N. Mkhize, P. Kiguwa, A. Collins (Lansdowne, South Africa: UCT Press, 2004), 26. See also Ifeanyi A. Menkiti, "Person and

As Ghanaian philosopher Kwame Gyekye notes, an individual's social status is measured by the following:

- A person's sense of responsibility, expressed, in turn, through his/her responsiveness as sensitivity to the needs and demands of the group.
- What a person has been able to achieve through his/her own exertions—physical, intellectual, moral.
- The extent to which a person fulfills certain social norms, such as having a marital life and bringing up children.[40]

One can see the hybrid of African and Western intellectual constructions of personhood defined by social achievement (Africa) and cognitive and intellectual capacities (Western). Such personhood constructions marginalize children. Children neither accumulate social capital nor evince any intellectual capabilities since the measurement standards for these criteria are designed for adults. It is not surprising that, in such constructions, the child is not classified as a person until she or he undergoes rites of initiation and is thereby introduced to the ancestors and the family. One can trace the conception and development of personhood attainment processes from the "it" status of the child to maturity of adult personhood.[41] To move from "it" status, the child must undergo some rituals of personhood attainment while the mother, who was defiled by this "thing" coming out of her, must also undergo a ritual of cleansing to purify her from the contaminations of the nonperson that she has produced. Such ritual traditions in many African societies are designed to "change one's status or social position."[42] As personhood is one of the statuses to be attained as one "goes along,"[43] children, since they have not yet achieved it, must undergo particular rituals in order to attain it. Nigerian philosopher Ifeanyi Menkiti (b. 1940) argues that such views of personhood mean that children are not regarded as full persons or fully human.[44]

Community in African Traditional Thought," in *African Philosophy: An Introduction*, ed. Richard A. Wright (Washington, DC: University Press of America, 1984), 171–182; cf. E. A. Ruch and K. C. Anyanwu, *African Philosophy: An Introduction to the Main Philosophical Trends in Contemporary Africa* (Rome: Catholic Book Agency, 1981).

[40] Kwame Gyekye, "Person and Community in African Thought," in *Philosophy from Africa: A Text with Readings*, 305.

[41] Gyekye, "Person and Community in African Thought," 301–304.

[42] Anne Nasimiyu-Wasike, "Christianity and the African Rituals of Birth and Naming," in *The Will to Arise: Women, Tradition, and the Church in Africa*, ed. Mercy Amba Oduyoye and Musimbi R. A. Kanyoro (Maryknoll, NY: Orbis Books, 1992), 40.

[43] Mkhize, "Psychology," 26.

[44] Cited in Mkhize, "Psychology," 23–26; Menkiti, "Person and Community," 171–181.

Debates among African philosophers on the nature of the personhood of children have exposed the problematic and widespread notion that personhood is attained or achieved. As philosopher Polycarp Ikuenobe asserts, "the developmental process of acquiring personhood in the community usually progresses from the status of an 'it' as a child through full personhood or elderhood to the status of an ancestor in the spiritual world."[45] When African thinkers declare that "man [sic] is part of nature, but also transcends it,"[46] it is a deliberate hierarchical comparison of personhood value starting from the gods, older men, younger men, older *women*, younger *women*, and lastly, children.[47] As Ulric Neisser and David A. Jopling emphasize, "Personhood is not always automatic in African societies, as it generally is in the West, but rather contingent upon such factors as gender, social position, age, and the production of offspring."[48] Neisser and Jopling seem not to realize that even in the West, personhood is not "automatic."[49] Personhood is only "conferred as a consequence of living out a proper life, which is realized only by overt participation in the social order,"[50] so personhood is not automatic but negotiated.

In many African cultures, children go through various personhood attainment rituals in order to become fully human. For example, in some Malawi tribes, because children are not classed as full human beings at birth, a particular birth ritual called *kutenga Mwana* has to be performed on the child in order to prepare them for personhood, which only becomes attainable at adolescence.[51] Of course, it depends on how one interprets these rituals, but some form of promotion from one state of being to another cannot be disputed. Among the Babukusu of Kenya, the child is given her or his temporary name at birth while awaiting the one she or he receives when attaining their full personhood at adolescence.[52] Among the Xhosa, circumcision is understood to be ritually important in becoming a man. When Jacob Zuma was elected president of South Africa in 2009, my Xhosa friends said in reference to Zuma, "How can we be ruled by a boy?" Zuma, a Zulu man, was most likely uncircumcised

---

[45] Polycarp Ikuenobe, *Philosophical Perspectives on Communalism and Morality in African Traditions* (Lanham, MD: Lexington Books, 2006), 64.

[46] Ikuenobe, *Philosophical Perspectives*, 64.

[47] There are, of course, exceptions to this rule. For example, if a young child in the family becomes the family ancestral medium, the matrix immediately changes.

[48] Ulric Neisser and David A. Jopling, *The Conceptual Self in Context: Culture, Experience, and Self-Understanding* (New York: Cambridge University Press, 1997), 43.

[49] It would be interesting to compare personhood constructions in specific Western and African contexts. In such a case, one would need to go beyond generalizing and offer a careful comparative social and anthropological analysis.

[50] Neisser and Jopling, *Conceptual Self in Context*, 43.

[51] Brian Morris, *Animals and Ancestors: An Ethnography* (Oxford: Berg Publishers, 2000), 75.

[52] Nasimiyu-Wasike, "Christianity and the African Rituals of Birth and Naming," 47.

in contrast to former president Thabo Mbeki, a Xhosa male, who most likely was circumcised. For the Xhosa, male circumcision is a ritual that is part of the attainment of full personhood, implying that without a traditional circumcision one is not recognized as a full human being.[53] Some African Christians object to baptizing infants or welcoming children to Holy Communion not only because of harmful missionary practices but also because they assume children are not human enough to receive "holy things."

Strengths and Limitations of Womanist and Feminist Critiques

African womanist and feminist theologians successfully exposed male hierarchies and gender-blindness in African theologies and culture and provided new insights into the human person but remained primarily adult-centered and child-blind. These protest and proactive theologies were largely informed by the experiences of African women. In their protest, African womanist theologians sought to show how a male-orientated African culture and many of its patriarchal features influenced and impoverished the outcomes of African theology. In their constructive dimensions, womanist theologies sought to create a "theological space for African women theologians to find and mentor each other on how to produce theological literature that is based on their experiences."[54] These theologians wanted to maximize the participation of women in mainstream African theological work.[55] The first wave of theologians—such as Mercy Oduyoye,[56] Musimbi Kanyoro, Nyambura Njoroge, Isabel Phiri, Madipone Masenya, and Teresa Okure—and the second wave—which includes Musa Dube, Sarojini Nadar, Fulata Moyo, and others[57]—all contributed various textures to this movement. The result of their collaborative work culminated in the establishment of the Circle of Concerned African Women Theologians.[58]

---

[53] See, for example, Sakhumzi Mfecane, "'Ndiyindoda' [I am a man]: Theorising Xhosa Masculinity," *Anthropology Southern Africa* 39, no. 3 (2016): 204–214; and Lubabalo Sheperd Mdedetyana, "Medical Male Circumcision and Xhosa Masculinities: Tradition and Transformation" (mini-thesis, University of the Western Cape, November 2018).

[54] Isabel A. Phiri, "The Circle of Concerned African Women Theologians: Its Contribution to Ecumenical Formation," *Ecumenical Review* 57, no. 1 (January 2005): 35.

[55] See, for example, Maluleke, "Half a Century of African Christian Theologies," 20–22.

[56] Mercy A. Oduyoye, *Hearing and Knowing: Theological Reflections on Christianity in Africa* (Maryknoll, NY: Orbis Books, 1986). In this book, Oduyoye focuses less on gender and more on the African religious outlook than she does in her later works.

[57] One can see some changes in the younger generation of African women theologians for whom culture is increasingly becoming problematic.

[58] Isabel A. Phiri, "Doing Theology in Community: The Case of African Woman Theologians in the 1990s," *Journal of Theology for Southern Africa* 99 (1997): 68–76.

What would be the working method and anthropological assumptions of these African women theologians? This can be gleaned from the individual and collaborative works of some of the leaders of this movement. For example, Phiri claims that the methodology of African women theologians should be appropriate to African culture, free of oppressive elements, and uphold what is of value, meaning that "whatever things uphold women's and men's humanity in the Bible, in African traditional religion, and in African culture are sources for this theology."[59] This critical reception of African culture goes back to Oduyoye's early work, when she would say, "We African women have to know our culture, our own rituals, challenge and change what needs to be changed, and appropriate what is of value and what upholds our humanity."[60] Oduyoye's perspective is only a slight change from Mbiti and his early community in that it seeks a more critical reception of the African culture but sees cultural personhood as one key element for doing theology.

This African womanist theological project succeeded in bringing gender to the fore as an important theological lens, but it did little to nothing to attend to questions of childhood. The gender dimension obviously made new important theological contributions, such as revising notions of the maleness of God. By introducing the feminine dimensions of the Divine, feminist theology enriched the field overall by highlighting the tenderness and motherly nature of God, consistent with such biblical depictions. Important as this contribution may have been, it was informed by the prevailing "adultism" that informed earlier contextual theologies. While such contextual theologies took seriously subjects' experiences as the starting point for theological reflection, it was mainly adults' experiences that counted; it was the experience of either the cultural, racial, economic, or gender exclusion of adults that really informed these theologies. The experiences of children were not seriously considered. Just as African feminist theologians had accused male theologians of being "gender blind,"[61] the feminist intervention also proved to be "child blind."

A Child-Attentive and Relational Theology of the Human Person

What are some elements of a robust theological anthropology that includes children? How might such a theology strengthen our view of children and the human person and community more broadly? How might it inform our

---

[59] Phiri, "Doing Theology in Community," 70–71.

[60] See also M. A. Oduyoye, "The Search for a Two-Winged Theology," in *Talitha, qumi! Proceedings of the Convocation of African Women Theologians*, ed. M. A. Oduyoye and M. Kanyoro (Ibadan, Nigeria: Daystar Press, 1990), 39.

[61] Nyambura Jane Njoroge, "The Mission Voice: African Women Doing Theology," *Journal of Theology for Southern Africa* no. 99 (1997): 80.

treatment of children and the church's advocacy role on behalf of children? Furthermore, if one recognizes the advances in African theologies on the basis of including excluded groups, then one should expect that an anthropology that includes children would also reshape and enrich other areas of African theology. What could be some of those theological advances? Let us consider the following foundational elements and practical and theological implications of a child-attentive theological anthropology.

Foundational Elements

First, a child-attentive theological anthropology must begin by recognizing the full dignity, integrity, and personhood of the child. This starting point avoids the pitfalls of adult-centered and achievement-oriented notions of the person and offers a corrective to African understandings of the child discussed earlier where the child's personhood could not be conferred until the child achieved something in life. Instead, a robust theology of the person recognizes children as full human beings from the start. Their personhood is given, not achieved.

Second, a child-attentive anthropology of personhood and community highlights the relational and nonhierarchical dimensions of being human. Of course, communitarian understandings of the human person are highly relational and have powerfully expressed the individual's integral relationship and interconnectedness to the community. Yet, as we have noted, and as is clear in studies of other cultural or postcolonial contexts, affirming communitarian and relational constructions does not automatically ensure equal regard for all persons.[62] Like individualistic notions, communitarian notions of the human person, although relational, can contain unethical and hierarchical features that undermine attention to children.

A robust notion of personhood as relational goes further than communitarian notions by assuming and explicitly drawing attention to the full humanity of each individual, regardless of age, and to the contribution of individuals to relationships and the whole of humanity. From this perspective, personhood is given. Children do not need to attain full personhood by either cognitive or social achievements or by simply growing up. Full status as a person does not depend on race, gender, intellectual capacities, or age. The value of the person does not depend on any other factor apart from the given reality that one belongs to the human race and the human race flourishes only through relationships.

---

[62] See, for example, Edwin Hui, "Jen and Perichoresis: The Confucian and Christian Bases of the Relational Person," in *The Moral Status of Persons: Perspectives on Bioethics*, ed. Gerhold K. Becker (Amsterdam: Rodopi, 2000), 95–117.

This relational understanding of personhood resonates with the move many twentieth-century and contemporary theologians and philosophers have made from a substance to a relational ontology. A substance ontology assumes that entities exist independently from one another whereas a relational ontology emphasizes the radical interconnectedness of all being. For example, German Lutheran theologian Gerhard Ebeling (1912–2001), building on Martin Luther, articulated a relational ontology as opposed to a substance ontology.[63] Ebeling (as summarized by Volker Rabens) criticized ontologies of substance for perceiving relations "as the weakest factor determining the nature of an essence" and proposed a theology in which primacy is given to being "as *relational*, as 'being together,' because relations have a constitutive character."[64] Many contemporary theologians also embrace a relational ontology and draw implications for our notion of the person and our relationships to one another, God, and the world. For example, as Catholic feminist theologian Catherine LaCugna (1952–1997) states,

> A relational ontology understands both God and the creature to exist and meet as persons in communion.... The meaning of to-be is to-be-a-person-in-communion.... God's To-Be is To-Be-in-relationship, and God's being-in-relationship-to-us *is* what God is. A relational ontology focuses on personhood, relationship, and communion as the modality of all existence.[65]

Although many theologians have embraced a relational ontology, they have not always considered children in their view of personhood. A robust relational view of the person that puts children at the center understands that all human beings—male, female, rich, poor, young, old—are gifts from the start. What needs to develop is the consciousness that relationality includes children.

Third, a robust theology of personhood recognizes the agency of children and their vital role in communities. Children are not only subjects of our care and concern but also valuable contributors to the joy, satisfaction, and hope of communities and the broader society. Children stimulate a sense of renewal and

---

[63] See, for example, Gerhard Ebeling, "Luthers Wirklichkeitsverständnis," *Zeitschrift für Theologie und Kirche* 90 (1993): 409–424; and Gerhard Ebeling, *Dogmatik des christlichen Glaubens*, vol. 1 (Tübingen: J.C.B. Mohr, 1979), 221–222, 228–230, 348.

[64] Volker Rabens, *The Holy Spirit and Ethics in Paul: Transformation and Empowering for Religious-Ethical Life*, 2nd rev. ed. (Minneapolis: Fortress Press, 2013), 138–139.

[65] Catherine M. LaCugna, *God for Us: The Trinity and Christian Life* (San Francisco: Harper Collins, 1991), 248–249; italics in the original. Cited by Gloria L. Schaab, *The Creative Suffering of the Triune God: An Evolutionary Theology* (Oxford: Oxford University Press, 2007), 152.

continuity for the community. Advances in neurosciences and social psychology are now helping us to understand that children, even from infancy, respond and contribute to the quality of community life. Babies have the capacity to give and to receive love. They interact with and engage others from the start. They are also affected positively or negatively by the stimuli around them. My observation of our own nine-month-old boy has shown me that he wants to participate where signals of positive gestures are expressed between father and mother. He can also express a face of disaffection where the atmosphere is tense.

A child-attentive theological anthropology honors the unique and critical agency of children and their growing moral capacities from infancy through youth. In recent years, especially, we have witnessed and become more aware of children's moral agency and their powers to mobilize positive social transformation. Brain studies highlight the early moral reasoning of children, and the news media show us the activism and leadership of young people in areas of social and environmental justice. The moral indignation of young people regarding the destruction of the environment, for example, partly comes from their realization of what such situations pose not only for their own future but also for the continuity of the human race in general. That children have gravitated to this existential issue across race, culture, and location is a testimony of something valuable in children that is a source of social conscience.

We also see the vital role of children in communities whenever we reflect on our common humanity and the continuity—as opposed to the end—of the human race. It is self-evident that, without children, communities would die out, and the human species would become extinct. Adults also have a difficult time even conceiving of the future without reflecting on children. We already see difficulties of imagining communities and humanity without children in those parts of the world where the population is aging faster than it is being replenished with youth. This problem is not limited to economic concerns of young people needing to support elderly populations. Rather, aging populations also reveal the existential difficulties of imagining hope, human flourishing, and a shared humanity without relationships to and the flourishing of children.

Practical and Theological Implications

This child-attentive theological anthropology has many wider practical and theological implications for church. For example, and most directly, if the church puts children at the center of what it means to be human, then it will more intentionally include children, more effectively advocate for them, and even see children as a test of the integrity of community. Children's sensitivity to a community's actions, good or bad, helps the faith community and the broader society realize that current social and political problems can have long-term impacts beyond present generations. We are told that some children who were conceived and born during World War II in Germany exhibited post-traumatic stress disorder and anxiety in their adult lives, even though they were not aware that a war was raging. What we do to children today can turn God from being a loving God to a God "punishing the children for the sin of the parents to the third and fourth generation" (Deut 5:9). An investment into peaceful communities for future generations is measured by how the present generation of children is treated.

Furthermore, a child-inclusive and relational understanding of the human person challenges us to expand our compassion for all people and come together to work across lines of difference for the common good. A child-inclusive relational understanding of the human person resonates with theologies that attend to culture, race, and gender yet expands their vision and attention to the children in our midst and around the world. Thus, once a child-inclusive notion of personhood becomes the basis for theological reflection, more attention can be given to the breadth, interdependence, mutuality, and quality of relationships across a host of barriers, including race, gender, culture, and age. A deeply relational and nonhierarchical understanding of the human person empowers persons of all ages and capacities to work together across lines of difference to advance the flourishing of human relations and the planet.

The notion that children, like adults, do not need to earn or grow into personhood also has implications for many other areas of theological reflection, including helping us to expand our conceptions of grace. Often we fail to extend the notion of God's grace, forgiveness, and mercy to children, because we are too focused on the image of children as sinners in need of discipline and instruction or who can only be redeemed by participating in the ritual of baptism or reaching a certain level of cognitive and confessional ability. Instead, we need to remember the words of grace prophesied by Jeremiah: "'Before I formed you in the womb I knew you, and before you were born I consecrated you; I appointed you a prophet to the nations'" (1:5). These words convey far more than God's foreknowledge of the professional route the child will take when grown up. It is based on the understanding that children are known and loved by God before they have done anything. The beginning of a relationship with God is assumed to happen before one is able to do anything to earn it. This confirms Paul's words: "For by grace you have been saved through faith, and this is not your own doing; it is the gift of God—not the result of works, so that no one may boast" (Eph 2:8–9). Such a view of children and their inability to make any contribution, either cognitively or by their actions, gives grace an emphasis that is not always evident in adult-centered reflections on grace.

Conclusion

This chapter has revealed how advances in African theology correspond with advances in the appreciation of different aspects of being human. We have shown that early African theology was shaped by understanding the African person as one who had culture and traditions. This was challenged by later African theologians who raised concerns of such uncritical acceptance of African culture where patriarchy marginalized and excluded women in defining the African person. Other African theologians raised concerns that the African person as an economic agent had not informed African theology. It has also been shown that all these African theologies had one thing in common: uplifting the African person as communitarian. Hence all their theologies had this communitarian leaning.

The chapter also noted that even though African theologies shaped by response to cultural domination, racial segregation, gender-based discrimination, and economic marginalization helped us draw methodological aspects of inclusive anthropologies, they had their own limits. These diverse African theologies made strides but were shaped by a communitarian framework of the human person that was hierarchical and adult-centered, thereby marginalizing children. These hierarchical anthropological frameworks continue to shape the exclusion of children in other areas of African theology.

The chapter therefore presented a child-inclusive and relational understanding of the human person and pointed out some of its wider theological and practical implications. A child-inclusive and non-hierarchical theological anthropology begins by recognizing children's agency, equality, dignity, and full personhood. A child-inclusive notion of personhood emphasizes, in turn, human interdependence and mutuality and the significance of working across lines of difference (whether of class, race, gender, culture, or age) and of fostering relationships based on mutual respect and cooperation rather than hierarchy. These relationships are founded on God's unconditional reaching out to all people. In other words, putting children at the center brings home a deeper understanding of grace. Children's moral capacities and their passion to translate moral indignation into transformative activism also benefit the community. As moral agents of transformation, children help build global networks of protest against social and environmental injustices. In these and other ways, putting children at the center of what it means to be human revitalizes the church, our com-munities, and our world.

4

CHILDREN'S EXPERIENCES OF EVIL IN THEIR MULTIPLE WORLDS

Ivone Gebara

Human beings across cultures and centuries have reflected on the problem of evil. Our perceptions of evil are personal and, at the same time, connected with our family, culture, and community. Our notions of evil shape, in turn, our visions of what "ought to be." As feminist theologian Rosemary Radford Ruether (b. 1936) explains, "The human being sets itself over against existing reality, names this reality as contrary to 'what ought to be' and thereby generates a vision of an ideal world that becomes the standard by which existing reality is judged as deficient."[1] The "what ought to be" functions like a benchmark delineating good and evil for individuals and communities.

Building on Jesus's vision of love, justice, and care for the marginalized, Christian ethicists and theologians address a host of contemporary evils. Whether theologians self-identify as liberationist, evangelical, or ecological, whether as Protestant, Catholic, or Orthodox, they address a range of injustices: racial, gender, ecological, socioeconomic, and so on. Whatever their context, they also seek ways for Christians to speak out and act on central Christian values of love, justice, compassion, and "what ought to be."

Although children both inhabit and inherit the same world as adults and have real experiences of evil and injustice, theologians and church leaders have neglected to take children's experiences fully into account, theologically and practically. This is the case even in my own work. Although I have explored the question of evil and written widely about ways the church can foster justice and solidarity with the poor and marginalized, I have not adequately attended to the problem of evil directly related to children. I have paid more attention to women and the poor, neglecting children's unique struggles and sufferings.[2]

---

[1] Rosemary Radford Ruether, *Womanguides: Readings toward a Feminist Theology* (Boston: Beacon Press, 1986), 81.

[2] See, for example, Ivone Gebara, *Out of Depths: Women's Experience of Evil and Salva-*

Furthermore, given children's experiences with evil and the multiple and often competing visions of what ought to be that surround them, the church has not adequately addressed how to support children, pass onto them Christian values and visions of what ought to be, and empower them to establish life-giving relationships among human beings in all webs of life. This is what I call educating children for solidarity, for compassion, and for reciprocity with all living beings. To educate for solidarity is to educate in a way that honors and protects human dignity and our planet.

This chapter reexamines the problem of evil by considering children's experiences. Specifically, I explore children's experiences of evil, outline contemporary obstacles to addressing evil and passing down the gospel and Christian values to children, and suggest ways to build more just societies that honor the needs and strengths of children. In the process, I address such questions as: How do children experience and perpetuate evil? What evils do they experience from their cultures and in their various worlds—with adults, with one another, at home, in community, and online? How do we pass onto them life-giving Christian teachings and values, particularly given their suffering and the growing presence of technology in their lives? Furthermore, how can we empower children to be both recipients and cultivators of such values, preparing them to face the evils of their time and to work with others to create a better world? Answering these and related questions requires new ways of seeking justice for all human beings of all ages. In addition, exploring solutions to these questions demands collaborating with children in ways that acknowledge their dignity and our mutual solidarity. Overall, by taking children's experiences of evil more seriously, we enlarge our understanding of evil and are better positioned to tackle the injustices facing children. Furthermore, we deepen our understanding of children's needs and strengths and develop new approaches to supporting and empowering them.

My reflection offers a new theological contribution regarding evil that includes children's experiences and is not attached to any philosophical or psychological theory about child development or children's experiences.[3] Rather, I describe and reflect on childhood experiences of evil based on my limited observations, current relationships with children, and personal reactions to some of their behaviors, as well as my own childhood, my Roman Catholic upbringing, and my philosophical and theological training. Since our understanding and experiences of good and evil are greatly shaped today not only by

---

tion (Minneapolis: Fortress Press, 2002), and Ivone Gebara, *Longing for Running Water: Ecofeminism and Liberation* (Minneapolis: Fortress Press, 1999).

[3] Melissa Freeman and Sandra Mathison, *Researching Children's Experiences* (New York: Guilford Press, 2009).

social and economic factors but also by technology and the virtual world, I also consider the role of technology in children's experience.

Reflecting on children's experiences of evil is a crucial yet difficult theological task. Children are suffering and deserve our attention, but describing their experiences of evil is difficult for a host of reasons. The encounter between adult subjectivity and child subjectivity is not simple. It includes mutual understanding and misunderstanding, proximity and distance, and merging and diverging emotions. The experiences and worlds of children and adults overlap yet are subjectively different. Furthermore, adults who write about children are no longer children and cannot fully recollect even their own childhoods.

My observations here are shaped by my life experience and context. I am a Roman Catholic nun who works mainly with young adults studying at colleges and universities. However, in my neighborhood of Camaragibe in northeast Brazil, I have frequent contact with children and families, many of whom live in poverty. Clearly, I miss important aspects and experiences in my context, and I cannot speak adequately to other contexts. Recognizing such limitations, I dare to believe that my observations speak meaningfully to Christians in other contexts, prompting them to reflect further on and address children's experiences of evil.

Children's Experiences of Evil

To reflect on evil in the child's world is to reflect on evil in the adult world. Children learn, react, repeat, and interpret the adult world in their own way. In this section, I share some reflections from my personal observation of children's behavior regarding the experience of evil in a time when economic and social realities are highly influenced by individualism, capitalism, and technology. I have organized my reflections around four central aspects of life that build on the work of French philosopher Paul Ricoeur (1913–2005), who wrote extensively on the problem of evil.[4] They include:

- the need to be protected, cared for, and nourished;
- the desire to have power;
- the desire to possess;
- the desire to be recognized.

---

[4] Paul Ricoeur, *Finitude et Culpabilité I, L'Homme Faillible* (Paris: Aubier/Montaigne, 1960), and *Finitude et Culpabilité II, La Symbolique du Mal* (Paris: Aubier/Montaigne, 1960).

These four broad aspects of life are not exhaustive and can be expressed in diverse ways, yet they aptly reflect basic needs and desires of human beings, regardless of age, that shape our experiences of good and evil.

The Need to Be Protected, Cared for, and Nourished

To be protected, cared for, and nourished are absolute needs of all living beings. When children fail to receive these basic needs, many other dimensions of their lives fail as well. Some children experience lack of care, food, and love from the day they are born and even before their birth. The lack of basic necessities undermines healthy child development and negatively affects their entire lives, influencing the ways they make choices and face difficulties, hopes, and joys. When a child reacts to hunger by stealing something to eat, he or she is immediately punished by their social environment. They are called thieves, vagabonds, "sons of bitches," and bad boys or girls. These children live in an evil situation, and others stigmatize them as producers of further evil. If they are Black or Indigenous, they are stigmatized even more. Prejudices against African descendants as well as Indigenous peoples are still realities in Brazil despite its claim to be a democracy.

Some children also experience sexual violence at home. They are sexually or physically abused, most often by relatives or family friends. As they are educated to obey adults, they accept sexual violence, harassment, and other abusive behaviors as acts of obedience. Children are not instructed to disobey adults when they are violent, and children do not know about laws protecting children from this violence. Children react to abuse in different ways, becoming silent, ill, aggressive, or all three. All children retain the marks of violence in their minds and bodies. They experience evil from others and in their own bodies, as well as a deep sense of guilt that manifests itself in different ways. Sometimes they are not welcome in their families. They often fail in school and must try to survive in their limited way. Most become marginalized young people and carry out on others the violence and victimization that they experienced.

Lack of adequate care and nurturing is a primordial experience of evil that diminishes self-esteem and has negative and lifelong consequences for children throughout the world. Given this tragic situation, in 1989, the General Assembly of the United Nations adopted the Convention of the Rights of the Child (CRC). Although this positive step was widely endorsed, many countries still do not observe or enforce children's rights. Furthermore, some actions that seek to protect children, especially girls, create other forms of violence against them. For example, in some parts of the world, adults believe that clitoris ablation of young girls or marriage of teenagers will protect girls, but they are forms of violence that furthers violence against them. Teenage girls' pregnancy from sexual abuse is also quite common in poor neighborhoods of the world, but many religious people and those who hold conservative values react with violence against abortion and accuse young girls of being murderers. This matter is particularly important at this time. In summation, common cultural practices worldwide are full of violent behaviors against children that harm them and violate their dignity and integrity.

The Desire to Have Power

Human beings desire power and need it to survive. Human power is a universal energy that can be used in either life-giving or deadly ways. I consider human power to be a "mixed power"—one that can go in multiple directions. We need power to stand up, walk, move, talk, eat, and drink. We can use this complex power either to kill, destroy, and harm ourselves and others or to love one another and build just relationships.

Human beings also need power to survive with dignity in a world where the strong often try to rob others of power. We need power to transform the world into what we believe it ought to be. When we experience a lack of power, our imagination creates heroes who can transform the world and fight for good. Most of the heroes presented in the media or video games today are loved by children. Superheroes can transform themselves from ordinary people into mighty beings. They have superpowers for creating good or evil. They fight in battles where only one emerges as the winner.

Children grow up learning from their social environment what power is. They do not need any theory to understand the need or desire for power. It is a strong and cherished human passion. They see how powerful people are often considered the winners and how this frequently results in power over others. In playing games with others, children experience how the winner takes pleasure in being a champion recognized by others; each child wants to be the hero, the powerful one, the winner, and the best. The affirmation of the ego is strongly present in positive and negative ways. Children's experiences reflect experiences in the adult world, in which the desire to win and impose one's will on others is often fed by competition or greed.

I observe how much some children react violently when they lose a game, or someone seeks to diminish or control their power. Some children keep silent or leave the place they were playing, holding within themselves a feeling of inferiority or vengeance. Sometimes they cry and accuse their peers of wrongdoing; they feel like victims. Mothers frequently defend their children, sending the message that evil and abuse of power come from the outside, from others. But children know, maybe by intuition and often better than adults, what goes on within and among them. Children notice their desire for power. They see that if you have power, you can have possessions and dominate others. The winner of a battle may take the best sandwich or the ice cream from someone else. As adults, we believe that they will learn better when they grow up, and frequently do not help them think about their actions.

I am not only observing the world of boys with these examples. Although the worlds of girls and boys differ socially, they are structurally quite similar and interdependent. Patriarchal values stress that women are the property of men and should please men by being obedient, pretty, elegant, and sexy. These patriarchal values influence the world of girls. Thus, girls compete among themselves, seeking to be the most glamorous, the most beautiful, and the most appreciated. They might lie to each other, gossip, or tell false stories to seek power and approval from others. Here, we see how gender stereotypes limit the power and place of girls as well as create experiences of evil among them.

Finally, poverty and the lack of power can also produce in children's lives a distinct deviation of their power. Consider the gangs of children found in Brazil and other countries. Children initiated into these gangs are taught at an early age how to use guns, rob, and kill. Adult drug dealers take advantage of them. These children experience violence and start committing acts of violence as young teenagers. Guilt, responsibility, and care for others are almost entirely absent in these gangs.

In Brazil, most of these kids regard themselves as Christian and express their faith in their own way. They pray for divine protection and wear crosses around their necks, signifying that protection. They believe—and doubt at the same time—that God, the Virgin Mary, or Jesus can help them. They live in a complex world in which they experience evil, carry out evil actions, and express a particular religious faith. Although they want to live and win, they learn from a very young age that life is a kind of daily warfare and that life and death always go together.

The Desire to Possess

Human beings also need the desire to possess in order to protect themselves. To possess is constitutive with being human. We need to possess clothes, food, and shelter to survive. We possess a sense of ourselves as individuals with certain rights as well as normative ideals about relationships among persons, institutions, and nations.

The desire to possess helps explain why some countries and individuals strive to accumulate excessive amounts of wealth and possessions, even when others live in poverty and without adequate food or clean water. The values of contemporary, consumer-oriented cultures and global marketing strategies feed this excessive desire for things. Adults and children alike are influenced by the widespread message that happiness and self-worth depend on how much money or property we possess. Such a message creates the desire to accumulate more money and possessions early on in children's lives.

From a young age, children in consumer-oriented and capitalistic societies, including Brazil, develop the desire to have what propaganda presents to them as good things. They want to have in their homes or on their bodies what marketers offer to them as sources of happiness. By acquiring or purchasing goods, they feel a sense of power, willfulness, and independence. This capitalist, individualist notion of independence is wrongly called "freedom" or even "children's individual rights." This consumer-oriented notion of independence promotes competition and aggressive behavior among children and between children and adults. Capitalism fosters consumerism particularly in this era of sophisticated technologies that bombard young consumers with ever more enticing messages. The consequences of consumerism in today's cyberculture are explosive.

We observe how the present model of consumerism creates violence among children and young adults. The desire to have is sometimes so strong that children rob their friends or their siblings or lie to their parents and teachers to get what they desire. Children can also become objects of desire by others who want to possess them. Consider, here, child sexual abuse perpetuated by adults, who promise rewards to children in exchange for sexual pleasure. Similarly, most young boys are socialized to oppress women and have them as their possessions. Boys and girls reproduce on a small scale what is present in their larger social context, including our global economy. They learn to desire what is proposed as valuable by international corporations that command the global market.

To possess fairly and justly is also a real human need, and children should be taught to share and live in solidarity with others. Therefore, adults have the responsibility to witness this behavior and are invited to live what they are teaching. This is a great challenge in our consumer-oriented societies where economic profits seem more important than human dignity and solidarity. As such, even violent actions against even one child or group of children require greater social and economic intervention to prevent the reproduction of those same acts and to educate our children to be responsible citizens from childhood onward.

The Desire to Be Recognized and Valued

All human beings need and struggle to be recognized. It is a widespread human need to recognize one's self and others and to be recognized and valued by others.[5] Individually, when some people are not valued or recognized, they

---

[5] Paul Ricoeur, *Parcours de la Reconnaissance* (Paris, FR: Editions Stock, 2004); trans. David Pellauer as *The Course of Recognition* (Cambridge, MA: Harvard University Press, 2005).

create distorted forms of self-recognition that diminish the value of others and try to convince themselves and others of their self-constructed truth. They might seek to force this exaggerated form of recognition on others in violent ways, dominating and imposing their will on others. Collectively, we have a long history of many forms of domination: one nation over another, one gender over another, one ethnic group over another, or one religion over another. We also see parents seeking to dominate their children, and more and more, inspired by the propaganda of consumerism and its heroes or celebrities, we see children seeking to dominate their parents. Whether in domestic or public spheres, dominated individuals or groups feel inferior. They are not valued for who they are, and they do not get what they need. They react in different ways and intensities, leading to various levels of conflict that we have seen in the past and still see today.

The desire to be recognized is present from early childhood. Children like showing adults that they can eat by themselves, count to ten, dance, or accomplish other tasks. The recognition they receive from adults helps them feel secure and encourages them to keep learning and developing their other capacities. This need for recognition continues throughout all stages of human development. Receiving recognition from others also helps cultivate self-understanding and the capacity to develop mutual recognition of other individuals and groups amid their differences and similarities. Children thrive when they grow up being valued, recognized, and respected, learning also how to value and respect others.

Unfortunately, we could write a long history about the lack of recognition that children receive, especially in marginalized communities. Some adults who grew up in poverty say that, when they were children, they heard their parents say that they were just another mouth to feed. They were not welcomed by their parents but rather treated as burdens. This cruel situation is still present in different countries where hunger caused by unjust economic development is a major problem. Only a small number of children manage to overcome this lack of recognition in their childhood.

Conversely, children in higher social classes frequently receive recognition but in a distorted form. Parents give their children clothes, candy, and toys but fail to be present for them. Psychologically, giving material things becomes the way of recognizing children's existence. This creates perverted relationships, greed, and a false self-image.

Children know whether they are valued for themselves or for their bodies, their work, or their possessions. When they fall into the trap of human trafficking and prostitution, teenage girls know that others only value them as sex objects. This value is short-lived because the human trafficking market always wants new bodies to feed it. Also, young boys used for physical labor know that they are not valued for themselves or even as much as young girls who work as domestic helpers. In the same way, children from the upper classes often know that their value is only measured by the possessions they are given by their parents and not for themselves. Depression and other forms of emotional diseases are prevalent in children of rich and middle-class families.

Children and their relationships suffer when they are valued too little or in perverted ways. Children who are not recognized and undervalued perceive themselves as inferior to others. They lose a sense of their own self-worth and easily depend on the opinions of others to build self-esteem. Children who are valued in excessive and distorted ways can begin to feel superior to others, leading them to treat others in a harmful and oppressive manner.

Obstacles to Empowering Children

In the face of children's needs and experiences of evil, churches have an obligation to find life-giving ways to support and empower children and their families. Children are socialized into worlds where consumption, greed, and individualism are strongly present. They need to be introduced to a Christian-centered vision of the world that speaks to the evils they experience and that emphasizes values of compassion, justice, and solidarity. Churches need to provide religious education that expands children's understanding of themselves as members of the global community—as interdependent beings called to love themselves and others.

At the same time, churches must expand Christian education to address not only individual suffering and sin but also systemic injustice and structural sin that create suffering for people of all ages. In seeking to address injustice, churches must work with people of diverse worldviews. This entails creating a form of education inspired by a dynamic Christian ethical and intellectual tradition. Such an education presents a rich understanding of what ought to be, provides critical thinking skills across disciplines, and empowers students to seek justice with people of diverse viewpoints. Such an education is also grounding and provides comfort and guidance amid the evils around and within us.

In other words, education seeking to foster mercy and compassion—to create a "heart of flesh"—must attend to individual experience and larger social and economic structures. After all, how can we educate to have mercy in a society where some children are dying by hunger and others by excess consumption? How can we love one another when many children have not had a real experience of being loved? Our answers cannot be limited only to an individual or to an exclusively formal religious perspective but must consider social, economic, political, and cultural structures. We must continually seek to make mutual love and freedom possible in contexts that prioritize consumerism and individualism. If we do not act regionally and globally, then Christian ethics, values, and traditions centered in the value of all lives will only be antiquated stories from the past without any relevance in today's common task of addressing injustice and creating a more humane world.

Sadly, many obstacles not only in society but also in the churches halt the support and empowerment of children toward embracing humane and environmental values. Religious education is often only a repetitive catechism of rote answers without any real challenge that invites children to seek greater meaning and to ask questions based on their own experience. Furthermore, existing models of faith formation both in the church and within Christian families fail to recognize the complex web of evil in which children live and the lack of adequate meaning of the role that Christianity can and should play in children's lives.

The following are my observations of some of the common, yet narrow and even oppressive, notions of religion and approaches to religious education that adults still impose on children. These notions not only fail to bring healing but often drive children away from the church and Christian tradition. Since we are dealing with complex social and cultural elements, some common trends across Brazil as well as challenges facing poor and middle-class people have been highlighted.

Children and the Role of Religion

What I observe from my limited view of the poor and lower classes in Brazil is that although some parents still pray with their children, they use religion primarily to regulate the behavior of children and young people. Parents hope that what they cannot do at home or teachers cannot do at school, religion and the church can do. From their perspective, religion passed down by the church with its powerful authority is linked directly to orders coming from God. I frequently hear mothers saying, "I always tell my child that if he does this or that, the Heavenly Father or the Blessed Mother will be very sad and can punish him." Sometimes parents speak even more harshly, such as when a child falls or breaks a leg, and parents say that God has punished the child.

Many parents say that the purpose of Sunday school for children or catechism classes for making one's First Communion in the Roman Catholic Church is to teach children morality, obedience, and the traditional prayers. Mothers and fathers are also happy when their children know stories from the Bible. Parents feel proud, but they rarely ask how biblical stories affect the lives of children or question how adults sometimes use these stories and religious content to coerce children to do what they want. Consequently, for many children, religion becomes something oppressive and boring, and many of them, when they become teenagers, leave the church. They do not like the religious instruction they receive from the church or from their parents and resent religion's oppressive role in their lives.

For many middle-class Brazilians, religious initiation becomes a cultural and social obligation connected more to social status than to leading a spiritual and ethical life. Parents feel obliged to baptize their children and host a reception for friends and family or to buy nice clothes for a child's First Communion, especially a beautiful white dress for a daughter. Some young brides and grooms dream of a marriage ceremony with a priest or pastor leading the service and finally declaring, "Now you are wife and husband, God bless you."

But how much of the deeper meaning of these religious ceremonies do young people really understand? How are these families and the church passing down life-giving values and practices to these children? Who can do it, especially when many parishes are controlled by very conservative perspectives or authoritarian leadership, or have scant respect for children as marvelous and complex persons?

Meaning, Dialogue, and Narrow Views of Children

Families and the church both seek to pass on Christian values to children, but in general, they hold outdated models of religious education as well as narrow views of children's capacities and creativity. Whatever the context, program, or setting, most children and young adults do not like Christian education. The language, aims, and teachings are not adjusted to our time or to their questions. They are boring and fail to challenge children or engage their questions and creativity. For instance, even in Bible studies, children are often not given a chance to engage the texts or ask questions. Thus, the texts have little meaning or value to them, and the children come away bored and forget what they have learned.

Generally, dialogue and mutual exchange between children and adults are not large parts of religious education programs or relationships in daily life. Frequently, adults do not explain the meaning or relevance of Christian beliefs and practices. They do not even clearly explain their own rules or orders. Adults do not open a dialogue that allows children to understand adult rules, what or why they are being taught, or why they are forbidden from doing something or obliged to do something else.

When parents or faith leaders do not take the time to explain their values or listen to children's own questions and ideas, they fail to recognize that children are creative and perceptive agents who are continually asking questions and seeking to find meaning in their world. Certainly, the child's world in some sense is conditioned by the adult world, yet children also have their own inner creativity that must be respected.

The process of socialization and moral formation is always the result of a complex process of interaction. Social and family environments shape children, and in turn, children shape these environments and themselves. Children are not only recipients of adult propositions; they are also creators, co-creators, and re-creators of their and our worlds.

Childhood is a short, basic, and intense time of human life in which meaning-making takes place in a host of ways, including play. Childhood is a period in which a person begins the process of becoming conscious of his or her own values and relationships with others. It is when sweet and bitter memories begin to build up and different seeds are planted. Childhood is when we begin to learn important thoughts and feelings about life amid play, jokes, and toys as well as troubling and even tragic situations. All these aspects mold our subjectivity and form our history as human beings.

Technology, Moral Formation, and Children's Creative Capacities

The lack of engagement with young people, a disrespect for their capacities, and outdated approaches to religious education are clear when we observe common responses of parents and church leaders to one of the major spaces in which children engage: the virtual world. Churches do not know how to deal with this attractive world where moral formation also takes place. Whether rich or poor, children are surrounded by computers, smartphones, and social media. These days, almost no one lives without a cell phone, and children are constantly on their devices either alone or with friends. Children are influenced by messages coming to them through technology and are actively interacting with it through video games, chats, and other online programs. A child's virtual world is filled with friends, enemies, reconciliation, wars, lovers, robbers, and images of good and bad. In this world, children are exposed to frameworks of good and evil, and they create their own heroes and villains. The virtual world is also central for playing with others, especially today, when so many children live in big cities with no possibility to play safely in the streets with friends or to run with others in a park after school.

The virtual world is a major factor in the formation of children's worldviews, yet parents and church leaders often fear or seek to control this virtual world without really understanding children's creativity or what they are experiencing online. We adults certainly recognize that children are using computers and other technologies sometimes better than we are. However, we are frequently afraid of this virtual world—a world mainly created by adults and offered to children. Thus, we seek to control children's online activities: how many hours they can play, what they can play, who they can play with, and so on. However, while adults are the creators of this world, we have no real control over it. Children are savvier and nimbler with technology than many adults, and thus our efforts to control children's use are often fruitless and make us feel even more inadequate.

When adults limit technology or seek to protect children from it without engaging or understanding them, children can experience this control as repressive. They feel their creativity, connection to others, and their own sense of discovery threatened. They resent the authority of adults and the repression of their own creative desires. They identify these gestures of control and protection as a lack of respect. This sense of adult repression undermines child-adult relationships.

While our fears are understandable because of the many violent pitfalls of the internet, we must be aware of our behavior. Instead of simply seeking to control children's use of technology, we should be opening more meaningful conversations with them to appreciate technology and the dangers as well as benefits of the virtual world. New technologies are not in themselves good or bad, but they are also not neutral. Thus, we are invited to respond to and use them in ways that align with our values. The new technology produced in our global culture has conditioned us all—adults and children alike—in multiple spheres of life. I say "conditioned" and not "determined," because we can always respond to our own creation and help children to do the same for their diverse interactions with technology.

We also need to respect children by understanding what they experience and enjoy through the virtual world. By doing so, we discover that it is not so different from what children experienced prior to the internet. Although I grew up long before social media and computers, I realize that elements of a child's experience in the virtual world parallel common experiences of childhood, including my own. Children of every generation seek to escape the world of adults and create their own adventures and worlds. In these worlds, good and evil are imaginatively at play. This is all part of self-discovery and meaning-making.

Insights from Alice in Wonderland

I came to respect and appreciate children's creativity and fascination with the virtual world when I reflected on my own previrtual childhood and the popular story *Alice's Adventures in Wonderland*.[6] This story helped me remember aspects of children's worlds and socialization that I had forgotten in my old

---

[6] Lewis Carroll, *Alice's Adventures in Wonderland*, illustrated by Sir John Tenniel (London: Macmillan, 1865).

age. Through this story, I discovered the same curiosity, love of adventure, and creation of new worlds that I saw in my own childhood and that we see in children's engagement with computers today. I highlight only some aspects of this popular story and what it teaches us about children and childhood. My reflections are not a literary analysis but rather a source for understanding the many worlds of children, their creative capacities, and their engagement with today's virtual world. My reflections on this story also invite us to think about other stories.

At the beginning of the story, Alice is bored. She is tired of sitting by her sister on the bank, having nothing to do. Once or twice she had peeked into the book that her sister was reading, but it had no pictures or conversations in it. "What was the use of a book," thought Alice, "without pictures or conversations?"[7] Alice is tired of the monotony of her situation without interesting things for her to do. She is in an adult world against her own wishes. She wants something more passionate and more moving.

She enters her own imaginary world filled with creativity, colorful images, and funny situations. Suddenly, "a white rabbit with pink eyes ran close by her." And it was not an ordinary rabbit but one with a watch it took out of its waistcoat pocket. "Alice started to her feet. She ran across the field after it and was just in time to see it pop down a large rabbit hole under the hedge." She goes down the rabbit hole into a new world far from adult control. She is curious and not afraid to explore this imaginary world. In this world, she can speak to animals and become friends with them. The rabbit's world has interesting messages and rules, and she can think for herself and about what she will do in this or that moment. She is far from an adult world, having new adventures and learning new lessons.

The adult world asks Alice: Why do you not stay on the bank with your sister? Why are you not reading a book as your sister does? The world of Alice's sister is the adult world, which is boring to children and, in a sense, painful, because it is ordained by a limited logic. Through their creativity and imagination, children can become small, enter a rabbit's house, talk with it, understand what it is saying, and use rabbit gloves.

Just like Alice, children of all eras and contexts love being in imaginary worlds seeking new experiences and adventures. For children today, computers have become a space where they can gather and discover a world of adventure. Computers have become their own "adventures in wonderland." Children are not afraid to explore new possibilities in their computers, open new links, find a rabbit hole, and begin a conversation with another creature. Children can go on

---

[7] Lewis Carroll, *Alice's Adventures in Wonderland*, ed. Robert Sabuda (New York: Little Simon, 2003), 1.

a colossal journey in a video game and be back in no time to drink orange juice together with adults. Their imaginary world is colorful, surprising, and empowering, whereas the adult world is often serious, repetitive, and authoritarian.

For children today, a primary culture that shapes children is cyberculture. We no longer live in an agrarian and precomputer age, and thus children's values and norms are shaped not only by their families, neighborhoods, and faith communities, but also by cyberspace and technology. Their engagement with and discoveries of good and evil now have new references. Computers shape their knowledge of themselves and others, notions of good and evil, and the contemporary world.

From a psychological and ethical perspective, elements of cyberculture are different and yet more or less the same as elements of moral formation in the past. If you ask older adults what they did as children, many might remember that they liked creating imaginary worlds with friends or alone. They also experimented with things that adults forbade or that adults did not like. We all entered risky situations and sought adventures as children. Some of us explored our bodies with other children, smoked a cigarette, tasted some whiskey, or robbed apples in a garden. All these actions were ways that we investigated good and evil to understand how much they are linked and interdependent. When adults took time to be there for us and showed us love and respect, we sometimes shared our adventures and imaginary worlds, and we had conversations with them about good and bad experiences in our lives or around us.

Strategies for Faith Formation and Social Transformation

In light of our reflections on children's experiences of evil and obstacles to religious formation today, how can we address the suffering and injustices they face? How can we more effectively nurture faith and pass on to children life-giving Christian teachings and values? How can we empower children to be both recipients and cultivators of such values, preparing them to face the evil of their time and to work with others to create a better world?

Building on a deeper understanding of the evils that children experience, here are a few strategies for strengthening approaches to religious formation and social transformation. Conscious of the limits of my present experience, they are offered with my strong belief in the right of children to their childhood, which means the right to taste the world, play in it, and learn from it as new inhabitants of this wonderful world. They have the right to receive the means with which to approach the tree of knowledge from their simple curiosity about all things. From this perspective, religious knowledges must be part of this world in a process of continuous discovery.

Let's be clear that changing some content in our religious education materials or building online platforms is a beginning, but not enough. A robust strategy for faith formation involves creating meaningful child-adult relationships, addressing unjust economic and social realities, and inviting and empowering children to help transform our world. The following strategies provide only a preliminary path, believing that we can all discover additional strategies in our contexts to help all children thrive.

Respecting and Acknowledging Children's Experiences of Evil

At the most basic level, we must acknowledge the suffering that children experience and respect them as human beings. As we have noted, children are caught up in a network of evil, and they suffer in often unacknowledged ways. We must also remember that children are complete and complex human beings with needs, wants, and longings, as well as vulnerabilities, agency, and creativity. Acknowledging children's suffering and full humanity can profoundly strengthen child-adult relationships, our approaches to faith formation, and our efforts to address injustice.

We must also respect children and strengthen religious formation by seeking to live out the Christian values that we are teaching our children. We pass on values by demonstrating them by our practice in our daily lives. We cannot ask children to respect others if we do not respect them. We cannot ask children to be kind to others if they do not see kindness in their own family or church. We cannot teach human rights with authority if every day we disregard children's rights.

Discussing the Bible in Solidarity with Children

If we respect children as persons, then our approach to studying the Bible will change from adults teaching children biblical stories in a top-down manner to children and adults discussing and reading the texts historically and in mutual solidarity.[8] Such an approach acknowledges the complexity of human life as well as the biblical texts. Given our human condition and the power of the biblical witness, we cannot create an effective method for religious formation without exploring how the Bible speaks to our situation and to the complex web of life—full of violence, lies, and disasters, as well as acts of compassion, love, and justice. This complex and continuous movement of life must be stressed in religious education and our reading of the Bible. We can no longer tell a simple

---

[8] Ivone Gebara, *O Que é Cristianismo* (São Paulo: Brasiliense, 2008), and Ivone Gebara, *La Trama de la Vida—Algunos Hilos Cristianos, Filosóficos y Feministas* (Montevideo: Doble Clic, 2011).

story that starts with a good creation, moves in the middle to sin, and ends with the joy of salvation, as we have done in traditional Christian education of children and adults. This simple story of sin and salvation does not capture the complexity of being human in the world. Given the various sources of sin and evil as well as goodness and justice, we must face the complexity of life and bring it to bear on our reading of the Bible.

We must also have lively exchanges about biblical stories with young and old. Biblical stories are complex, and they invite our mutual conversation and reflection on our own lived experience. Once we honor children's own challenges and experiences of evil as well as their capacities to think and imagine, we can more effectively engage them, listen to their questions and insights, and learn from them.

Telling Our Stories

We can also connect more deeply with children and one another in our discussions of the Bible and Christian teachings if we tell stories from our own lives and the lives of those who have worked for justice and sought to follow Jesus's model of compassion. We can make a practice of inviting everyone, young and old, at home and in church, to tell new stories stirred by the gospel. Such stories help make the teaching and example of Jesus real to young people. The gospel read in our times is also the gospel with narratives for our times. This approach creates meaningful connections among one another and between the past and the present.

We can also expand our discussions of the significance of the biblical texts and strengthening educational materials generally by listening to the stories, concerns, and experiences of children and young people, including what they witness and experience in the virtual world. Children make sense of new ideas by drawing analogies to their own experience and to stories they encounter through movies, video games, and social media. We can create new and engaging materials for children only by listening carefully to their stories, questions, ideas, and experiences.

Appreciating Stories of Solidarity from Diverse Worldviews

Reading the gospel in our time also means that we need to listen to and tell stories about people from diverse Christian denominations, as well as from different religious traditions and worldviews that are promoting love and justice. For many centuries, Christians have primarily valued models of compassion and justice from the Bible or their own denominations. It is time for Christians to recognize people from diverse faith traditions and worldviews who are making a positive difference locally and globally. They are diverse icons for a better world.

They are Christians, people of all faiths or no religious faith, and people from diverse countries, cultures, and generations. They are addressing multiple violations of human rights and dignity and inspiring movements for peace, climate justice, gender equality, racial equality, interreligious cooperation, and justice for the poor and marginalized. Christians need to recognize those who are seeking love and justice and leading such movements as the faces of the mysterious God in today's world.

By telling such stories in our homes, Sunday schools, and other religious education classes, Christians can help children and adults learn from and be in solidarity with people from diverse backgrounds who are seeking justice in our neighborhoods or around the world. Solidarity with people from diverse worldviews is vital in our world today, especially when we are so deeply connected to one another economically, socially, politically, environmentally, and virtually. We need to help children understand that there are justice-seeking people in their own milieu with whom they can be in solidarity. Children need to know about others who do not scorn people based on their economic status, skin color, nationality, or religious tradition. We need to tell children stories from our time as well as from the past about those who have sought to build just relationships and societies. Telling such stories helps to build hope and a new generation of young people who seek to work in solidarity with others. Given the many challenges we face in our contexts and around the globe, and given the foundational values of Christianity, telling such stories of compassion and justice should be part of the moral and spiritual formation of Christians today.

Stories of people from diverse worldviews who are seeking to promote compassion and justice should influence not only approaches to religious education and formation but also Christian thought and practice. The church as a community needs a new theological paradigm that helps us discover the presence of love and justice in diverse cultures, religions, historical periods, and geographical regions of the world. Opening ourselves to plural manifestations of love and justice helps Christians uncover multifaceted dimensions of God, ourselves, and the world and empowers action. What I am proposing is not easy, especially when many religious leaders and communities are dominated by fear of losing their privileges and power. However, each of us—individually and in our circles of responsibility—can spark small revolutions for building a better future for our children and grandchildren.

Intergenerational Invitation to Building a Just Society

Inviting children to work in solidarity with other children and adults to help build a just society is a concrete part of educating children in the way of Jesus. Jesus taught and lived out the message of treating others fairly, compassionately, and justly, and he invited people to care for one another so that all might flourish. Adults and children are all invited to participate in building together a fair and just society in a collective, responsible way. Central to Jesus's message and the Christian life is the ongoing cultivation of just and life-giving relationships and social structures. Some children might ask us why, if Jesus was a good man, some people crucified him, and we must be honest with them. Let us reveal what they know by intuition: that in human history, sometimes wonderful people are killed.

As feminists and liberation theologians have expressed in various ways, Jesus did not just talk. He acted with love, justice, and solidarity. Good preaching and teaching come from the authority of love in us, which is more than simply discourse. It is acting justly and showing compassion. Such actions reflect aspects of the face of the mysterious God. No one has seen God, yet those who love their brothers and sisters experience a glimpse of the mysterious energy called God.

Children live in a time very different from the childhoods of adults, but we can help one another investigate the world, learn from it, and make a difference. For example, children can help us explore urgent questions that we all must ask regarding the ability for people and our planet to thrive. In many ways, children and young people today are leading the way in helping us to address a host of questions, such as: How should we be addressing climate change? How can we work together to address systemic racism? How can cyber technologies help individuals and communities thrive? How are the practices of global corporations affecting the lives of poor people and our planet? Such questions are most essential to the future well-being of children. We must therefore explore these questions and others with children and young people to find ways to collectively build shared values and effective initiatives for protecting one another and the planet. Furthermore, we must honor and build on the creativity, confidence, and courage young people display in their contributions to the common good.

Conclusion: Challenges and Hopes

Building on a fundamental respect for children and a clearer understanding of their experiences of evil, in these and many other ways, churches and families can strengthen faith formation and transform society. Of course, many Christians in my country and around the world experience a host of obstacles, even in the church, to supporting children, nurturing their faith, and bringing about justice and solidarity in our world. Although children's needs are real, we know how hard it is to transform not only society but also religious institutions, religious traditions, and the content and approach to religious education. Many churches, regardless of denomination or history, acknowledge that change can be slow, and even the most transparent and well-intended ecclesial structures of power cannot eliminate abuses.

Many forms of liberation theology seek to address systems of injustice in church and society, and we can build on their insights to support and empower children. These theologies have exposed destructive hierarchies based on race, gender, and socioeconomic status, and they point us to new and more inclusive notions of power that seek to help all people and our planet thrive. Now, building on and inspired by their work, the church can move forward globally in all areas of theology and practice to attend to and learn from one of the largest marginalized groups on the planet: children. We can find ways both to create meaningful and engaging approaches to religious education and to work with children and adults from diverse backgrounds and worldviews to address the social, economic, and age-biased hierarchies and injustices that affect children.

Churches are not alone in this work, and they cannot work alone. Indeed, the church is called to work in solidarity with people from diverse worldviews to address individual and systemic injustices and to support and empower children. Evils and injustices arise from many sources, and we can and must work locally and globally to create just societies, cultivate the moral lives of children, and educate new generations for compassion and solidarity. This means working not only with religious leaders and communities but also those engaged in a host of fields: the arts, humanities, sciences, and technology.

Such hopes are realistic. They do not reflect some sort of search for a romantic, happy ending in human history and the complete alleviation of children's suffering. By respecting children as human beings and becoming more aware of the evils they face and their own creative capacities, we can all strengthen our commitment to children and develop new approaches in our diverse contexts to helping children thrive, cultivating their moral sensibilities, and empowering them to help both people and our planet to flourish.[9]

---

[9] With thanks to John Collier for translating this chapter from Portuguese to English and to Marcia J. Bunge, Megan Eide, and Judith Ress for their editorial assistance.

5

The God-Child Paradigm and Paradoxes of the Incarnation

Wanda Deifelt

One of the central themes in Christian theology is the incarnation. This theme explores the significance of Jesus Christ's embodiment as a human being and the meaning of the claim that "the Word became flesh" (John 1:14). Theologians over the centuries have offered various interpretations of the relationship between Jesus's humanity and divinity, often termed the "God-man" or "God-human" relationship. The incarnation also raises important questions about our own humanity and God's relationship to humanity and the world. It places a question mark on God's omnipotence, challenging human logic and revealing God's intimate relation to the world. As German liberation theologian Dorothee Sölle (1929–2003) once stated, God came into our lives to become discoverable, making visible and disclosing that which is invisible.[1]

Although the incarnation has been a central topic for centuries, the focus of theological reflection has primarily been on God assuming a human nature (becoming the "God-man"), but less attention has been given to God's embodiment as a child. Even if the church recognizes that Jesus was an infant and celebrates the Christmas story, the significance of this divine incarnation has often been ignored or misrepresented. In modern times, for instance, the sweet baby Jesus has been domesticated to produce a theology of endearment and consumerism. This not only shortchanges incarnation but misses the mark in terms of God's radical message about the reign of God and the role of the most vulnerable in its proclamation.

Certainly, many theologians have highlighted God's embodiment as a human being, even as an infant, and several theologians have built on the incarnation to illustrate the relational aspect of the Divine, particularly God's

---

[1] Dorothee Sölle, *Creative Disobedience*, trans. Lawrence W. Denef (Cleveland: Pilgrim Press, 1995), 66.

immanence. For example, Martin Luther wrote and preached about the significance of Jesus's birth and what it tells us about God's grace in the midst of human tribulations.[2] Contemporary theologians such as John Cobb (b. 1925) have reminded us that the incarnation is an affirmation of the Divine in Jesus and the Divine in us.[3] Some have revisited the Chalcedonian formula of 451 (Jesus Christ as truly God and truly human) through a Trinitarian lens, drawing from the mutuality in the Trinity to emphasize the self-disclosure and approachability of God in human form.[4] Liberation and feminist theologians, such as Kristin Johnston Largen and Vítor Westhelle, have also reflected on the incarnation and Jesus's birth to address the paradoxes of God's vulnerability and power as well as what God's embodiment says about our own embodiment and treatment of the most vulnerable among us.[5]

Building on such insights, this chapter aims to deepen theological reflection on the incarnation by focusing directly on Jesus's incarnation as a child—a particular focus that I term the "God-child" paradigm. Various authors have paved the way for attention to children in theological thought, and the ideas presented in this chapter are in continuity with their work.[6] I address the incarnation and its significance for Christian theology by focusing on the God-child paradigm and exploring the consequences of this shift. Drawing attention to God entering the world as a child both sharpens our understanding of the incarnation and expands the horizon of the role of children in theology. This chapter

---

[2] Martin Luther, *Luther's Works: The Sermon on the Mount and the Magnificat*, vol. 21, ed. Jaroslav Jan Pelikan, Hilton C. Oswald, and Helmut T. Lehmann (St. Louis: Concordia Publishing House, 1999), 299.

[3] John Cobb, "Does It Make Sense to Talk about God?" in *Essentials of Christian Theology*, ed. William C. Placher (Louisville, KY: Westminster John Knox Press, 2003), 75.

[4] See Nancy E. Bedford, "Speak, 'Friend,' and Enter: Friendship and Theological Method," in *God's Life in Trinity*, ed. Miroslav Volf and Michael Welker (Minneapolis: Fortress Press, 2006), 40, and Cynthia L. Rigby, "Scandalous Presence: Incarnation and Trinity," in *Feminist and Womanist Essays in Reformed Dogmatics*, ed. Amy Plantinga Paw and Serene Jones (Louisville, KY: Westminster John Knox Press, 2006), 62.

[5] Kristin Johnston Largen, *Baby Krishna, Infant Christ: A Comparative Theology of Salvation* (Maryknoll, NY: Orbis Books, 2011), represents a landmark for the intentionality in addressing Jesus's infancy as well as its comparative approach. See also Vítor Westhelle, *The Scandalous God: The Use and Abuse of the Cross* (Minneapolis: Fortress Press, 2006).

[6] Bonnie Miller-McLemore is quoted throughout this chapter, but I want to call attention to the contribution by Marcia J. Bunge that serves as a "state of the art" on children and theology: Marcia J. Bunge, "Beyond Children as Agents or Victims: Reexamining Children's Paradoxical Strengths and Vulnerabilities with Resources from Christian Theologies of Childhood and Child Theologies," in *The Given Child: The Religion's Contribution to Children's Citizenship*, ed. Trygve Wyller and Usha S. Nayar (Göttingen: Vanderhoeck and Ruprecht, 2007), 27–50.

illustrates this point by highlighting three paradoxes inherent in the God-child paradigm: divine vulnerability in light of God's power, human vulnerability and our capacity to be agents of transformation, and finally, the paradoxical reality that all—whether adult or infant—are children of God.

Divine Vulnerability in Light of God's Power

The God-child paradigm is soaked in tension and paradox because it juxtaposes apparently contradictory elements: divine and human, adult and child, immanent and transcendent. The biblical narrative of Matthew 1:18–25, introducing Jesus's genealogy and the events preceding his birth, brings further theological reflection to this paradigm. It explains one of the most puzzling, invigorating, and awe-inspiring faith statements: that the Word became flesh and dwelt among us (John 1:14). The fact that God becomes flesh, fully assuming a child's body, reveals a God who rejoices and suffers with the whole creation, embodying both power and weakness to redefine the human-God relationship. The incarnation of God as an infant strengthens this statement, for a child is a fragile creature, and such vulnerability clashes with the view of an omnipotent God.

The Gospel of Matthew tells us that Joseph and Mary were engaged (practically married). According to the Jewish tradition, this was a two-step process:[7] one was the legal procedure; the other was the actual living together. The first part of the ceremony had been performed but, apparently, not the second. When Mary is found to be pregnant, Joseph decides to divorce her quietly, for the child is not his. In Matthew 1:19, Joseph is described as a just man, unwilling to put Mary to shame. We do not know if he was just because he wanted to divorce her quietly (if he did not want to shame her) or because he did not follow the legal procedures.[8] He is a respectable Jewish citizen and highly regarded by his community. But he is also a man and, as such, a beneficiary of a cultural and social system that privileges males. In line with Joseph's ancestors listed in the genealogy, he too could play the role of the omnipotent patriarch.

Conversely, the text does not refer to Mary as being just, although Luke, in the Magnificat, describes her prophetic voice. Little is said about Mary's agency as a young pregnant girl or about her motivation for pursuing this endeavor. Being already betrothed, Mary's pregnancy was a concrete sign of adultery, a crime punishable by stoning. Divorcing Mary in public was not only a shame,

---

[7] Jane Schaberg, *The Illegitimacy of Jesus: A Feminist Theological Interpretation of the Infancy Narratives* (San Francisco: Harper and Row, 1987), 20–77.

[8] Schaberg, *Illegitimacy of Jesus*, 55–62.

but a threat. In fact, Mary could have been stoned to death and Jesus would never have been born!

Seeing Mary as a potentially adulterous woman might seem shocking. However, a closer look at the other women in Jesus's genealogy shows that his lineage is far from pristine. Tamar (Matt 1:3) is a woman best remembered for her cleverness in handling a patriarchal system. She dressed up as a prostitute and became pregnant by having sexual intercourse with her father-in-law, Judah. Under the accusation of adultery, she was able to produce her father-in-law's staff and ring, proving that he was the father, thus assuring her survival through the law of levirate (cf. Gen 38).

Another woman of questionable reputation in the genealogy of Jesus is Rahab (Matt 1:5). A prostitute, Rahab is described in the book of Joshua as a woman who played an instrumental role assisting the Israelites in capturing the city of Jericho on their way to the promised land. Ruth is also mentioned (cf. Matt 1:5). She is a foreigner, remembered for her faithfulness and love toward her mother-in-law, Naomi. With her help and strategy, Ruth developed skills that ensured their survival and the birth of children. Next is the wife of Uriah (cf. Matt 1:6), better known by her name Bathsheba. This is a sordid story of how David arranged for Uriah to be killed in battle so that he could keep his wife, having previously seduced and impregnated her. The child dies, but eventually Bathsheba gives birth to another one, Solomon, who becomes a link in the genealogy of Jesus.

Matthew's genealogy closes with startling information: the Messiah had to be born from the house of David. This lineage, however, is given through Joseph, not Mary. If Jesus is not the biological son of Joseph, how can he be a descendent of David? The answer is given by divine intervention. Because Joseph plays an important role (among other things due to his lineage), the narrative has a twist: an angel appears to Joseph in a dream, telling him to take Mary. That which is conceived in her is of the Holy Spirit. She will bear a son, and Joseph is to name him Jesus, for he will save the people from their sins. By naming the child, Joseph officially assumes his responsibility as a father. By becoming Jesus's father, Joseph assures the messianic lineage, removes the danger of Mary's ill reputation, casts away the threat of her being stoned, and assures that Jesus will be born safely.

All these life stories constitute the history of Jesus's family tree. Through so many twists and turns, it is clear how fragile, dependent, and seemingly insignificant human beings are in the overall scheme of great events. The biblical narratives about these women and their children are not included accidentally. They make explicit how messy and cruel human affairs can often be. Each person in Jesus's genealogy is there because God acts in strange and mysterious ways, and we do not always understand how human meddling can convey anything about the Divine or how God can mend human wrongdoings. Yet, it is precisely this wonderment that also opens us to the God-child paradigm. It destroys the wisdom of the wise and frustrates the intelligence of the intelligent. Sometimes, only a child's sense of awe can capture this mystery and surprise.

Martin Luther, commenting on the first chapter of Matthew and Jesus's heritage, also noticed the women of questionable reputation listed in the genealogy. He concluded that this was just another way for God to show proximity to us. God could have chosen to be born in a palace, and yet God chose a humble stable. God could have chosen any woman to give birth to the savior, and yet God chose a young woman called Mary. God could have chosen somebody rich and powerful, and yet God delighted in a maid. In his commentary on the Magnificat, Luther stressed Mary's *humilitas* (humbleness) and identified Mary as a role model for all Christians because of her humility. The women in Jesus's genealogy are there to show that God did not choose perfection but real life and real people. Jesus's family is just like yours and mine.[9] It reveals the fragile, messy aspects of human history.

The God-child paradigm temporarily upends social structures and expectations. British cultural anthropologist Victor Turner (1920–1983) explains that, in general, social structures are conditioned by a hierarchical dichotomy that separates sacred and profane, ascribing value to human beings according to their role and function. But there are moments in which these structures are temporarily suspended to render such differences void.[10] God's incarnation as a child topples the hierarchy of social structure, because through it, God subverts all structures of powers as we know them: God is born through a woman, in a stable, among barn animals, in poverty, and as a child. The incarnation, then, is a complete reversal of power, as sung in the Magnificat:

> When the holy virgin experienced what great things God was working in her despite her insignificance, lowliness, poverty, and inferiority, the Holy Spirit taught her this deep insight and wisdom, that God is the kind of Lord who does nothing but exalt those of low degree and put down the mighty from their thrones, in short, break what is whole and make whole what is broken.[11]

---

[9] Susan C. Karant-Nunn and Merry E. Wiesner-Hanks, *Luther on Women: A Sourcebook* (Cambridge: Cambridge University Press, 2003).

[10] Victor Witter Turner, *O Processo Ritual: Estrutura e Anti-Estrutura* (Petrópolis, Brazil: Vozes, 1974). Turner analyzes rituals, religious festivals, and the symbolism of space. His work on liminality (to be "betwixt and between") has been used by theologians to address ambiguity and the role of the *communitas*.

[11] Luther, *Luther's Works*, 299.

Paradox is present even before Jesus's birth. The God-child paradigm suspends the idea of the almighty God when God's very destiny is hinged on human action. Mary's fate, her reputation, the danger of being stoned to death, and the concrete peril that this pregnancy might never come to fruition depend on a man, Joseph, following a dream. The biblical text reminds us that the dangers Jesus encountered were present even before his birth. They do not begin with Herod's murder of other infants or with Jesus's adult ministry. Rather, Jesus is a vulnerable God-child who is at risk from the very beginning of his incarnation.

While the incarnation teaches us that, in Jesus Christ, God reconciles justice and mercy, holiness and love, the fact that God comes to us as a frail human being escapes our understanding. As German Reformed theologian Jürgen Moltmann (b. 1926) notes, in the story of Jesus there is an "irreducible historical contingency which cannot be reconstructed by theological systems."[12] God's freedom within the polarity of human need and divine redemption from that need present something new and unique: God comes to us as a child, moving us to see the world through the eyes of children and taking a risk by leaving matters in their hands.

By coming to us a child, God prepares earth like a cradle. Creation is re-signified, for it is now not only the result of God's hardworking hands (cf. Gen 2) and organizational skills (cf. Gen 1), but creation is also the very place that God will inhabit. As the place that sustains human beings and all God's creatures, it is also the place where God will be embraced and supported. God comes to us and for us as a child in beauty, purity, and love, but this God-child is also helpless and already threatened even before coming into this world. These insights into creation and God's vulnerability connect us closer to God and the children we know, whether our own offspring, the children in our neighborhood, the children in a distant country, or the child within us.

Through the God-child paradigm, the Divine becomes the most immanent, down-to-earth, quotidian, and embodied faith experience that we, as human beings, can have. Children keep us grounded precisely because they ignite in us what also keeps us human: caring for and protecting those who are in need and being receptive to the contagious joy in life. By becoming a child, God changed the power dynamics and suspended social hierarchies. God's incarnation draws on human capacity to depend on others, to trust one's dreams, and to rely on the cooperative efforts that make life possible.[13] This is not merely survival but

---

[12] Jürgen Moltmann, *Theology of Play*, trans. Reinhard Ulrich (New York: Harper and Row, 1971), 25.

[13] Luiz Carlos Susin, "Proximidade na Marginalidade: Uma Interpretação do Bom Samaritano," in *Pastoral de DST/AIDS, Igreja e AIDS: Presença e Resposta* (Porto Alegre: CNBB, 2004), 64–81.

superlative life, with quality and abundance, which draws from a dialogical and more humble approach to human existence.

Human Vulnerabilities and Capacities

The incarnation also reminds us of paradoxes regarding the human condition. On the one hand, we possess certain powers and capacities. We can care for ourselves and others, living in mutuality and fruitful relationships. On the other hand, we are also limited, riddled with contradictions, and ailing with pain and loss. Our basic needs are not consistently met, and our desires for meaningful lives and relationships can be hampered by fear, anxiety, and loneliness.

The irony is that, due to our human condition, we attempt to overcome our ambiguous situation by either overcompensating and stressing our capacity for self-sufficiency and independence, sinking into despair and dwelling in self-pity, or becoming apathetic. Security is one of the basic human instincts, but we strive for and emphasize self-reliability instead of interdependence. Acknowledging weakness is bitter. It seems sweeter to inflate human expectations with emotional, sometimes religious, yet always artificial scaffoldings that give us false illusions about who we are.

Although vulnerability in itself is not a virtue, it is a fundamental reality of our human existence and must be re-signified through the lens of faith. In fact, faith, hope, and love refashion human weakness and vulnerability precisely in the light of our tendency to affirm human knowledge, power, and pride. Our hubris is replaced by vulnerability not to render us powerless, but to redefine and reshape us in light of Christ's message of incarnation.

Vulnerability and our capacities to address our needs and seek security are intertwined. However, either experiencing excessive vulnerability or seeking excessive security for one's self alone is problematic. From a religious perspective, overemphasizing false or self-centered security can lead to a theology of prosperity, justification by works, or a spirituality that denies God as ultimate. To overstress one's own security is to deny our dependence on God and the fact that, as human beings, we are bound to a finite reality. In other words, we see a dual danger for theology. On the one hand, a theology that solely stresses one's own security does not need to rely on God's grace, because it is sure of its own merits. On the other hand, a theology that only preaches vulnerability can easily portray its members solely as victims and not as agents of transformation. Stressing vulnerability alone may prevent accountability, responsibility, and active participation. Therefore, interpreting the God-child paradigm as an option for vulnerability does not mean enforcing passivity or resignation. Similarly, recognizing the need for security does not mean being complicit with power structures. How can our vulnerability and need for security along with our capacities and powers to address vulnerabilities be maintained in such creative tension?

Christ's cross and resurrection offer a compelling message. Despite the trials and tribulations that can lead to despair, God's own option for vulnerability can comfort and encourage us. As German American theologian Paul Tillich (1886–1965) aptly stated, "An act in which courage accepts risk belongs to the dynamics of faith."[14] Every existential truth carries an element of insecurity that needs to be acknowledged. As doubt is experienced, faith will accept this insecurity and view it as an act of courage. Faith, then, encompasses both doubt and courage.[15] Doubt allows us to continually pose questions, as children do who have curiosity and openness to learn. Courage is to act from our core, being true and honest to our human existence and condition.

Vulnerability has been addressed particularly in light of Jesus's incarnation: only a God who becomes flesh can fully experience life and death. Such a message renders void our feeble attempts of false security. Jesus's birth as a child, his ministry in solidarity with the sick and socially outcast, and his death on the cross are at the core of this inversion of power. Liberation theologians such as Jon Sobrino (b. 1938), Leonardo Boff (b. 1938), and Ivone Gebara (b. 1944) have written poignant accounts relating the suffering of Christ to the suffering of the poor and marginalized on the Latin American continent.[16] The blood of the innocent shed by military powers, the blood of the poor shed by economic injustice, and the blood of women and children shed by famine or disease are as painful and concrete as the death of Jesus on the cross. Liberation theologians have long stressed that the role of Christianity is to comfort the afflicted and afflict the comfortable.[17]

In child development, it is known that children deprived of their basic needs grow up less confident and self-assured. A study conducted in northeast Brazil among workers in the sugar cane plantations discovered that many parents locked their children up in small shacks when they left early in the

---

[14] Paul Tillich, *Dynamics of Faith* (New York: Harper, 1957), 23.

[15] Tillich explains this more thoroughly by saying, "If doubt appears, it should not be considered as the negation of faith, but as an element which was always and will always be present in the act of faith. Existential doubt and faith are poles of the same reality, the state of ultimate concern.... Many Christians feel anxiety, guilt and despair about what they call 'loss of faith.' But serious doubt is confirmation of faith. It indicates the seriousness of the concern, its unconditional character" (Tillich, *Dynamics of Faith*, 25).

[16] Jon Sobrino, *Christology at the Crossroads* (Maryknoll, NY: Orbis Books, 1978); Leonardo Boff, *Jesus Christ Liberator* (Maryknoll, NY: Orbis Books, 1978); Ivone Gebara, *Out of the Depths: Women's Experience of Evil and Salvation* (Minneapolis: Fortress Press, 2002).

[17] See Sturla Stalsett, *Discovering Jesus in Our Place: Contextual Christologies in a Globalised World* (Delhi: ISPCK, 2003).

morning to do seasonal work cutting cane. When the children cried because they were hungry, soiled, or simply scared, there was no adult to care for them. They were left under the supervision of a slightly older child (one not old enough to work in the fields), who would usually resort to spanking to keep them quiet. Their need for security—translated in this particular context as having access to food, shelter, clothing, and love—was never satisfied. This creates generation after generation of passive human beings.[18]

The physical and emotional vulnerability of these plantation workers' children reflects their parents' social and economic precariousness. The apparent security of the older sibling (who can spank the younger ones) compensates for the insecurity of being left at home in charge of others. Being made responsible does not empower the older children, since they do not have the appropriate means to feed, clothe, or protect the siblings. Children themselves employ violence to resolve conflicts, since it is the only model they know. It masquerades their sense of inadequacy and gives the strongest ones a feeling of control. They know that they are vulnerable and at the mercy of the larger powers. They repeat, on a smaller scale, the power dynamics between their parents, who are poor and underemployed, and the large landowners and their thugs, corrupt politicians, and century-old oligarchies. The story of these small children is a microcosm that reflects a broader picture.

The socially disadvantaged in the global South can hardly rely on the government to assure welfare. One does not presume that the social, political, or economic system will work for the well-being of those who are outcast or at the margin of society. In general, as we look at our own countries and around the world, the state is often not created for a common good as it ought to be. Rather, political laws and policies aim to develop systems in which goods can be better appropriated by the financial and political oligarchies.[19] This brings us to yet another facet of the paradox: the vulnerability of the secure. The more that vulnerable people fear, the more they search for security. Socially, the paradox between vulnerability and security is thus constructed: the security of some is the vulnerability of many, and the vulnerability of a few—in those aspects that affect power, might, status, and stability—leads to the lack of security for all.[20]

---

[18] Similar accounts are documented in Beatriz Camargo dos Santos et al., *Maus-Tratos e Abuso Sexual Contra Crianças e Adolescentes: Uma Abordagem Multidisciplinar* (São Leopoldo, Brazil: CEDECA, 1997); José Adair Santos da Silva et al., *"Rua que Te Quero Criança." Meninos e Meninas de Rua: Quem São e Por Que?* (São Leopoldo, Brazil: CEDECA, 1997).

[19] Eduardo Galeano, *Open Veins of Latin America: Five Centuries of the Pillage of a Continent* (New York: Monthly Review Press, 1973).

[20] A more comprehensive reflection on the paradox between vulnerability and security

Being aware of our vulnerability makes us humble, and the awareness of the vulnerability of others empowers us to be agents of transformation. This basic Christian principle has influenced scholars such as Paulo Freire, who emphasized consciousness-raising—that is, the capacity of each human being to read reality critically and transform it.[21] We can learn how to rely on each other, to create alternative networks, and to devise ways to ensure that the basic needs of all are met. Focusing on vulnerability when articulating a theology of incarnation based on the God-child paradigm is not done in order to foster passivity or resignation. Rather, it reclaims the core of what makes and keeps us human. Vulnerability is not only our most human characteristic; it is also the ethos of Christian love, as embodied in a theology of incarnation.

God's incarnation as a child is a reminder of our own vulnerability. Because vulnerability is an inescapable human condition, it is also an indisputable condition for acting humanely. Being vulnerable is what connects us to other human beings and returns us to our own humanity. Coming to terms with our own humanity and the humanity of others is a catalyst for ethical capacity and responsibility. Reminded of our own limitations, we are freed to rely on others for acceptance and forgiveness and to undertake collective efforts to overcome shortcomings. As the Church of Norway stated so well, "Vulnerability implies an openness to one's surroundings, to one's fellow human beings, to specific others, which enables people to recognize the pain of others as their own and accept responsibility for alleviating the distress of others."[22]

Recognizing our own vulnerability and weakness allows us to come to terms with and accept the weakness of others. It is an invitation to place ourselves in a community of believers who follow not a God of revenge but a God of love, mercy, and acceptance. With others, then, we create a fellowship that is not based on domination but on the power of vulnerability and self-emptying that Jesus modeled in his birth as a child and in his death on the cross. American biblical scholar and theologian Walter Wink (1935–2012) called this "God's dominion-free order." Wink notes that, as Jesus announced the reign of God, he also announced a new charter of reality:

> Jesus does not condemn ambition or aspiration; he merely changes the values to which they are attached: "Whoever wants to be first must be last of all and servant of all." He does not reject power, but only its use

---

can be found in Wanda Deifelt, "Vulnerability and Security: A Paradox Based on a Theology of Incarnation," *Journal of Lutheran Ethics* 5, no. 6 (June 2005).

[21] Paulo Freire, *Pedagogy of the Oppressed* (New York: Continuum, 1970).

[22] Church of Norway Council on Ecumenical and International Relations, *Vulnerability and Security: Current Challenges in Security Policy from an Ethical and Theological Perspective* (Oslo: Commission on International Affairs, 2002), 13.

to dominate others. He does not reject greatness, but finds it in identification and solidarity with the needy at the bottom of society (Matt 5:3 // Luke 6:20–23). He does not renounce heroism, but expresses it by repudiating the powers of death and by confronting unarmed the entrenched might of the authorities.[23]

Christians use models in Jesus's life and ministry, particularly in the language of the reign of God, to imagine and work toward a just society.

With salvation assured in Christ, Christians are free to redirect their reason and good works toward serving their neighbor. Martin Luther captured the consequences of divine incarnation and justification by faith by expressing his ethics in the paradoxical nature of Christian freedom, which accepts both liberation from bondage and God's invitation for human service. We are our brothers' and sisters' keepers, willingly in faith and begrudgingly in rebellion. "Since the Christian is at once righteous and sinful, his enforced service aids his self-discipline while his voluntary service meets his neighbors' needs."[24]

The imitation of Christ, then, is to be able to bear, accept, and embrace vulnerability as God's own path. God's incarnation as a child transforms us because we see the world and ourselves in a different manner, not self-sufficient but codependent on God's love. Through the God-child paradigm, we engage in a process where we become more and more aware of our own shortcomings and weaknesses, relying on each other to be nurtured and encouraged to grow in community. Incarnation incites us to live in truth and honesty, acting in courage to promote justice. Although amid our struggles we are tempted to abide by this world's model of domination and to give into its demons, God's love and Spirit strengthen us.[25]

All Are Children of God

God comes to us as a child, which changes our perception of the Divine and how we relate to each other. The God-child paradigm paradoxically identifies us all (old and young) as children of God. In his preaching and teaching, his life and resurrection, and his personal ministry and invitation to discipleship, Jesus

---

[23] Walter Wink, *Engaging the Powers: Discernment and Resistance in a World of Domination* (Minneapolis: Fortress, 1992), 111.

[24] Martin Luther, *Luther's Works: The Christian in Society I*, ed. Jaroslav Jan Pelikan, Hilton C. Oswald and Helmut T. Lehmann, vol. 44 (1966; repr. Philadelphia: Fortress Press, 1999), 44n13.

[25] See Walter Wink, *Unmasking the Powers: The Invisible Forces That Determine Human Existence* (Philadelphia: Fortress, 1986).

treated us all as brothers and sisters. What does that say about our role as God's children? What does it say about human agency and growing into maturity? And how does it define our relationship with God?

German Lutheran theologian Rudolf Bultmann (1884–1976) said that we cannot understand God apart from the concrete events of our lives. Because human life resides in space and time, God's encounter with us can only be an event in the particularity of the here and now.[26] It makes sense, then, that God would reveal Godself as a child, in a manner that is familiar to every human being, for we all have a shared experience of being children—albeit the understanding of childhood and what entails a child is itself a social, cultural, political, and economic construct.

It is equally logical, then, that Jesus's way of addressing God as a parent would not only redress the experience of the child but also creatively redefine the notion of parenthood. Swiss Reformed theologian Karl Barth (1886–1968) stated that we can only understand God from the perspective of revelation. Thus, we can only talk about God if God starts the talking. This revelation comes, then, through the incarnation and the message that a God becoming human impinges on us. But it is also revealed, as Barth reminds us, through Jesus's way of addressing God, by employing a parental language and making us all God's children:

> On the basis of the eternal will of God we have to think of *every human being*, even the oddest, most villainous or miserable, as one to whom Jesus Christ is Brother and God is Father; and we have to deal with him on this assumption.... On the basis of the knowledge of the humanity of God no other attitude to any kind of fellow man [sic] is possible. It is identical with the practical acknowledgment of his human rights and his human dignity. To deny it to him would be for us to renounce having Jesus Christ as Brother and God as Father.[27]

It is not surprising that this parental metaphor became so widespread in Christianity. German Lutheran theologian Joachim Jeremias (1900–1979) tracked the usage of "God-the-father" language in the New Testament and over time.[28] Psychologists have explained the preference for the divine father metaphor as a coping mechanism once we realize the limitations or absence

---

[26] Rudolf Bultmann, *New Testament and Mythology and Other Basic Writings* (Philadelphia: Fortress, 1984), 110–119.

[27] Karl Barth, *The Humanity of God* (Louisville, KY: Westminster John Knox Press, 1996), 53.

[28] Joachim Jeremias, *O Pai-Nosso* (São Paulo: Paulinas, 1976).

of our human father. A childlike faith might draw from the notion of God as protector, capable of making sure that nothing will harm us.

However, as feminist theologians have long recognized, the language of God as father can and has been misused. This language can mislead us to remain in a state of blissful ignorance, unwilling to grow and be challenged. The predominance of paternal language (God as father but never as mother, for example) to address God can also be misappropriated to justify patriarchal structures. American feminist philosopher and theologian Mary Daly (1928–2010), for instance, claimed that naming God as father was, in fact, a deification of the father. For Daly and many other feminists, if God is father, then the father becomes god.[29]

Both those who agree and disagree with Daly's work recognize that she and other feminists point to a perennial problem in theology regarding language about God. Once a metaphor becomes domesticated and can be manipulated, it is necessary to deconstruct it. The domestication of God was one of the subjects the prophets addressed. Along with critiquing the system that oppresses widows, orphans, and the poor, the prophets also criticized idolatry as an attempt to make God in our image. Instead of being made in the image of God, we try to make God in ours—and this is idolatry. Any God-talk language runs this risk, but its danger needs to be spelled out. Theologians such as James Cone (1936–2018), Leonardo Boff (b. 1938), Clodovis Boff (b. 1944), and Rosemary Ruether (b. 1936) have helped us address this danger, particularly when the name or image of God is used to justify racism, sexism, class structures, and systemic violence.[30] They remind us that Christianity is often attached to human reason, individualism, and the privatization of religion. A predominantly masculine terminology for the Divine contributes to these problems.

Nevertheless, we can only address the Divine through metaphors. Reducing God to a single metaphor is, indeed, idolatry. But the metaphor of God as parent and humanity as children can be redefined through a paradoxical approach. It is possible to relate to God as parent without reinforcing patriarchal stereotypes and to understand humanity as children without assuming that it implies a debilitating dependence.

Against this background, we reinterpret Jesus's teaching us to pray by addressing God not as a patriarch but as "Abba." The father figure in the

---

[29] Mary Daly, *Beyond God the Father: Toward a Philosophy of Women's Liberation* (Boston: Beacon Press, 1973), 143.

[30] James Cone, *A Black Theology of Liberation* (Maryknoll, NY: Orbis Books, 1986, 1990); Leonardo and Clodovis Boff, *Introducing Liberation Theology* (Maryknoll, NY: Orbis Books, 2005); Rosemary Radford Ruether, *Sexism and God-Talk: Toward a Feminist Theology* (Boston: Beacon Press, 1983).

Greco-Roman tradition was the progenitor, who, as a free citizen, had absolute power over wife, children, slaves, and all his property. Jesus addresses God as "Abba," which could be better translated using the intimate language of "Daddy." This is radically different from the Greco-Roman concept of the *paterfamilias*. In the Jewish context, addressing God in the familiar, intimate manner that "Abba" entails is quite novel. Its novelty is often lost to contemporary followers of Jesus who, accustomed to it, do not perceive the creativity in his communication. By being a child of God himself, Jesus expanded this condition to all believers, even telling us to receive God's reign as children (cf. Mark 10:13–15). In addressing God as a beloved parent, Jesus creatively inaugurated a new way of addressing God that allows proximity, protection, reassurance, and comfort.

American feminist theologian Sallie McFague (b. 1933), in particular, considers the possibilities and limitations of addressing God as father and our self-identification as children.[31] Relying on a grand protector can prevent us from growth. To what extent does God as parent allow human agency? What happens if God does not intervene to save us from harm, even if we beg? McFague poses questions that allow us to see the perils of romanticizing the God-child paradigm by reducing children to a perpetually infantile stage. The answer to this quandary is not to abandon the metaphor that we are all children of God but to rediscover what being a child means. Unless we see the child in the God-child paradigm as a moral agent, capable of responsibility, change, and growth, the paradigm falls flat.

The key to this rests in discipleship as children who sit at Jesus's feet and follow in his footsteps. By addressing God as "Abba" and making us all God's children, Jesus presents a caring God who wants us to extend the same care to others, in responsibility, solidarity, and hospitality. In his interpretation of the Lord's Prayer, English theologian N. T. Wright (b. 1948) agrees that the church that prays the Lord's Prayer thereby claims an eschatological status of the people of God.[32] In addition to the eschatological dimension, to address God as a divine parent has concrete consequences already for the here and now, because it defines us all as God's children. We are compelled to extend compassion to others independent of class, race, sex, or religion. By imitating Christ, we stretch our arms beyond the limits of confessional identity and nationality so that all can be in God's embrace.

---

[31] Sallie McFague, *Metaphorical Theology: Models of God in Religious Language* (Philadelphia: Fortress Press, 1985).

[32] N. T. Wright, "The Lord's Prayer as a Paradigm of Christian Prayer," in *Into God's Presence: Prayer in the New Testament*, ed. R. L. Longenecker (Grand Rapids: Eerdmans, 2001), 132–154.

When Jesus told us to receive the reign of God as children, he unveiled for us a dimension of grace. A key feature of Christian life is the transformation from an alienated, estranged, sinful, and self-sufficient self to a new being. The divine is at work in us, through us, and in others, imparting transformative creativity. As Sölle observed, we are given a capacity to create, set in motion, and experience the joy of new beginnings. As we grow older, this capacity becomes lost or hidden. Because this creativity depends not only on us but also requires transformation, it entails risk. Only through the risk of faith and the courage to be faithful can we find fulfillment. However, this creative spontaneity is threatened by the false notion that fulfillment can be achieved through acquisition, ownership, or consumption. To be named a child of God allows us to drink from the divine creativity and find fulfillment in a manner that subverts the powers of dominance:

> The new and more noble being, the person for whom the fullness of selfhood has become a reality, not only consumes that which falls to his or her lot, but also brings into being a new and different world. Such a sense of fulfillment will one day be named in accordance with its spiritual source. It will be called a son or daughter of God.[33]

To receive the reign of God as children is to reclaim the joy of life amid trials and tribulations. To be like children does not mean immunity from the pains and sufferings of this world or a naiveté regarding one's care and responsibility toward the world. To be like children, rather, is to be able to play, laugh, cry, and sing, even if things are not perfect. Moltmann summarizes this in his theology of play: "*Life* as *rejoicing* in liberation, as *solidarity* with those in bondage, as *play* with reconciled existence, and as *pain* at unreconciled existence demonstrates the Easter event in the world. *But can believers play?*"[34] His answer is that only children and those liberated from guilt are able to do so. This is also a breakthrough for a theological view of the incarnation that takes the God-child paradigm into account.

Only when we understand children, too, as moral and religious agents can we fully understand the richness of the God-child paradigm. American theologian Bonnie Miller-McLemore (b. 1955) reminds us that, although we tend to stress either children's innocence or passivity in decision-making, children are neither wholly depraved nor wholly innocent. Drawing from the ideas of art historian Anne Higonnet (b. 1959), Miller-McLemore states that children "have valuable and increasingly complicated moral and spiritual lives. They are

---

[33] Sölle, *Creative Disobedience*, 48.
[34] Moltmann, *Theology of Play*, 31 (Moltmann's italics).

as much about 'difficulty, trouble, and tension,' as they are about 'celebration, admiration, and passionate attachment.'"[35] The idea of children as spiritual and moral agents allows for a new window of interpretation when describing ourselves as children and addressing God as parent. Children's agency, responsibility, and ambiguity are additional configurations of the novelty that incarnation presents.[36]

The child in the God-child is a *knowing child*—one who, in growth, assumes agency and encounters a place in the world.[37] The knowing child confronts adults, because she is eager to learn and not afraid to pose questions. Her curiosity is not barred by a false sense of pride and self-sufficiency. And yet, she too can become entrapped by power games and cruelty:

> Capacity for sin develops gradually, incrementally, over time. Adults who care for children need better understanding of this dynamic within children and within themselves, including the recognition that adults possess greater power and knowledge and therefore increased responsibility and guilt.[38]

Although children are vulnerable and in constant need of care or attention, they also hold immense power. The parent-child relationship is not a one-sided exercise of power. A child also exerts power over her parents. The parental bond goes beyond "giving life" and touches on the notion of "giving up life" for the well-being of one's child. Theologically, this gives us food for thought and presents even further possibilities for interpreting the God-child paradigm. When Jesus beckons us to be born anew, we are constantly being transformed. Through that renewal, we each bring to the world the child of God that we are. The incarnation is to allow Jesus's filial reality to take shape and form also in us, to embody itself in our humanity.

When Jesus told the disciples to receive the reign of God as children, he not only emphasized the childlike attitude that one is expected to have but also

---

[35] Herbert Anderson and Bonnie Miller-McLemore, *Faith's Wisdom for Daily Living* (Minneapolis: Augsburg Fortress, 2008), 42. Chapter 3, titled "Facing Frailty," was originally written by Miller-McLemore.

[36] For further reading on children and theology, see Bonnie J. Miller-McLemore, *Let the Children Come: Reimagining Childhood from a Christian Perspective* (San Francisco: Jossey-Bass, 2003); Joyce Ann Mercer, *Welcoming Children: A Practical Theology of Childhood* (St. Louis: Chalice Press, 2005); Bonnie J. Miller-McLemore, *In the Midst of Chaos: Caring for Children as Spiritual Practice* (San Francisco: Jossey-Bass, 2007).

[37] I am indebted to Bonnie Miller-McLemore for the concept of the "knowing child" and the complex ways moral agency is fostered in children.

[38] Anderson and Miller-McLemore, *Faith's Wisdom for Daily Living*, 42.

brought up a criticism of hierarchical power. The child is the "other," outside the realm of decision-making and agency. Jesus's attitude toward children is similar to his treatment of all those who are at the fringes. It is precisely to them that God's loving care and attention are turned. God chooses those who are not chosen (the outcast). In addition, Jesus framed this invitation in light of discipleship—as an ongoing process of growth, of already and not yet.

The God-child paradigm is an exercise of displacement for adults: it makes us aware of a reality that no longer is or that is present in another (in the encounter with children). This displacement is equally paradoxical. On the one hand, it is a journey into oneself: the experiences of the past, a reality that no longer exists and yet continues to have its impact. We carry the marks of our own upbringing, of the childhood we had. On the other hand, it is also a journey into another: a human being, a self that is different and yet somewhat similar to me, an invitation and opportunity for encounter, of meeting Christ in the other.

Recognizing that we are children of God gives us freedom to explore new ways of expressing our faith and to relate it to our lives. There is a radical, subversive, and creative novelty in God becoming incarnate as a child, echoed in Jesus's words to the disciples: "Whoever does not receive the kingdom of God as a little child will never enter it" (Mark 10:13–15). The God-child paradigm invites us to receive God's reign with a childlike attitude: through curiosity and playfulness, through taking risks and posing questions, through seeing life with wonderment, through openness to ask for help when needed, and through a willingness to perhaps not take ourselves so seriously.

Conclusion

God's option for vulnerability, the recognition of our own fragility, and understanding human beings as children of God are just a few of the ways that the church might strengthen its understanding of the incarnation by focusing on the God-child paradigm. Remembering that God embodied a human form in its most fragile stage—a child—reminds us that God participates intimately in human affairs. God comes to us amid danger and in and through the messiness of life. Although we might expect God's revelation in grandeur and pomp, the God-child paradigm reveals the Divine in the mundane and ordinary. Taking Jesus's embodiment as a child seriously also exposes more clearly God's option for vulnerability: Jesus became a vulnerable child, and in his ministry, he focuses on those who are most marginalized in society.

This view of the incarnation challenges us, in turn, to be practitioners of solidarity and hospitality, caring for those who are most vulnerable and in need.

The paradox of God's vulnerability and power helps us live out the paradox of our own vulnerabilities and capacities, thereby seeing more clearly the needs of others, inspiring courage, and empowering us to be agents of transformation. We also see more clearly the needs of children. In the state of our world today, we cannot deny that children are among the most vulnerable. The God-child paradigm is a reminder that we are Christ's body on earth and are to care for the most disenfranchised, including children. We are serving God by loving our neighbor, and we see Christ in those who are in need.

Finally, attention to Jesus's embodiment as a child as well as his example and message of the reign of God remind us that adults and children are paradoxically all children of God. Jesus placed us all under the same protective care and confidence, even telling us to receive God's reign as children. The God-child paradigm invites us to receive the reign with a childlike attitude. This strengthens our awareness of children's role in the body of Christ and offers adults a different outlook on our own lives, with burdens shared and greater cheerfulness in the care of God. The God-child paradigm also helps us take children seriously, compelling the church both to respond to their needs, well-being, and moral and spiritual development and to respect children's equality, agency, and relationship to God.

For these reasons and more, future theologies of the incarnation that attend to the God-child paradigm and Jesus's embodiment as an infant are bound to cultivate robust theologies that honor more fully the humanity of children, ourselves, and Jesus Christ.

6

SOTERIOLOGY AND CHILDREN'S VULNERABILITIES AND AGENCY

Rohan P. Gideon

Soteriology or the study of understandings of salvation is a central theme in Christian theology and religious thought more broadly. Theological discussions on salvation have ranged from understanding salvation as eternal salvation and *saving* one's soul to contextually *liberating* oneself or a community from oppression and injustice. In contemporary pluralistic and multireligious contexts, the focus for some theologians has shifted from the biblical imagery of the "narrow gate" to the belief that everyone is part of God's "wide embrace" without being rejected.[1]

The diverse forms of liberation theology around the world have done much to highlight the significance of salvation as liberation from oppression and injustice. In India, for example, Dalit, tribal, feminist, and womanist liberation theologies have exposed various forms of suffering and discrimination based on class, gender, religion, and caste. These theologies have worked alongside secular and religious movements to improve the social and economic status, sense of personal dignity, and human rights of exploited and oppressed communities.[2] Like many Christian theologies seeking to address social injustices, liberation theologies in India emphasize that all people are made in the image of God and that Jesus Christ identifies with the oppressed.

Although liberation theologies in India have addressed the suffering and salvation of many marginalized groups, they have not given adequate attention to children. Ironically, many of the marginalized groups that liberation theolo-

---

[1] Kajsa Ahlstrand, "Salvation in Theology of Religions: Some Preliminary Considerations," *Swedish Missiological Themes* 99, no. 2 (2011): 211.

[2] See Rohan Gideon, *Child Labour in India: Challenges for Theological Thinking and Christian Ministry in India* (New Delhi: ISPCK, 2011), 77–79. See also Sathianathan Clarke, *Dalits and Christianity: Subaltern Religion and Liberation Theology in India* (Delhi: Oxford University Press, 1998), 20.

gians identify include children, yet their plights are often ignored or reduced only to data. Children suffer and are exploited in multiple and unique ways, and their rights and dignity have been continually and unacceptably violated.[3] Furthermore, like all human beings, children's identities and forms of suffering are complex and intersect. For example, millions of children suffer from a lack of education, proper health care, or a safe living environment. The plight of migrant and refugee children is compounded by war, violence, border crossings, and separation from families. Many children are also forced into slavery or practices similar to slavery, such as the sale and trafficking of children, debt bondage, serfdom, or forced or compulsory labor, including forced or compulsory recruitment of children for use in armed conflict. Legal definitions for child labor in the relevant international treaties also include using children as prostitutes, for the production of pornography or pornographic performances, and for other illicit activities, such as the production and trafficking of drugs. All of these contexts of suffering are defined under "Worst Forms of Child Labor."[4]

Without attention to children's unique suffering, theological understandings of "liberation" and "salvation" often narrowly exclude and diminish children, even though children are part of God's salvific plan. For example, as we see in India, liberation theologies have not extended their notion of liberation and social transformation broadly enough to include attention to violation of children's rights and dignity or other forms of children's suffering and exploitation. They have not recognized children's complex and intersectional identities. More conservative theological traditions focus on salvation as deliverance from individual sin and the promise of eternal life, yet they fail to recognize fully that salvation offered through Christ also applies to this life here and now. Christian communities across the theological spectrum certainly include children and seek to address their basic needs, yet their notions of both salvation and children do not reflect children's full humanity, the unique challenges they face, nor the multifaceted thinking about salvation found in the Bible and the history of Christian thought and practice.

Given common but thin understandings of salvation that disregard or diminish children's full humanity in God's reign, and given the multilayered forms of suffering that children experience in our immediate and wider contexts, the primary question of this chapter is to explore how attention to children might strengthen and expand Christian theologies of salvation. This

---

[3] Gideon, *Child Labour in India*, 77.
[4] These were adopted by the International Labor Organization (ILO) in 1999 as ILO Convention No. 182. See Yoshie Noguchi, "ILO Convention No. 182 on the Worst Forms of Child Labour and the Convention on the Rights of the Child," *International Journal of Children's Rights* 10 (2002): 355–369.

study requires revisiting Christian theological and biblical understandings of salvation and children. It is therefore based on an intersectional analysis of the situation and agency of children as well as deeper and wider views of salvation. Deeper ideas of salvation lead to more robust ideas of children. Similarly, deeper and existential explorations of the place and dignity of children lead to expanding and evolving notions of salvation.

This chapter is organized into three main sections. First, "Locating and Relocating Salvation" briefly reviews and evaluates various understandings of salvation in the history of Christian thought to discover resources for articulating an expansive and holistic concept of salvation that attends to children as well as adults. This approach to salvation includes the notion of the agency of children as articulated in child-related theologies. Second, "Salvific Promises and Conflicts" revisits some familiar and some not so familiar biblical passages to identify biblical promises of a dignified childhood and breaches of those promises. Building on these ideas, the third section, "A Holistic Approach to Soteriology," articulates a more holistic and expansive understanding of salvation that takes into account the vulnerability and suffering of children as well as their own agency.

This expanded notion of salvation builds on ideas of salvation as humanization and liberation yet more intentionally acknowledges children's full humanity, vulnerabilities, and agency and emphasizes three guiding principles: the rooted solidarity of the caring community, the mystery of children, and cooperative social transformation. This broader view of salvation calls the church to affirm the humanity and dignity of all children, recognizes their unique forms of suffering, and honors their agency, hopes, and contributions. Carrying out this task requires the church to expand its understanding of both children and salvation and to work collaboratively across interdisciplinary, intergenerational, ecumenical, interreligious, and religious-secular lines to liberate, protect, and honor children.

Locating and Relocating Salvation

Soteriology is a subject of real people in real historical contexts. Therefore, while formulating an understanding of salvation with attention to children, one must consider liberative resources emerging from different biblical and theological traditions. Like searching for the ingredients of a nourishing recipe, we need to search for elements of biblical and theological traditions that help us envision how children's dignity is rightfully restored and maintained. We need to draw from liberative sources and motifs that honor children's full humanity and help the church play a proactive role in analyzing injustices and contributing to social transformation for all of God's children, not just metaphorically or euphemistically, but for actual children. Such liberative sources help the church understand the meaning of God's salvation more broadly than just ensuring a place in heaven or carrying out select political activities.

Conventional Christian Understandings of Salvation

Several conventional Christian understandings of salvation focus on assuring a place in heaven. This notion is usually derived from Jesus's sermon in Matthew 7. The passage indicates a way (a "narrow gate," and a "hard road," vs. 13–14) to a destination ("heaven," v. 21). Many of these conventional views also associate salvation with Jesus's death on the cross to save us from our sins. Such questions as "Why did Jesus have to die on the cross?" and "What is the outcome of Jesus's death on the cross?" are answered in what is classically known as "atonement theories."

While traditional atonement theories recognize the dimension of salvation as forgiveness from sins, they have some limitations. For example, these atonement theories limit the source of salvation to the act of Jesus's death on the cross. They also do not consider other ways of salvation that the biblical texts suggest, such as salvation through *belief* in the Lord Jesus (Acts 16:31), salvation through *belief* and *baptism* in the resurrection of Jesus (Mark 16:16), and salvation by *confession with the mouth* that "Jesus is Lord" and *belief in the heart* that God raised Jesus from the dead (Rom 10:9). Furthermore, many classical atonement theories focus solely on a spiritual or transcendental dimension of salvation and do not offer practical responses to daily troubles.

Canadian feminist theologian Grace Jantzen (b. 1948) highlights the problem with notions of atonement that disconnect practical problems from transcendental solutions in her reflections on the question of the Philippian jailor and the response of Paul and Silas in Acts 16. To the jailor's question as to what he should do to be saved from an embarrassment of the failure of duty, a fear of being reprimanded, and therefore, an attempted suicide, Paul and Silas firmly replied that he and his household should believe in the Lord Jesus Christ. As Jantzen explains,

> The jailor was not asking how he could be assured of a place in the next world, or how he could be reconciled to God or have his sins forgiven. His was a cry of quite unreligious desperation: was there any alternative to suicide, now that his prison was no longer secure and he had failed in his duty?[5]

---

[5] Grace M. Jantzen, "Human Diversity and Salvation in Christ," *Religious Studies* 20, no. 4 (1984): 579.

Jantzen suggests here that salvation means providing practical and timely responses in a crisis. While Paul and Silas focus on saving one's soul in Jesus's name, the jailor would probably have been happier with a practical and legal way out of his desperate situation. Therefore, salvation, in its qualified sense of liberation, is rooted in sociopolitical resolutions and answers to the immediate needs of a person for a holistic life.

Liberation Theologies

Understandings of salvation take a significant turn toward addressing real-life contexts with the advent of liberation theology. Here salvation is translated as reclaiming the voice, place, and dignity of the oppressed. It calls for a committed bias for those without an agency. Peruvian theologian Gustavo Gutiérrez (b. 1928), with his radical call for a praxis-based theological reflection, continues to base some of his arguments on salvation in the context of day-to-day human life. For Gutiérrez, the "history of Salvation is the very heart of human history."[6] Liberation is at the heart of the Christian *kerygma*, and many notions of salvation or liberation have to be understood integrally.

This integrated approach can be understood on three levels: political, psychological, and liberation from sin.[7] Political transformation envisions overhauling power structures to include rightfully those in the margins. Psychological or anthropological transformation addresses deep-rooted issues that have taken the form of a consciousness. For example, a psychological transformation would be a movement from a fearful consciousness toward affirming one's agency and power in history. Gutiérrez also talks about liberation from sin, where liberation is achieved by making space for God's act in history through the death and resurrection of Jesus Christ; salvation becomes integral with each aspect awaiting the fulfillment of the other. This idea also incorporates the integration of the activities of God and human beings toward a holistic salvation.

Salvation as Freedom

Another person who meaningfully connected the "transcendental" to the real or "categorical" is German theologian Karl Rahner (1904–1984). Rahner begins his theology of salvation by exploring the notion of "freedom." For Rahner, while salvation is brought about by "created and uncreated grace," it is grounded in the "categorical" because it is fundamentally coupled with ethical resolutions

---

[6] Gustavo Gutiérrez, *A Theology of Liberation: History, Politics, and Salvation*, rev. ed. (Maryknoll, NY: Orbis Books, 1988), 86.

[7] Gustavo Gutiérrez, *A Theology of Liberation*, 21–42.

and events in a historical space and time.⁸ His understanding of salvation is based on the immediate connectedness to our own humanness, especially our views on how our lives are made meaningful and fulfilled. Consequently, divine agency is a mediated intervention into human existence, drawing a connection to the rest of human experience. According to Rahner,

> [Salvation] means rather the final and definitive validity of a person's true self-understanding and true self-realization in freedom before God by the fact that he accepts his own self as it is disclosed and offered to him in the choice of transcendence as interpreted in freedom.⁹

Essentially, Rahner's understanding takes us to a theology of acceptance and inclusion by emphasizing God's grace working in real contexts. Salvation accomplishes the ethical task of including persons in the fold of a community that enjoys freedom and acceptance.

Salvation as Humanization

Salvation as freedom and liberation where spiritual-historical dichotomies are overcome was strongly proposed by renowned Indian theologian M. M. Thomas (1916–1996). In his quest to make salvation understandable, he equates salvation with "humanization." For Thomas, salvation is essentially spiritual and material and therefore holistic. He promotes justice as a key to understanding salvation, as unjust situations deprive human beings of their personhood, equality, and dignity. He notes that "the mission of salvation and the task of humanization are integrally related to each other even if they cannot be considered identical."¹⁰ He is firm that Christianity cannot overlook humanization and justice by preaching only about the salvation of the soul.¹¹ Thomas presents Christian faith as living out the model of the "Cosmic Lordship of Christ" that emphasizes holistic human development and questioning unjust social structures that conflict with the way the Spirit of God leads us in history. Thomas speaks to contexts in which people of different faiths work together for the common good of liberation of humankind.

---

⁸ Gasper Martinez, *Confronting the Mystery of God: Political, Liberation, and Public Theologies* (New York: Continuum, 2001), 7–9..

⁹ Karl Rahner, *Foundations of Christian Faith: An Introduction to the Idea of Christianity*, trans. William V. Dych (New York: Seabury Press, 1978), 39.

¹⁰ M. M. Thomas, *Salvation and Humanization: Some Crucial Issues of the Theology Mission in Contemporary India* (Madras: The CLS, 1971), 8.

¹¹ For a fuller treatment of the theme, see Heilke T. Wolters, *Theology of Prophetic Participation: M. M. Thomas's Concept of Salvation and the Collective Struggle for Fuller Humanity in India* (Delhi: ISPCK, 1996).

Salvific Promises and Conflicts

Although these various perspectives on salvation in the Bible and across Christian traditions rarely mention children, they provide resources for formulating a more expansive and holistic view of salvation that includes children. They show that the notion of salvation is not monolithic or one-dimensional. Rather, conceptions of salvation in the Bible and theology are multifaceted, expanding, and evolving. They develop within contexts and are both transcendental and historical. They are broad enough to include attention to the next life as well as liberation, freedom, humanization, acceptance, inclusion, safety, and cooperation in this life.

We can now begin to mine further resources for a robust understanding of salvation that includes attention to children by revisiting biblical narratives about children. An exploration of the biblical texts helps us to "humanize" children, especially by identifying promises of a dignified childhood and breaches of such promises.

The Bible exposes several perspectives on children, ranging from children as divine expressions in the world to that of economic commodities in the hands of adults. These passages help us to incorporate children's dignity and their rightful agency into a more robust notion of salvation. They also help us to avoid a common error—a "paradigmatic problem"—in theological discourse: theology that is articulated by adults from the perspective of adults in a "wordy, propositional, and argumentative" style and focused on adults.[12] In other words, theologians can be hierarchical, assuming that children are not important in the "superior" field of systematic theology but only in practical theology. Furthermore, even in the latter field, discourses on children are often "age-biased," written through the parents' or community's perspectives, and consider children as "peripheral." Thus, the following exploration closely reexamines biblical texts in order to reaffirm the dignity of children and transform the structures that stifle their existence, opening up spaces for the needs and contributions of children in understanding salvation.

Children as Fully Human and Made in the Image of God

Several biblical texts help underscore the full humanity of children. For example, the Bible claims that all human beings are made in the "image of God" (Gen 1:27). This is not restricted by age or other distinctions that we sometimes use to discriminate, such as gender, class, race, or culture. Human beings in all their diversity are made in God's image.

---

[12] Israel Selvanayagam, "Children Laugh and Cry: Authentic Resources for Christian Theology," *Asia Journal of Theology* 9, no. 2 (1995): 352.

The biblical texts also highlight the significance of children. They are "gifts from God." Children are also viewed as a "means of God's activity." They are a "symbolic assurance of the Covenant between God and the people of Israel," inclining the Hebrews to have children and to place them in high esteem.[13] The psalmist notes that young children are capable of worshiping God and participating in the community of faith affirmations (Ps 8:2–3).

Salvific Role of Children in Messianic Discourse

Other biblical texts emphasize the role that children themselves play in bringing about salvation or providing hope. For example, the image of "child" plays an important part in messianic expectations in the Old Testament. The prophet Isaiah speaks of a future *child* of David's line who will be the hope of his people despite much suffering (Isa 7:14, 16; 9:16). The same prophet also describes this future in terms of an idyllic return to the childlike innocence of the Garden of Eden (11:8–9). The prophet Zechariah has a vision of the messianic era as a time of peace and joy when "the streets of the city shall be full of boys and girls playing in them" (8:5).

Children as Central to and Aligned with the Reign of God

The centrality of children is further strengthened by aligning them with the reign of God. While the thought of "kingdom of God" as a "kingdom of children" has attracted various perspectives, the helplessness of children has prompted John Dominic Crossan to state pointedly that this "kingdom of children" is the "kingdom of nobodies," for "to be a child was nobody."[14] Biblical scholars Judith Gundry-Volf and Hans Reudi-Weber emphasize this proposition. Children are the inheritors of the reign of God; they are the models of entering the reign of God; they are the paradigms of greatness in the reign of God; receiving children is as significant as receiving Jesus; and the exemplary humility of children is required of any person in God's reign.[15] Weber draws

---

[13] Joseph A. Grassi, "Child, Children," in *Anchor Bible Dictionary*, vol. 1, ed. David Noel Freedman (New York: Doubleday, 1992), 904–907. See also the etymological description of children in the Hebrew Scriptures and the New Testament under the titles "Yonek" and "Tap" in *New International Dictionary of Old Testament Theology and Exegesis*, vol. 2, ed. William A. VanGemeren (Grand Rapids: Zondervan, 1997), and "Helikia," "Pais," and "Nepios" in *New International Dictionary of New Testament Theology*, vol. 2, ed. Colin Brown (Grand Rapids: Zondervan, 1986).

[14] John Dominic Crossan, *The Historical Jesus: The Life of a Mediterranean Jewish Peasant* (San Francisco: Harper, 1991), 265–302.

[15] Judith M. Gundry-Wolf, "The Least and the Greatest: Children in the New Testament,"

additional lessons from Jesus's attention to children for the "adult Christian life" and discipleship.[16] Jesus specifically invites the little children to come to him (cf. Matt 19:13–15; Mark 10:13–16; Luke 18:15–17) and vehemently reverses the disciples' intentions to keep children at the margins (cf. Mark 10:14). His indignation suggests the gravity of the exclusion of children from God's blessings. Jesus uses novel ways to teach disciples about the kingdom of God and entering the same. Welcoming children to be "among them" (Luke 9:36) would also mean welcoming Jesus and the One who sent him.

The Adult-Child Dichotomy

The biblical texts also help expose how easily children's full humanity can be dismissed. For example, viewing children as blessings or signs of the covenant can lead to narrow views of children as validating the worth of adults. In several biblical texts, the worth of a woman was measured by her ability to bear children. Childlessness was shameful, and measures were taken to overcome this situation. The story of the conception of Isaac presents God as helping out a woman from a shameful situation (Gen 21). Sarah and Abraham are so advanced in age that the birth of a son appears impossible, yet God's promise to them is fulfilled by divine intervention, even after Abraham had already worked toward immortalizing his lineage by having Ishmael through Hagar. In instances of childlessness, the Levirate law provided for carrying on the family name and for continuity through the nearest relative (Deut 25:5–10).

In the biblical texts, we also see examples of children treated as economic entities who, with the least idea of what happens around them, compete to give in meekly to the adults' world. During the economic crunch of the Israelites during Nehemiah's leadership, some members of the community had to pledge their children for debt-slavery.[17] They belonged to landless classes and had to mortgage whatever little property they owned. In helpless circumstances, they traded their children as exchange goods, and the phenomenon of converting a child into a commodity seemed acceptable, according to adult logic. Indeed, the process had already begun, as some of their daughters had already been "enslaved" to sexually gratify the creditors' lusts as payment for delaying foreclosure on the loans. This word in Hebrew has sexual overtones (as in Esth 7:8),

---

in *The Child in Christian Thought,* ed. Marcia J. Bunge (Grand Rapids: Eerdmans, 2001), 29–58.

[16] See, for example, Hans-Reudi Weber, *Jesus and the Children: Biblical Resources for Study and Preaching* (Loveland, OH: Treehaus Communications, 1979).

[17] H. G. M. Williamson, *Word Biblical Commentary: Ezra, Nehemiah*, vol. 16 (Dallas: Word Books, 1998).

where singling out of daughters adds a gender dimension to the severe treatment of debt-slavery.[18]

The narrative of the barren Hannah and the birth of her son, Samuel (1 Sam 1), also reveals elements of the commodification of children. As Naomi Steinberg explains, Hannah's prayer for the gift of a child appears to be religiously as well as economically motivated. In the passage, the adult motivation is legitimized as God's own interest; who, it appears, needs a replacement for Eli's sons. Thus, in this instance, the "property paradigm" of childhood is well explicated: infant Samuel is merely a pawn. He can "be bartered away by his mother to Yahweh in exchange for the gift of fertility, followed by her expected subsequent rise in status in the family of her husband Elkanah."[19] Steinberg continues,

> In an economic sense, a child's value and identity was formed based on membership in a family, i.e., a patra-lineage, and what the child owes the parent based on this family identity. The economic value of a child is seen, e.g., in 2 Kgs 4:1, when children are taken by a creditor to pay off a debt. Control over a child's fate resides in the hands of the child's parents when the child is viewed as property. By the same token, in the case of Samuel, his dedication to Yahweh at Shiloh requires making a sacrifice as his parents fulfill Hannah's vow. Individual actions, in a context such as this one, where family values address economic production and reproduction, represent collective family interests.[20]

The above analysis helps identify many unseen forms of entrapment that children unknowingly enter even today.

Additional examples of biblical texts that diminish the full humanity of children can be found in the New Testament Epistles. Here, a common perception is that a child symbolizes a stage that one grows out of (i.e., the present stage as a stage of immaturity) or a state of being where one's potential is not completely accomplished (cf. 1 Cor 13:11; 14:20; Jam 1:6; Heb 5:13; 1 Pet 2:2). The difference between Jesus's teaching about children and that of the Epistles is an interesting point of theological and historical musing. Paul's use of the theological metaphor of children as someone to mature toward adulthood (cf. 1 Cor 4:14–15; Gal 4:19; 1 Thess 2:11), and the impression of the writer of

---

[18] Williamson, *Word Biblical Commentary*.

[19] Naomi Steinberg, "1 Samuel 1, the United Nations Convention on the Rights of Children, and 'The Best Interests of the Child,'" *Journal of Childhood and Religion* 1, no. 3 (2010): 12.

[20] Steinberg, "1 Samuel 1," 13.

the Johannine epistles about children (1 John 2:1, 18, 28; 3:7, 18; 5:21; 3 John 4) represent the authors' spiritual association with social reality. They deprive children of their sacramental presence as full members of the body of Christ and as images of God.

Even when biblical stories appear to honor the role of children, scholars and the biblical authors themselves appear to diminish their role. For example, Matthew derogatorily introduces the "insignificant" presence of children in religious gatherings, such as the feeding of the "five thousand" (14:21, cf. Matt 15:38). However, the story itself points directly to the "sacramental" sharing of the food by a young boy, whose actions provided nourishment and sustenance. In this incident, scholars have associated sacramental significance to the prayer and act of Jesus in distributing the food. They substantiate it by noting that "Jesus is the messianic provider" and that the "Messianic blessing also appears to be intended in the overabundance of food."[21] Grossly forgotten is the boy as the "provider" and that the abundance of the food had its beginning in the sharing of the boy's food! Therefore, a dichotomy of "earthly" and "heavenly" is subtly present here. Even scholars could not see a messianic act in the child's act of sharing. This identifies the negligence of biblical scholarship in taking attention away from a significant act of a child. Therefore, salvation through sacrament is attested to an adult Jesus in this passage.

The Epistemological Dynamics

Jesus challenges the paradigm that equates "wisdom" with "adults" when he praises his Father: "I thank you, Father, Lord of heaven and earth, because you have hidden these things from the wise and the intelligent and have revealed them to infants; yes, Father, such was your gracious will" (Luke 10:21; Matt 11:25). While it is argued that the use of the word "infants" (according to the Latin etymology, infant means "the one who cannot speak" or "voiceless"[22]) here—as elsewhere in many of the elucidated passages—can only have metaphorical significance, the prayer offers readers a new epistemological dynamic. The purpose of raising children is commonly understood as helping them reach adulthood, where adulthood is epitomized by maturity, rationality, and power. According to this conventional view, childhood is only a passage to adulthood and not a valuable stage of life in itself, and a child's process of acquiring knowledge is moving toward the knowledge that adults possess. However, the above-cited praise strikes down this prerogative. The passage implies a new

---

[21] Donald A. Hagner, *Word Biblical Commentary: Matthew 14-28*, vol. 33b (Dallas: Word Books, 1998), 418–419.

[22] François Bovon, "The Child and the Beast: Fighting Violence in Ancient Christianity," *Harvard Theological Review* 92, no. 4 (1999): 382.

methodology where the movement of knowledge happens from children to adults—and not just from adults to children as conventionally believed. The passage underscores that adults are not the only custodians of knowledge and wisdom. Rather, Jesus opens a bilateral and intergenerational notion of wisdom and epistemology. This new methodology presents children as subjects who also provide ways and means of attaining wisdom. Hence, the tag of "ignorance" is detached from children, and children are made equally important in the construction of knowledge systems and in meaning-making. Children are posited with certain knowledge that can be explored in ways that do not denigrate their existence and distinctiveness.

To summarize, although biblical traditions honor the full humanity, contributions, and agency of children, we see how easily children are considered less than human or valuable only in relation to adults—both today and in the past. Furthermore, Christian theology has tended to emphasize only a few of these biblical traditions: the Epistles' teachings and more prominently Pauline teachings on the subordination of children. Christian theology must pay more attention to the notion of children made in the image of God and to gospel messages of the centrality of children in the reign of God and their wisdom for adults. Doing so would help the church address the plight of children and the many contexts in which their rights and dignity are violated.

A Holistic Approach to Soteriology

With this broader perspective of both salvation and children, we can now articulate a more holistic theological understanding of salvation than conventionally expressed or practiced. Our theology of salvation must pay particular attention to when and where children's dignity is honored, thus adding a significant dimension to the question of the personhood of a child and in the understanding of "image of God." Likewise, our theology of salvation must also consider when and where children's agency and their rightful place in the kingdom of God are recognized, as well as when and where an important framework of discrimination—the adult/child dichotomy—is exposed. This necessitates that our theology of salvation remains attuned to multiculturalism so that it can equip us to work toward social transformation for and alongside people of diverse worldviews.

Child-related theologies of salvation need to build on notions of salvation as humanization, liberation, and social transformation that we have seen in various forms of soteriology. Yet the unique situation and suffering of children and the dangers of highly adult-centric theologies of salvation require a more nuanced and holistic perspective of salvation. Building on the previous multifaceted biblical exploration of salvation and liberation with attention to children, we now explore a holistic and child-related soteriology formulated by expanding humanization and liberation to recognize children's vulnerabilities and agency and by emphasizing three additional guiding hermeneutical principles: the rooted solidarity of the caring community, the mystery of children, and cooperative social transformation.

Expanding Humanization and Liberation

A robust and child-attentive concept of salvation clearly builds on the notions of salvation as humanization and liberation and ensures that children are included. In regard to children, salvation as humanization means an understanding of children as full human beings with complete dignity and agency and thus as beings entitled to participation, protection, and provision. Children's vulnerable position demands preferential protection in church and society. The parallel theological grounds for the humanization of children emerge from notions of their personhood as endowed with the image of God, their rightful place in the kingdom of God, and their agency in leading humankind to the kingdom of God. Humanization of children initiates them into human societies, religious organizations, and other communities. Humanization also reminds the church of its responsibility to safeguard children's dignity whenever it is violated. To address the plight and demeaning position of children, a robust understanding of salvation must also recognize children's agency and their centrality in the reign of God. Children are not merely beings in need of salvation, they are also agents of salvation. They are unique, complex beings who are as much recipients of the kingdom of God as they are keepers of it. Therefore, we must open up spaces for children's voices, participation, and contributions in our world and in our efforts to liberate and care for children. After all, salvation's promises of freedom and acceptance belong especially to our children, so a "wide embrace" of children in our understanding of salvation necessitates a wide embrace of children and all they have to offer and teach.

Possibilities and Limitations of Child Advocacy

One of the primary vehicles for ensuring the humanization and liberation of children, as for adults, is advocacy. Advocacy is commonly understood as a powerful tool for addressing the needs of the marginalized. Generally, advocacy seeks to speak on behalf of marginalized communities, raise awareness of and address the injustices they face, and empower them. Advocacy is fundamentally didactic in nature and its objective is to conscientize and empower the marginalized.²³ In the case of child advocacy, adults who have power and a voice typically raise awareness of children's suffering, seek political and social changes that address their suffering, and strengthen children's own agency. Such advocacy efforts certainly help to realize salvation and liberation for both children and adults. Through such efforts, adults from adult-privileged communities renounce their cultural and religious entitlements in the best interest of the children and create new spaces for the advancement of children's centrality. Child advocates are mindful of the differences between the worlds of children and adults, and they strive to be responsible for representing children through adult-language systems.

While advocacy is a powerful tool for liberating a marginalized group, it has its downsides. Advocates for the marginalized can misjudge their power to represent. Thus, as some scholars have shown, the marginalized community sometimes takes up the language of those who have power to speak on their behalf, and in the process, their own voices and experiences are not clearly heard. This is sometimes the case in child advocacy. Adults seek to advance the cause of children, yet children are rarely given an opportunity to speak or even to find their voice. Furthermore, even when they are given the space, they often use the adult-privileged language. To complete this vicious circle, the adult representatives re-hear their own language to make it easier for them to represent their own perspective of the narrative, many a time wrongly presented as the voice of children. Thus, advocacy may not always be truthful to the narratives and experiences of the oppressed, particularly in the case of children. Advocacy seeks to lift their voices, yet in the end sometimes strangles their narratives, thereby failing to advance the centrality and the situations of children.

An additional difficulty in depending too much on advocacy as the primary tool of the liberation and salvation of children is that advocacy can quickly move from deep listening and narratives of experience to an important yet narrow type of discourse focused almost exclusively on rights. Listening and representing in advocacy often then take a legal turn. In the case of children, their suffering can be narrowly framed in the language of violation of their rights. While attention to children's rights is crucial, adult advocates may tend to resort to a counterlegal language that is caught up in philosophical debates. Consequently, the unique narratives, concerns, and hopes of children are often lost. Children do not find an authentic place of discourse.

---

²³ I have further explained the limitation of the didactic nature of theologies and mission in the context of children in my "Children's Agency and Edinburgh 2010: The Great Commission or a Greater Omission?" in *Teaching All Nations: Interrogating the Matthean Great Commission*, ed. Mitzi Smith and Jayachitra Lalitha (Minneapolis: Fortress Press, 2014): 195–213.

Rooted Solidarity of the Caring Community and Intergenerationality

In an unequal world of adults and children that privileges adults, advancing salvation for children cannot be restricted to child advocacy alone. A more relevant, broader approach for the liberation of children requires a "rooted solidarity of the caring community." Rooted solidarity calls adults to listen empathetically and actively to children and take time to responsibly listen and discern. Careful listening and discerning are important because it is difficult to hear and understand the experiences of children in a predominantly "adult" world of language. Adults have all been children, which can help them empathize with but also "mishear" them. While adults have experienced deprivation and biases in their own childhoods, children's experiences are different from their own. Thus, as adults seek to understand and sympathize with children who face injustice and vulnerability, adults must balance the dual and difficult task of listening to children as well as recalling their own narratives of vulnerability and deprivation. This dual focus and attention create "rooted solidarity." Such solidarity helps adults deeply sympathize with and understand a child's narrative and experience to a greater extent than when adults seek merely to represent children as child advocates. Rooted solidarity involves a redefined responsibility of not just representing but also listening to children to a degree that, finally, what adults as individuals and as members of communities hear is converted into communities actively listening to children and creating spaces for their voices to be recognized and heard. Such community "active listening" develops authentic narratives of the experiences of both children and adults, and thereby fosters a deeper sense of intergenerationality.

The Mystery of Children

A special dimension of a child-attentive view of salvation in addition to rooted solidarity is appreciating the mystery operating in child advocacy and in the lives of children themselves.[24] Among several theologians who have spoken about mystery in ontological terms, Mark Lewis Taylor and Martin Marty provide two prominent perspectives.[25] Taylor speaks of a fertile "region of

---

[24] See reference to children and mystery in Jan Grobbelaar and Gert Breed, *Theologies of Childhood and the Children of Africa* (Durbanville: AOSIS, 2016), 59. My own thoughts on children and adult-centric Christologies can be found in "The Challenges of Subjectivity of Children to Christology," *Bangalore Theological Forum* 51, no. 2 (2019): 168–180.

[25] Mark Lewis Taylor, "Subalternity and Advocacy as Kairos for Theology," in *Opting for the Margins: Postmodernity and Liberation in Christian Theology*, ed. Joerg Rieger (Oxford: Oxford University Press, 2003), 23–44; and Martin Marty, *The Mystery of the Child* (Grand Rapids: Eerdmans, 2007).

mystery" in discourse between often entitled advocates and the marginalized that deepens understanding of the "other," and his ideas can be applied to challenges and power differentials in child advocacy. Through his discussion of mystery, Marty clarifies aspects of God and Christ that also encourage child advocacy and underscore children's agency, complexity, and the ways God is already moving in their lives. The following are just a few examples how notions of mystery expressed in the works of these two thinkers can be fruitfully applied to children.

Taylor sees mystery as helping advocates, who stand in entitled and privileged positions, to become more authentic and effective advocates for the marginalized and exploited. Although Taylor does not directly address the situation of children, his reflections on the challenges of "entitled advocates" seeking to work or speak on behalf of "subaltern peoples" and his proposals for "authentic advocacy" apply to child advocacy. His ideas help foster a more sophisticated awareness of the complexities and power differentials at work when adults seek to advocate for children. Among his suggested modes of "authentic advocacy," Taylor mentions mystery. For him, mystery is a fertile space of engagement where binaries of the "advocate" and "subaltern" might begin to break down and real sharing might evolve. Mystery creates a new and challenging space of self-other interplay. By being open to this mystery, child advocates might more nimbly reorient their own self-understanding and relationships to children; more carefully listen to children; more easily appreciate the wisdom and worldviews of children; more precisely name children's distinctive, diverse, and complex forms of suffering; and more proactively work with children toward liberation from injustices. Such openness is a movement away from adults' authoritative selves toward creative solidarity and cooperation with children.

Taylor's thoughts on mystery can be augmented by turning to Marty's elucidation of mystery. Marty discusses the mystery of children themselves, pointing out their complexity and "apparently limitless depth."[26] Building on Marty, conceptualizing children as mystery demands an openness to see them beyond any one category, such as their physicality or vulnerability. Their significance cannot be restricted simply to biblical notions of the child as a gift of God or as the source of covenant—notions commonly promoted in child-related theologies. Nor can their significance be restricted to the mysterious silence of the child who points the way to the kingdom of God. Marty compels us to ascribe the stature of mystery to children—a stature that our traditional theologies often reject or ignore. Furthermore, Marty takes up the idea of mystery in the context of three existential realities: finitude, contingency, and transience. Thus, caring for a child involves engaging a double mystery: the child's depth and its vulnerabilities. As they care for children,

---

[26] Marty, *The Mystery of the Child*, 13, 52–69.

caregivers and advocates must reflect not only children's possibilities and potentials but also human mortality and unforeseen cir-cumstances.

Marty's central argument is that if we seek a radically improved way of understanding and interacting with children, then we must make an equally radical shift from viewing children as simplistic or problematic to seeing them as "mystery surrounded by mystery" and thereby relating to them with compassion, wonder, and joy.[27] The biblical mandates of understanding children as made in the image of God, as signs of the covenant, as messiahs, and as ways to the kingdom of God can be translated as mystery. Mystery, here, is not elusive or slippery but represents the surprise, wisdom, and new directions that children offer us and that reflect the presence of the Divine.

Cooperative Social Transformation

Mystery helps adults more fully realize that children, just like adults, are agents in God's creation with complex intersectional identities. Thus, salvation with attention to children must seek wide-ranging social transformation and restoration that engages cooperation with people across many lines of difference. Since children, like adults, are complex beings, they matter in all ways: socially, politically, religiously, and intergenerationally. Therefore, our efforts to honor and uplift children's dignity, identity, and agency must happen on an intersectional level. For example, adults of all backgrounds must work together to pursue liberation and social transformation for children. Salvation as social transformation seeks social and political liberation from injustices. Yet child-attentive notions of salvation must pay even more attention to the need to work across religious and political boundaries to liberate children in various contexts—such as home, schools, religious communities, society, and refugee camps—from unique and often neglected forms of oppression and exploitation that result from to their vulnerability.

This means our efforts to honor and uplift children's dignity, identity, and agency must happen on an intersectional level. Here, the church and society work with fluid boundaries but also creative and various approaches to care for the children by addressing issues that threaten their basic existence.

Consequently, the theology of salvation becomes one of liberation, which in turn takes seriously the language of sociocultural, religious, and political discourses. When these possibilities are explored, they work positively to include children's issues that are beyond any one theological theme.

An ecclesiology along these lines makes the church a crucial agent in bringing about salvation, as the boundaries of the church cannot be confined

---

[27] Marty, *The Mystery of the Child,* 1.

to a few political activities.²⁸ Therefore, churches are called to care for children and address injustices that threaten their basic needs and rights in various collaborative and creative ways. In my context in India, for example, Christian communities must take an active stance against child labor and a caste system that dehumanizes children as lesser beings with inadequate rational and physical ability.²⁹ Thus, the church in India must also stand against other forms of systemic injustice that merge with the caste system to compel children into the labor force. Such unjust systems include gender bias, generation bias, and globalization. Moreover, the church must work to reaffirm the dignity of children and also transform structures that stifle their existence and humanity.

While our discussion is primarily Christian in its approach, it also adds to the ocean of interdisciplinary thoughts on children's dignity and liberation. Therefore, as Christians and as a global church, we must work closely alongside child advocates from other schools of thought and religious traditions. In doing so, we must be willing to offer our distinctive Christian view of children's humanity and agency while opening our minds and ears to other approaches to honoring, liberating, and protecting children.

Conclusion

Paying attention to the rightful place of children in our theologies and world reveals our restricted, exclusive notions of salvation. A more holistic and expansive notion of salvation that attends to the vulnerabilities and agency of children builds on notions of salvation as humanization, liberation, and social transformation yet more intentionally includes children as persons and is guided by a configuration of special principles, including the rooted solidarity of the caring community, the mystery of children, and cooperative social transformation. This approach builds on biblical texts and contributes to dynamic and ever-expanding notions of salvation and liberation in Christian theology. A more child-attentive and broader understanding of salvation also helps the church honor the humanity of all of its members, young and old, as well as strengthen its advocacy for and solidarity with all children. Indeed, at the intersections of these child-attentive principles are fertile spaces for further exploration of the theology of salvation as well as more intentional advocacy for, rooted solidarity with, and effective social transformation on behalf of all people.

---

²⁸ An understanding of the wider implications of salvation and some interconnected thoughts in the discussions of Karl Rahner, Johann Baptist Metz, Gustavo Gutiérez, and David Tracy can be found in Martinez, *Confronting the Mystery of God*.

²⁹ Gideon, *Child Labour in India*.

7

CHILDREN AND THE
SPIRIT IN LUKE AND ACTS

Amos Yong

Despite the doctrine of the Holy Spirit—pneumatology—being one of the classical theological loci, the Spirit has traditionally been a neglected topic of theology, even to the point of being known as the "shy" or "hidden" member of the Trinity.[1] However, in the second half of the twentieth century, there was a renaissance of Trinitarian theology and, along with that, a resurgence of pneumatology. The latter has brought with it not just advances related to the doctrine of the Spirit but also a pneumatological revisioning of other traditional doctrines.[2] Theologians are not only exploring the person and work of the Spirit but are also considering how a rethinking of other theological or dogmatic themes might emerge by beginning with the Spirit. It is also increasingly clear that the doctrine of the Spirit is concerned not with ethereal, spiritual, or otherworldly dimensions of Christian faith, but is eminently connected with the embodied, social, and environmental nature of human life in this world.[3]

Pentecostal theologians have been contributing to this renewed interest in the Holy Spirit. Global Pentecostalism is a diverse phenomenon and irreducible to one definition.[4] However, central to the movement is an emphasis on the

---

[1] Editor's note: A version of this chapter was originally presented at the "Child Theologies: Perspectives from World Christianity" consultation (organized by Marcia J. Bunge and held at Valparaiso University) and later revised and published as chapter 6 in Amos Yong, *The Hermeneutical Spirit: Theological Interpretation and the Scriptural Imagination for the Third Christian Millennium* (Eugene, OR: Cascade Books, 2017). With slight revisions, the chapter is reprinted here with permission of the author and publisher.

[2] For example, Clark H. Pinnock, *Flame of Love: A Theology of the Holy Spirit* (Downers Grove, IL: InterVarsity Press, 1996).

[3] For example, Eugene F. Rogers Jr., *After the Spirit: A Constructive Pneumatology from Resources outside the Modern West* (Grand Rapids: Eerdmans, 2005).

[4] See, for example, Allan Anderson, *An Introduction to Pentecostalism: Global Charismatic Christianity* (Cambridge: Cambridge University Press, 2004).

Spirit, and a core biblical text for Pentecostals is the Day of Pentecost narrative (Acts 2), which includes an explanation of what was happening regarding the outpouring of the Holy Spirit upon all peoples. Pentecostal theologians have traditionally focused on developing the doctrine of the baptism in the Holy Spirit or on a theology of the spiritual gifts (*charismata*), both of which are central to the vibrant spirituality of Pentecostalism. They are also, however, thinking creatively and constructively out of their experience and reconsidering various traditional and ecumenical theological themes and even doctrines.[5] These reflections have been important not only for their churches and their self-understanding but also for the ecumenical church worldwide in large part because Pentecostalism and charismatic movements have sparked the most vigorous growth of Christianity in the global South.

As a pentecostal theologian,[6] I am sensitive to the global expansion of pentecostal, charismatic, and related movements and to the diversity of its expressions. My own work in pentecostal theology has been intentionally global and thoroughly pneumatological, both materially regarding the doctrine of the Spirit (pneumatology) and methodologically in terms of doing theology from the standpoint of the experience of the Spirit. I have consistently taken a pneumatological approach to exploring many areas of Christian thought and practice.

Although pentecostal theologians, myself included, have contributed to new developments in pneumatology and published widely on a number of subjects, we have said little about how attention to children might inform our understanding of the Spirit. Indeed, despite the flurry of new and creative work about the Spirit in many areas of theological reflection, it seems that "children" is a neglected theme in pneumatology. Theologians across denominations who have reflected on the Holy Spirit say little about children. Among pentecostal theologians, attention to children might be limited to identifying how the Holy Spirit might touch or form children, and this task is understood to be relegated preeminently to applied theology. Children have played active roles in the pentecostal movement since its beginnings, and they are welcome participants in pentecostal worship experiences today based on a core notion in Acts 2 that the Spirit is poured out on "all flesh." However, Pentecostals have not yet developed robust theologies of childhood that reflect their rich perspectives on the Spirit, and the general upbringing and treatment of children among many

---

[5] For example, Frank D. Macchia, *Justified in the Spirit: Creation, Redemption, and the Triune God* (Grand Rapids: Eerdmans, 2010).

[6] Throughout this chapter I capitalize "Pentecostalism" and "Pentecostal" as nouns but do not capitalize "pentecostal" used adjectivally. For discussion of the diversity of Pentecostalisms and the problem of nomenclature, see my *The Spirit Poured Out on All Flesh: Pentecostalism and the Possibility of Global Theology* (Grand Rapids: Baker Academic, 2005), 18–22.

Pentecostals today often reflects a harsh and rigid view of children borrowed from some strands of Protestant fundamentalism that focus on obedience, training, and discipline, including physically punishing children, based mainly on narrow interpretations of the book of Proverbs.

Current developments in pneumatology and theologies of childhood, however, have potential for expanding our understanding of the Spirit and children in new ways. So the question this chapter addresses is twofold: How can attention to children contribute to the task of rethinking theologies of the Spirit, and how can attention to the Spirit illuminate theologies of childhood? Given my own pentecostal grounding, let's begin, first, with a pneumatological approach to scripture and children. Second, building on this pneumatological approach, we explore references to and narratives about the Spirit and children in Luke–Acts. Finally, this chapter presents some practical and theological implications of this programmatic exercise of doing theology in the light of children and the Spirit. Theologically, we demonstrate how a pentecostal and pneumatological approach provides insights for theological conceptions of children, especially by emphasizing that children are Spirit-filled agents and central citizens of the reign of God.[7] It also illustrates how attention to the experiences, perspectives, and realities of children can enrich and transform pneumatology as well as Christology and theological methodologies. Practically, this chapter uplifts the need for inclusive ecclesial environments *for* children (the church as a fellowship of the Spirit), empowered ministries *with* children (the people of God as inspired by the Spirit to bear witness), and a world that is more compassionate *toward* children (the cosmos as the dwelling place of the Spirit). For those from diverse theological traditions, this chapter provides an example of how a pentecostal approach to reading the Bible with attention to the Spirit and children can strengthen Christian theology and practice.

Pentecostal Approaches to Scripture and Children

Pentecostal scholars and theologians have gradually arrived at the academic roundtable.[8] As such, pentecostal contributions to theological conversations across the board are still very preliminary. Take any theological topic, and there is probably a dearth, if not absence, of pentecostal reflection. This is no different

---

[7] There are obviously nonpentecostal pneumatological theologies, and these applied to the task of child-related theologies would undoubtedly highlight different emphases. In this essay, I use "reign of God" instead of "kingdom" language primarily because I wish to avoid the patriarchal and kyriarchical connotations of the latter.

[8] The inaugural volumes were Donald W. Dayton, *Theological Roots of Pentecostalism* (Peabody, MA: Hendrickson Publishers, 1987); and Steven J. Land, *Pentecostal Spirituality: A Passion for the Kingdom* (Sheffield: Sheffield Academic Press, 1993).

from the developing discussions of theologies of childhood, particularly since this theme and undertaking itself are also somewhat recent. Furthermore, since pentecostal theologians are relatively new to the academic scene, their methods are not widely understood. Thus, before offering a rereading of Luke and Acts with children in mind, let us first outline current pentecostal notions of children and approaches to reading scripture.

Pentecostal Experiences

Of course, Pentecostals have and raise children, and these youngsters, in turn, become adults. So it is not as if Pentecostals lack perspective on children—we have all been children at some point in our lives. In the extant literature, of course, children have been an explicit part of the pentecostal experience from the beginning. At the historic Azusa Street Revival (1906–1909), for example, there were testimonies of miraculous healings involving children.[9] In addition, typical of many evangelical and conservative Protestant movements of the first part of the twentieth century, pentecostal evangelism and missionary ventures have always been concerned with the plight and welfare of children, often establishing orphanages for their care in order to raise and form children within a distinctive pentecostal ethos.[10] Furthermore, children have always participated in pentecostal revivals, church services, and other religious activities. For example, there were child evangelists from the very beginning of the Azusa Street mission,[11] and they have always been expected to manifest the unique elements of pentecostal spirituality in their personal lives. Not surprisingly, then, it has been an ongoing pastoral question about how to nurture children so that they may be open to and actively embrace these pentecostal expressions, including the all-important experience of receiving the baptism of the Holy Spirit subsequent to Christian initiation.[12]

---

[9] Sister Dundee, "Suffer the Little Children," in Tom Welchel, *Azusa Street: They Told Me Their Stories*, rev. ed. (Mustang, OK: Dare 2 Dream Books, 2008), 107–112.

[10] Keith J. White, "Insights into Child Theology through the Life and Work of Pandita Ramabai," *Dharma Deepika: A South Asian Journal of Missiological Research* 12, no. 2 (2008): 77–93.

[11] Grant Wacker, "Living with Signs and Wonders: Parents and Children in Early Pentecostal Culture," in *Signs, Wonders, Miracles: Representations of Divine Power in the Life of the Church—Papers Read at the 2003 Summer Meeting and the 2004 Winter Meeting of the Ecclesiastical History Society*, ed. Kate Cooper and Jeremy Gregory, Studies in Church History 41 (Woodbridge, UK: Published for the Ecclesiastical History Society by the Boydell Press, 2005), 423–443, esp. 427. See also Thomas A. Robinson and Lanette D. Ruff, *Out of the Mouths of Babes: Girl Evangelists in the Flapper Era* (Oxford: Oxford University Press, 2012).

[12] Barbara J. Rostrup, "Teaching Children about the Baptism in the Holy Spirit," and William R. Myers, "Encouraging Youth to Receive the Baptism in the Holy Spirit," both in

In many respects, however, pentecostal beliefs about and practices relating to children, especially in the North American context, have been characteristic of those to whom they were closest: their conservative Protestant and fundamentalist cousins. Parents were strict, and children were disciplined, in accordance with such scriptures as, "He that spareth his rod hateth his son: but he that loveth him chasteneth him betimes" (Prov 13:24, KJV), which were believed to be consistent with the overall portrait of the fatherhood of God as one who "disciplines those whom he loves, and chastises every child whom he accepts" (Heb 12:6, KJV; cf. Prov 3:12). Certainly, some pentecostal parents used these texts as justification for what in other contexts would be child abuse, and, in doing so, they provoked their children to wrath and failed to "bring them up in the nurture and admonition of the Lord" (Eph 6:4, KJV). In general, however, Pentecostals took child-rearing seriously, because they sought to raise their children in the ways of the Lord. Inevitably, their methods were also informed by the strictest mores of the time, in hopes that their children would adhere to the Christian way for the rest of their lives.[13]

Times are, of course, changing, and in our contemporary context, this has also involved the complex dynamics of globalization. Migration has meant that the customs and conventions for child-rearing have shifted—even within pentecostal communities—so that nonnegotiables of a previous generation are now being adjudicated in various contexts.[14] As such, we can no longer presume a homogeneous view regarding children among Pentecostals. There are probably many different contemporary understandings of children among lay Pentecostals just as there are many forms of child-rearing practices across the global renewal movement.

Pentecostal Theology and Scriptural Interpretation

Our task is not merely phenomenological or historical but theological. Despite what Pentecostals might believe or what their practices are regarding children,

---

Conference on the Holy Spirit Digest: A Condensation of Plenary Sessions and Seminars of the Conference on the Holy Spirit in Springfield, Missouri, August 16–18, 1982, ed. Gwen Owens (Springfield, MO: Gospel Publishing House, 1983), 174–179 and 180–184, respectively; and Richard L. Dresselhaus, "Can Children Receive the Baptism?" in *Questions and Answers about the Holy Spirit*, ed. (Springfield, MO: Gospel Publishing House, 2001), 105–108.

[13] For fundamentalist theologies of the family, see John R. Rice, *The Home: Courtship, Marriage and Children* (1945; repr. New York: Garland, 1988), and William L. Hendricks, *A Theology for Children* (Nashville: Broadman Press, 1980).

[14] For example, Stephen Hunt and Nicola Lightly, "Work in Progress: The Religious Beliefs of Young Nigerian Pentecostals," *International Journal of Children's Spirituality* 5, no. 1 (2000): 103.

our aim is to explore how pentecostal theology might contribute to a theology of the Spirit that is attentive to children as well as a theology of childhood more attentive to the Spirit. Of course, this raises methodological questions about the nature of pentecostal theology. Essentially, pentecostal spirituality correlates intuitively to a pneumatological orientation, for three interrelated reasons. First, as noted earlier, Pentecostalism derives its name from the Day of Pentecost narrative in Acts 2. The outpouring of the Holy Spirit, signified by the speaking of many tongues and languages, has been intrinsic to the modern pentecostal movement from its beginning. Second, from this follows the fact that not just glossolalia but the entire range of charisms or spiritual gifts are embraced by pentecostal believers as characteristic of the Spirit-filled life. For most Pentecostals, being filled with the Spirit is to be fully and authentically Christian. Last but not least, Pentecostals are bound not by any creed (in fact, many, like other restorationists, are anti-creedal) or by institutional bonds. Rather, as a protean and global movement, what unites pentecostal Christians is their spirituality, particularly their openness to the ongoing manifestation of and interaction with the Holy Spirit.

The preceding overview is suggestive not only for pentecostal theological methodology but also for its hermeneutical orientation, that is, how Pentecostals read the Bible and the particular portions of scripture to which they are most immediately attracted. Regarding the latter, as already noted, Pentecostals focus first and foremost on the book of Acts, desiring to experience the fullness of God as did the apostolic leaders and early followers of the messianic Way. It is the Acts narrative that has thus functioned intuitively as the pentecostal canon-within-the-canon, in contrast to the Reformation focus on St. Paul, in general, and the Epistle to the Romans, in particular.[15] This has given impulse to a unique pentecostal approach to scripture, one that might be characterized as a form of reader-response hermeneutic, although I prefer to call it a soteriological and even eschatological mode of reading the Bible.[16] In other words, Pentecostals spend much less time worrying about historical-critical matters. Rather, Pentecostals take what the Bible says at face value in terms of its descriptions of what happened and are much more concerned that they enter into and experience for themselves the realities of the "Word of God." Consequently, it becomes clear why the book of Acts captures the attention of Pentecostals more than the New Testament Epistles. Narrative genres invite reader self-identification with the described events in ways that the more propositionally framed discourses of the early Christian letters do not.

---

[15] See Roger Stronstad, *Spirit, Scripture, and Theology: A Pentecostal Perspective* (Baguio City, Philippines: Asia Pacific Theological Seminary Press, 1995).

[16] See Yong, *Hermeneutical Spirit*.

Consequently, Pentecostals, in general, read the Bible as they do the early Christian account in Acts—pneumatologically and soteriologically.[17] What they seek—indeed, what initially led them to scripture—is a living encounter with the Holy Spirit, which means that they both read "in the Spirit" and in anticipation and expectation of deeper and more intense experiences of the Spirit. These pneumatic occasions are soteriological through and through, involving regeneration, justification, and sanctification. What the scripture witnesses to in terms of the work of the Spirit among the apostles and prophets is also expected, even prevalent, today.

Pentecostal Narratives about the Spirit and Children in Luke–Acts

From this pentecostal approach to scripture, what do we discover about children and the Spirit that might strengthen theologies of both the Spirit and childhood? Let's begin with the book of Acts and then turn to its prequel, the Gospel of Luke.

Children and Households in Acts 2

Meditating momentarily on the primordial pentecostal narrative—the Day of Pentecost, the outpouring of the Holy Spirit in Acts 2—two key passages may be suggestive for thinking pneumatologically about children. These are the beginning and the end of Peter's apologia to the crowd for what was happening. The former is recorded by Luke as involving reference to the prophet Joel, wherein Peter says,

> This is what was spoken through the prophet Joel: "In the last days it will be, God declares, that I will pour out my Spirit upon all flesh, and your sons and your daughters shall prophesy, and your young men shall see visions, and your old men shall dream dreams. Even upon my slaves, both men and women, in those days I will pour out my Spirit; and they shall prophesy. And I will show portents in the heaven above and signs on the earth below, blood, and fire, and smoky mist. The sun shall be turned to darkness and the moon to blood, before the coming of the Lord's great and glorious day. Then everyone who calls on the name of the Lord shall be saved." (Acts 2:16–21)

---

[17] For example, Veli-Matti Kärkkäinen, *Toward a Pneumatological Theology: Pentecostal and Ecumenical Perspectives on Ecclesiology, Soteriology, and Theology of Mission*, ed. Amos Yong (Lanham, MD: University Press of America, 2002).

Here, two elements are noteworthy for preliminary consideration. First, the visitation of the Spirit involves both sons and daughters, young men and young women, as manifest in their activity of prophesying, dreaming divinely appointed dreams, and seeing God-given visions. Visions and dreams are to be taken in verse 17 as part of the parallelism between young and old men and thus as making the mutual point that "God will be accessible to and direct his people."[18] This is, of course, the basis for pentecostal expectations that children will be involved in any pentecostal revival and that they will be participants in and recipients of the gracious visitation of God whenever the Spirit is present in any extraordinary manner.

Second, and more importantly, is the eschatological horizon of the apostolic understanding. Here, Peter and Luke understand the gift and outpouring of the Spirit upon all flesh as an eschatological event, one that inaugurated "the last days" (Acts 2:17). (From a pentecostal perspective focused on the soteriological dimension of the biblical text, there is less of a need to sort out historical-critical issues about whether Peter really said this or if it is merely Luke who puts this in Peter's mouth.) According to this exposition of the prophet Joel, these last days are the days of God's visitation, manifest through a variety of media—tongues, prophecies, visions, dreams, and so on—and they accomplish, or at least begin to bring about, God's salvation. These salvific works of God (2:21) portend, if not precipitate, "the Lord's great and glorious day" (2:20).

Modern Pentecostals often read these verses through the lens of dispensational eschatology, although there are other ways to understand the eschatological significance of this text.[19] What is undeniable, however, is that modern Pentecostals have embraced this eschatological message and have been thereby inspired to respond to the Great Commission and urgently take up the evangelistic mandate of the church.[20] For them, to experience the Spirit of Pentecost is not merely to manifest charismata-like glossolalia but to be consigned into the "last days" apostolic mission to the world. The Spirit of Pentecost is the eschatological Spirit, and the Spirit of the last days is the Spirit of Pentecost.

Keeping in mind these two elements from the beginning of Peter's sermon in Acts 2, what else then can or should we notice about children and the Spirit from the end of his sermon? Here, he holds an altar call, one in response to a crowd eager to make a commitment:

---

[18] Darrell L. Bock, *Acts: Baker Exegetical Commentary on the New Testament* (Grand Rapids: Baker Academic, 2007), 114.

[19] For example, Larry R. McQueen, *Joel and the Spirit: The Cry of a Prophetic Hermeneutic* (Sheffield: Sheffield Academic Press, 1995).

[20] See D. William Faupel, *The Everlasting Gospel: The Significance of Eschatology in the Development of Pentecostal Thought* (Sheffield: Sheffield Academic Press, 1996).

> Now when they heard this, they were cut to the heart and said to Peter and to the other apostles, "Brothers, what should we do?" Peter said to them, "Repent, and be baptized every one of you in the name of Jesus Christ so that your sins may be forgiven; and you will receive the gift of the Holy Spirit. For the promise is for you, for your children, and for all who are far away, everyone whom the Lord our God calls to him." (Acts 2:37–39)

Again, we find the pneumatological and soteriological self-understanding of the apostolic church: salvation at least culminates, if it does not also consist centrally, in the gift of the Holy Spirit.

What is further noteworthy for our purposes, however, is the reference to children. In this case, the apostolic response was that the promised gift of the Spirit was going to be liberally available. The crowd, who had already been indicted for the murder and crucifixion of Jesus (Acts 2:36), was promised full salvation in Christ by the power of the Spirit. Not only that, salvation was also accessible to their children, near and far, geographically close by and distant. From an eschatological perspective, "far away" means not those removed from Jerusalem but descendants separated by generations in time.[21] To be sure, "children" in this context means more literally descendants than it does those youngsters who remain under the oversight of their parents. However, my point is that the metaphorical reference to "children" in the broader context of Peter's (and Luke's) explanation of the Pentecost event does not exclude those who are not adults. Rather, the thrust of the pentecostal message here involves "all flesh" being included in the soteriological and eschatological work of the Spirit of God. Furthermore, the children whom Peter (and Luke) discusses are eschatological agents and subjects who have not only encountered the Spirit but also participated in the salvation-historical events of the last days.

After chapter 2, sons and daughters are rarely mentioned in the book of Acts.[22] There are references to Moses's sons (7:29), the sons of Sceva (19:14), and the daughters of Philip (21:9).[23] Acts also rarely refers to children as a group: once metaphorically regarding the people of Israel (13:33) and then at Paul's departure from Tyre to Jerusalem. Interestingly, on this latter occa-

---

[21] For this reading of the "last days," I am indebted to Lutheran theologian Vítor Westhelle, "Liberation Theology: A Latitudinal Perspective," in Jerry L. Walls, *The Oxford Handbook of Eschatology* (Oxford: Oxford University Press, 2008), 311–327, esp. 320–323.

[22] As noted also by Joel B. Green, "'Tell Me a Story': Perspectives on Children from the Acts of the Apostles," in *The Child in the Bible*, ed. Marcia Bunge (Grand Rapids: Eerdmans, 2008), 215–232.

[23] All scriptural references here and in these next few paragraphs are to the book of Acts, unless otherwise noted.

sion, it is said, "When our days there were ended, we left and proceeded on our journey; and all of them, with wives and children, escorted us outside the city. There we knelt down on the beach and prayed" (21:5). Luke, the narrator, is obviously present, but so are entire households in saying goodbye to Paul.

Although specific children are seldom mentioned, households with children appear frequently. Cornelius's household is said to have feared God (10:2), and entire households are visited with the salvation of the Spirit (Cornelius's in 11:14) and then initiated into faith through baptism (Lydia's and the jailer's in Philippi, 16:15 and 16:31–34, and Crispus's in Corinth, 18:8). So, although children are not talked about explicitly in these accounts, some understanding of the social structure of first-century Mediterranean families helps us to realize that they were included in these households. Children traveled with their parents (the father being the head of household). They often participated in the faith practices of adults in the home, and it was not surprising that when the head of household—who could be a woman (like Lydia)—converted religiously, the children would also follow suit.

More importantly for our purposes, the universal scope, eschatological reach, and soteriological promises of God—that all flesh, including sons and daughters, would be visited by and receive the gift of the Holy Spirit—are anticipated in Luke and find their fulfillment even in the Acts narrative within the context of the household.[24] Children are saved and baptized, just as Peter indicated would happen in this assuring response to the anxious crowd on the Day of Pentecost. Nowhere, though, does Luke mention that children, as toddlers or whatever, received the fullness of the Spirit. However, it is recorded that Philip the deacon "had four unmarried daughters who had the gift of prophecy" (21:9). We are not told how young they were at the onset of these gifts, but, given the understanding of the Spirit in both Acts and Luke, when that happened is not as important as that it happened. Whereas during the Second Temple period, the major formative rites for children were in the synagogue, for the earliest Christians, these events, particularly those associated with the coming and even present reign of God, happened within households as their heads and families responded to the presence and activity of the Spirit of God.[25]

---

[24] David Lertis Matson, *Household Conversion Narratives in Acts: Pattern and Interpretation*, Journal for the Study of the New Testament Supplement Series 123 (Sheffield: Sheffield Academic Press, 1996).

[25] See John H. Elliott, "Temple versus Household in Luke–Acts: A Contrast in Social Institutions," in *The Social World of Luke–Acts: Models for Interpretation*, ed. Jerome H. Neyrey (Peabody, MA: Hendrickson, 1991), 211–240.

Children in Luke

For Pentecostals, the book of Acts has principally been the entry point into the scriptural canon. For anyone seeking to formulate a robust pneumatology, entering into a sustained dialogue with the Gospels and the book of Acts is a good place to begin. St. Luke the theologian is the most charismatically oriented of the Gospel writers. The gift of the Spirit most prominently highlighted in the Day of Pentecost narrative (Acts 2) is not just an incidental event in the life of the early church but is central to Luke's understanding of the life and ministry of Jesus and of church as a charismatic and missionary fellowship of the Spirit.[26]

I suggest, then, reading Luke's account of the life of Christ (the Third Gospel) from the standpoint of the Spirit's outpouring on all flesh.[27] The same Spirit that was given without measure to the apostolic community also empowered the life and ministry of Jesus (see Luke 4:18–19; Acts 10:38). For Luke, the life of Christ is not a detached historical account but a theological understanding deeply informed by the apostolic experience as that unfolded through the expansion of the early church around the Mediterranean world.[28] More particularly, considering Luke's own major themes, Jesus is not merely presented as a risen savior but understood as one anticipating and then enacting the outpouring of the Spirit. Acts states explicitly that the Spirit is given by Jesus (see 2:32–33). In other words, this is not merely a post-Easter perspective but a post-Pentecost one as well.

When we turn to Luke's account of the life of Christ, four noteworthy references to children become apparent.[29]

First, John the Baptist, the forerunner of Jesus, is also said to be pneumatically empowered to prepare the way for the salvation-historical events to come. More precisely, it is said of John: "With the spirit and power of Elijah he will go before him, to turn the hearts of parents to their children, and the disobedient to the wisdom of the righteous, to make ready a people prepared for the Lord" (1:17). Is the issue, here, intergenerational conflicts? Perhaps. More probably, the "disobedience" of the fathers needs to be aligned with the holiness of God

---

[26] See James B. Shelton, *Mighty in Word and Deed: The Role of the Holy Spirit in Luke–Acts* (Peabody, MA: Hendrickson, 1991).

[27] See Amos Yong, *Who Is the Holy Spirit?: A Walk with the Apostles* (Brewster, MA: Paraclete Press, 2011).

[28] That Luke is no mere historian but also a theologian in his own right is now established, the picture of Luke the theologian emerging, interestingly, during a similar period of time as that of modern pentecostal scholarship; see François Bovon, *Luke the Theologian: Fifty-Five Years of Research (1950–2005)* (Waco, TX: Baylor University Press, 2005).

[29] Unless otherwise noted, all scriptural references throughout this section are to the Gospel of Luke.

the Father, so that redemption might be effected for all, parents and children, the latter in all of the innocence with which they are taken up into the reign of God.[30] The goal is clear: that the renewal and restoration of Israel can occur and that the people of God can be revitalized and reinvigorated as the dwelling place of the Spirit. Hence, John "grew and became strong in spirit, and he was in the wilderness until the day he appeared publicly to Israel" (1:80). This should not be surprising: both of his parents, Elizabeth and Zechariah, also experienced charismatic visitations of the Spirit (see 1:41, 67). Should not the son of two Spirit-filled parents also be nurtured in the ways of the Spirit, especially one with his own charismatic vocation before him? Should not one whose task it was to effect a ministry of reconciliation between parents and children also be bonded together with his parents, even from his mother's womb (1:41, 44)?

Second, Jesus's childhood certainly deserves comment. Conceived through the Holy Spirit (1:35), he was recognized, even as an infant, through the revelation of the Spirit, as symbolically representing and even embodying the promised salvation not only of Israel but also of the world (2:25–32). Alongside his cousin John, Jesus also "grew and became strong, filled with wisdom; and the favor of God was upon him" (2:40). At the age of twelve, Jesus had already developed spiritually enough to recognize that, while he needed to remain obedient to his parents, Mary and Joseph (2:51), he had also become sufficiently sensitive to spiritual and religious matters that he sought out the teachers of Israel to learn more about God as the Father of Israel (cf. 2:46–49).[31] This divine fatherhood is later revealed as merciful (6:36), as a caretaker and provider (12:30–32), and as patient and longsuffering (the parable of the Prodigal Son), although it is unclear at this point if Jesus recognized all of these theological qualities. Yet clearly, the Spirit was with Jesus, even during these years, as he "increased in wisdom and in years, and in divine and human favor" (2:52). He honored his earthly parents so that his mother "treasured all these things in her heart" (2:51b). One wonders to what degree his mother was able to recognize and be supportive of her son's youthful mission since she herself was probably not much more than a teenager when she responded to the divine call and even prophesied then (see the Magnificat; 1:46–55), as if anticipating the Pentecost unleashing of the Spirit's "prophesying daughters"—even as Jesus related to his heavenly Father as one intent on fulfilling, rather than falling short of, his vocational call.[32] By stepping into his vocational calling at the age of twelve, Jesus

---

[30] See Joel B. Green, *The Gospel of Luke* (Grand Rapids: Eerdmans, 1997), 76–77.

[31] Wilfrid L. Hannam, *In the Things of My Father: A Study of the Purpose of Luke the Evangelist* (London: Epworth Press, 1953), 45–49.

[32] Adrienne von Speyr, *The World of Prayer*, trans. Graham Harrison (San Francisco: Ignatius Press, 1985), has a short section (290–291) on Jesus's sonship being shaped as a

anticipates the Spirit-filled younger generation of Acts, when young men shall see visions and shall prophesy in the power of the Spirit.

Third, then, Jesus as the Spirit-empowered agent of redemption is clearly also recorded as having uttered some hard sayings that set off, rather than reconciled, parents with children and vice versa. Representative of these are the following four passages:

> Then his mother and his brothers came to him, but they could not reach him because of the crowd. And he was told, "Your mother and your brothers are standing outside, wanting to see you." But he said to them, "My mother and my brothers are those who hear the word of God and do it." (8:19–21)

* * *

> "Whoever comes to me and does not hate father and mother, wife and children, brothers and sisters, yes, and even life itself, cannot be my disciple." (14:26)[33]

* * *

> And he said to them, "Truly I tell you, there is no one who has left house or wife or brothers or parents or children, for the sake of the kingdom of God." (18:29)

* * *

> "You will be betrayed even by parents and brothers, by relatives and friends; and they will put some of you to death." (21:16)

From a child-attentive theological perspective, these four pericopes might appear to suggest that Jesus advocated not honoring one's parents or that he exonerated parents for neglecting their children for the sake of the reign of God. However, we need to keep in mind that Jesus was aware of the commandment to honor one's parents (18:20), and there is no clear indication that his way of life was dishonoring to them. Furthermore, and more importantly, from

---

child through pneumatic participation in the divine love. In other words, Jesus was able to pursue his father's will without deviation because of his own Spirit-filled life.

[33] To "hate" means not to abhor, detest, or loathe, but to love less in comparison to something else, in this case, the call of discipleship; so notes F. F. Bruce, *The Hard Sayings of Jesus* (Downers Grove, IL: InterVarsity Press, 1983), 120.

within the eschatological horizon of the outpouring of the Spirit, these texts bear witness consistently to Jesus's commitment to do the work of establishing the reign of God to restore, renew, and redeem Israel. From this perspective, there can be no partial allegiances since the oppression of Israel has persisted for far too long, and any stragglers will simply perpetuate the wandering of the people of God in the wilderness.

Fourth, and most importantly, as a counter to more fundamentalist readings of the previous litany of texts related to family relationships, all of Jesus's explicit teachings about children as well as his dispositions toward, behaviors regarding, and treatments of children are compassionate and positive.[34] For instance, when Jesus's disciples were bickering among themselves about who was the greatest, "Jesus, aware of their inner thoughts, took a little child and put it by his side, and said to them, 'Whoever welcomes this child in my name welcomes me, and whoever welcomes me welcomes the one who sent me; for the least among all of you is the greatest'" (9:47–48). Later, in rejoicing with his disciples about their experiencing the manifestation of God's saving power in their itinerant ministries, he exclaimed in the Holy Spirit, "I thank you, Father, Lord of heaven and earth, because you have hidden these things from the wise and the intelligent and have revealed them to infants; yes, Father, for such was your gracious will" (10:21). The reference to "infants" here is, of course, metaphorical, but the metaphor works precisely because of the point that was being made: that the reign of God would arrive not among the wise or intelligent, but to and through those who were most intimate with and dependent upon the goodwill of the Father.

Then, on the road to Jerusalem, it was said of him, "People were bringing even infants to him that he might touch them; and when the disciples saw it, they sternly ordered them not to do it. But Jesus called for them and said, 'Let the little children come to me, and do not stop them; for it is to such as these that the kingdom of God belongs. Truly I tell you, whoever does not receive the kingdom of God as a little child will never enter it'" (18:15–17). In these instances, Jesus established children, even infants, as being the central citizens of the reign of God. The "least of these" are thus neither merely tolerated nor only recognized as only potential contributors to the divine will and work. Instead, they are part of the people of God whom God promises to care for as God's own, even to the point of promising (24:49) to give them fully of God's own self in the Holy Spirit (cf. 11:11–13).[35]

---

[34] See Ma. Marilou Ibita and Reimund Bieringer, "(Stifled) Voices of the Future: Learning about Children in the Bible," in *Children's Voices: Children's Perspectives in Ethics, Theology, and Religious Education*, ed. Annemie Dillon and Didier Pollefeyt (Leuven: Uitgeverij Peeters, 2010), 73–115, esp. 90.

[35] See Jeremy Worthen, "Babes in Arms: Speechlessness and Selfhood," in *Children of*

There are other Lukan accounts of Jesus's responses to other children like the son of the widow of Nain (7:11–17), Jairus's daughter (8:41–56), and the demon-possessed son (9:37–45), and further child-theological considerations with Lukan perspectives need to look at these as well as other aspects of the above materials of which we have only scratched the surface. Suffice it to say that Jesus's interactions with children as well as his teachings about them are all messianic activities accomplished under the inspiration and empowerment of the Holy Spirit (4:1, 14, 18). In fact, Jesus's understanding of children was thoroughly soteriological and eschatological, having to do with the coming reign of God inaugurated with his charismatic and messianic-prophetic life and ministry. If the outpouring of the Spirit in Acts serves to herald the present realities of the coming reign of God, then the words and deeds of the Spirit-filled Christ in Luke prefigure and precipitate this eschatological event to the point that some—for example, the son of the widow of Nain—ultimately experienced the power of the Spirit of the last days, the coming to life from the dead!

Theological and Practical Implications

In this last section, we briefly outline some of the broader implications from the preceding discussion for strengthening theologies of the Spirit and childhood and our views of and interactions with children in families, congregations, and communities.[36]

An Eschatological Perspective

Consideration of children and the Spirit in Luke and Acts invites, as we have seen, an eschatological perspective. From this "last days" vantage point, the normal lives of children persist to some degree: they are shown as being cared for by parents and thus in submission to parental authority (i.e., being present with their parents for Paul's departure to Jerusalem). However, nothing is conventional about life in the reign of God. The activation and enablement of sons and daughters by the Spirit, and the presence of children, even infants, at the heart of the coming kingdom, signals that Jesus in the power of the Spirit is bringing about another form of sociality, one oriented not around the values of the world but around the reign of God. This is a world, as was noted of the

---

God: Towards a Theology of Childhood, ed. Angela Shier-Jones (Peterborough, UK: Epworth, 2007), 41–61, esp. 56–57.

[36] The following section is based on my reflections on the theology of the family. See Amos Yong, "Sons and Daughters, Young and Old: Toward a Pentecostal Theology of the Family," *PentecoStudies: An Interdisciplinary Journal for Research on the Pentecostal and Charismatic Movement* 10, no. 2 (2011): 143–173.

apostles, turned upside-down (Acts 17:6).[37] It was an in-between time, during the last days inaugurated by the Spirit-filled Christ and his outpouring of the Spirit on all flesh while still awaiting the final consummation. In this time and space, children symbolized both the innocence and the potential of a new order, one redeemed from sin and not contaminated by fallen conventions.

It might be thought then that Luke (in his two-volume work) has nothing to say about children in the "real world." After all, it seems to be too far-fetched to think that children only live in the eschatological time and space of the Spirit of God. Yet, as we have shown, Luke and Acts helps us see the radical and generous outpouring of the Spirit to all flesh, including children. The Spirit is liberally available to all. Furthermore, the texts remind us that children are not just simply present in the midst of adults or to be taught by adults. Rather, children are open to and embraced by the Spirit. They are Spirit-filled and eschatological agents who can bear witness to the gospel and awaken adults to the possibilities of the present experience of God's eschatological reign.

Pneumatological Aspects

What then about pneumatology? That the Spirit is poured out upon young and old highlights the freedom of the Spirit to give of herself as she wills. St. Paul perceived as much in his thinking about the charismatic dimensions of ecclesial life and congregational worship: "All these are activated by one and the same Spirit, who allots to each one individually just as the Spirit chooses" (1 Cor 12:11). A further refrain throughout Paul's interactions with the Corinthians is that the Spirit empowers not the strong but the weak; the Spirit elects not the elite but the marginalized; the Spirit works through not the wise but the foolish, and so on.[38] This is consistent with how Luke understands the central role of young men and women in the eschatological work of the Spirit. In short, the workings of the Spirit highlight the normativity of prophesying daughters as well as visionary adult males, although perhaps the former more clearly depict the Spirit's unconventional methods in bringing about the reign of God.

Note, though, that in Luke, the divine Father not only wants to give good gifts but desires also to give of deity itself. In Jesus's words, "'If you then, who are evil, know how to give good gifts to your children, how much more will the heavenly Father give the Holy Spirit to those who ask him!'" (Luke 11:13).[39]

---

[37] See John T. Carroll, "'What Then Will This Child Become?': Perspectives on Children in the Gospel of Luke," in *The Child in the Bible*, 177–194, at 194.

[38] See my "Disability and the Gifts of the Spirit: Pentecost and the Renewal of the Church," *Journal of Pentecostal Theology* 19, no. 1 (Spring 2010): 76–93.

[39] See also Amos Yong, *Spirit of Love: A Trinitarian Theology of Grace* (Waco, TX: Baylor University Press, 2012), esp. chapter 6.

The Spirit actually becomes the promise of the Father (Luke 24:49; Acts 1:4), which begins to be fulfilled on the Day of Pentecost (Acts 2:33, 39). In other words, the promise of the Father and the outpouring of the Spirit on all flesh—sons and daughters, young and old—is not only what enables the reconciliation of parents and children but also restores their relationship to Yahweh. From this pentecostal, eschatological, and pneumatological perspective, then, children become central to the salvation-historical intention of God to renew Israel and to redeem the world. It may even be that children are the most receptive of the human species to the dawning of the reign of God.

Christological and Methodological Implications

This leads also to more systematic theological considerations. To be sure, there is no space for a full explication across the loci, much less any in-depth reflection in any one locus. Nevertheless, let me suggest two strands of inquiry: the christological and methodological.

Christologically, thinking about children ought to return us, again and again, to Jesus.[40] Both Jesus's teachings about children and his reception of them are theologically potent. Note, in particular, those aspects of the Gospel accounts that are pneumatological and, especially for Luke, eschatological. Jesus's teachings and actions are Spirit-anointed, precisely the meaning of his messiahship. As such, what is said of children is just as much pneumatological as christological. What we need, then, is a Spirit-christological theology of childhood. Further, as already intimated, Jesus's teachings about and interactions with children must be understood in an eschatological plane. In that case, then, his salvific message and actions bring about the reign of God, at the center of which are the children of the world.

Perhaps this means that at the heart of the reign of God are both vulnerability and play. I return soon to the former; for the moment, I concentrate on the latter. If children are the point of entry into the reign of God and if the reign of God is characterized at its core by children, what does this tell us about how God not only sees but wishes to structure the world? What children do is play, at least if they are healthy, cared for, and properly nurtured.[41] In that case, the reign of God is also characterized fundamentally by play rather than by any pragmatism, utilitarianism, or even instrumentalism. If play reigns, then

---

[40] See also Judith M. Gundry-Volf, "The Least and the Greatest: Children in the New Testament," in *The Child in Christian Thought*, ed. Marcia J. Bunge (Grand Rapids: Eerdmans, 2001), 29–60.

[41] See also Peter Privett, "Play," in Anne Richards and Peter Privett, *Through the Eyes of a Child: New Insights in Theology from a Child's Perspective* (London: Church Publishing House, 2009), 101–124.

calculative and instrumental logic do not. The image of God then becomes most deeply manifest in the playful nature of *homo ludens*.

Pentecostal theologian Wolfgang Vondey has argued at length that the pentecostal spirit—in effect the Spirit of Pentecost—is essentially and primarily playful.[42] For Vondey, the work of the Spirit is liberating, creative, and playfully unpredictable. Children exhibit these qualities. However, adults have been "trained" to grow up, and play is transformed into work. Not that work is bad, but human rationality in the case of work without or apart from play becomes rationalism when driven by calculative goals. Instead, the imagination ought to be permitted, and we should be encouraged to engage in and exercise imaginative play, even amid our work.

What Vondey's argument does not consider is the perspective of children. When that is added into the mix, reason is directed toward a playful kind of creativity. Children reason imaginatively and intuitively in their playful interactions with one another. They help remind us of the proper role of creativity, spontaneity, and novelty in our thinking, regardless of age. The theological imagination, then, would not work first and foremost deductively or inductively, but perhaps abductively—by provisionally drawing and exploring affective sensibilities and instinctively formulating hypotheses and inferences—in a creative hermeneutical circle that connects the dots in an attitude of playful reverence.

While play ought to be central to the theological task and our understanding of the reign of God, we must also be vigilant of the vulnerability of children. As noted by practical theologian Joyce Ann Mercer, when talking about children, "It's not 'child's play'!"[43]

Children are vulnerable to all kinds of threats, from poverty to war. Their needs are manifold—physical, economic, social, educational, and spiritual—and they are reliant on the provision of adults. But they are even more at risk because of the asymmetry between adults and children. Hence, the latter are susceptible to adults who have power and authority over them and are defenselessly exposed to those who might prey on their unsuspecting nature. Child abuse happens in many forms, and each time it happens, the child's capacity to play, create, and imagine a better world is compromised.[44]

Adults, theologians included, have the moral obligation to look out and care for the vulnerable in our midst, children included. Practical theologian

---

[42] See Wolfgang Vondey, *Beyond Pentecostalism: The Crisis of Global Christianity and the Renewal of the Theological Agenda* (Grand Rapids: Eerdmans, 2010).

[43] Joyce Ann Mercer, *Welcoming Children: A Practical Theology of Childhood* (St. Louis: Chalice Press, 2005), 71–116.

[44] See Janet Pais, *Suffer the Children: A Theology of Liberation by a Victim of Child Abuse* (New York: Paulist Press, 1991).

Adrian Thatcher has insisted, "The Christ Child is the foundation of children's rights! God became a Child."[45] Furthermore, it is not just the Christ Child who symbolizes our obligations to children but the Spirited Christ Child that exemplifies what it means to be people who abide according to the coming reign of God: the young Jesus of Nazareth who was doing his father's work, because he was full of the wisdom, grace, and leading of the Spirit. In that case, the Spirit of the last days is the Spirit that empowers young men and young women—sons and daughters—to prophetically call the church to her moral responsibility for these same children.

Practical Dimensions

These insights from Luke and Acts have further practical implications for our interactions with children at home, in our faith communities, and in the world.

Regarding the life of the church, seeing children as participants in and recipients of the Spirit calls us to create a welcoming ecclesial environment *for* children (seeing the church as a fellowship of the Spirit) and empowered ministries *with* children (knowing that the people of God are inspired by the Spirit to bear witness). We are not only to welcome children to worship and make formative liturgies accessible to them but also to honor their experiences and contributions to the faith community. Simply including children could end up only training them to be no more than "consumers" of these central Christian rites.[46] As important as participating in these rites is, it is more important to involve and engage children so that they experience how their lives, actions, and words contribute to the constitution of these Christian practices. In turn, adults may also come to expect this as a normative part of Christian celebration. In other words, if the Spirit is poured out indiscriminately upon all flesh, children included, then they also become the prophetic witnesses—sometimes using words, other times not, perhaps simply in and through the way they are present to us—to the eschatological judgment, renewal, and salvation of God. To involve children in the central Christian practices is to allow their presence to be felt, their voices to be heard, and their lives to be a conduit of the Spirit's work in the ecclesial community.

This view of children, the Spirit, and Jesus's own life also has practical ramifications for inspiring Christians to create a more just and compassionate world

---

[45] Adrian Thatcher, "Beginning Again with Jesus," in *Children's Voices: Children's Perspectives in Ethics, Theology, and Religious Educatio*, Annemie Dillen and Didier Pollefeyt, ed. (Leuven: Uitgeverij Peeters, 2010), 137–161, at 159.

[46] See Gertrud Mueller Nelson, "Christian Formation of Children: The Role of Ritual and Celebration," in *Liturgy and Spirituality in Context: Perspectives on Prayer and Culture*, ed. Eleanor Bernstein (Collegeville, MN: Liturgical Press, 1990), 114–135.

for all children (understanding that the whole cosmos is the dwelling place of the Spirit). This involves attending to the vulnerabilities and needs of children and ensuring their safety, protection, and well-being. Such commitments require guaranteeing that their basic needs are met and responding effectively to and preventing child abuse and neglect whether in our homes, faith communities, or larger social contexts. Creating a more just and compassionate world for children also means honoring the agency and capacities of children by respecting them, listening to their ideas, recognizing their contributions, encouraging them as they grow and take on new responsibilities, and advancing children's rights.

Pentecostals, mainline Protestants, and other Christians across traditions also have much to gain from a close reading of Luke and Acts for strengthening family relationships and spiritual life. For mainline Christians, for example, Luke provides a fresh and often neglected understanding of children as Spirit-filled agents. Although mainline Christians seek to welcome children in their congregations, having an understanding of children as Spirit-filled could encourage more parents to carry out spiritual practices in the home and listen to and learn from their children's religious questions and spiritual experiences. Luke's vision also challenges mainline Christians to critique models of healthy child development that ignore the significance of religious and spiritual life. For Pentecostals who already respect children as Spirit-filled, they are reminded by Luke of Jesus's care and compassion for children and that the work of the Spirit is not limited to the worship space but radically alters our relationships to one another at home and in the world. Once Pentecostals or Christians of any affiliation take Jesus's life and eschatological relationality to heart, how can they blindly follow popular yet narrow and rigid views of children borrowed from strands of Protestant fundamentalism that neglect the freedom of the Spirit and Christ's compassion and focus instead on training and disciplining children, including with physical blows? In other words, rather than measuring Luke's eschatological reality according to conventions of the family espoused by some contemporary fundamentalists, Christians across the ecclesiastical spectrum must rethink child-parent relationships in light of Jesus's life and the images of children associated with the coming reign of God. This means trusting that the Spirit moves among us all, therefore empowering us to respect, show compassion toward, and participate with children in the Spirit-filled life.

Conclusion and Transitions

This brief pentecostal reading of Acts and Luke expands our understanding of both the Spirit and children, yet so much more theological work can and needs to be done. This study invites us to explore many more biblical texts with a pneumatological and child-attentive lens. We could explore, for example, the implications of St. Paul's charismatic theology for family life and child advocacy. We could examine how the references to children function in the passages discussing the Day of Yahweh in the Hebrew prophets or in the eschatologically dominated message of the Apocalypse. Meanwhile, we will not too soon exhaust ourselves in thinking about how children must be honored and cared for as those at the center of the workings of the Spirit of God in these last days.[47]

---

[47] I am grateful to Marcia J. Bunge for her editorial work on this chapter through many iterations.

8

PLACING ETHICS AND CHILDREN AT THE HEART OF ECCLESIOLOGY

Agbonkhianmeghe E. Orobator

The Christian community in sub-Saharan Africa is growing at a phenomenal rate, and its visibility and influence in public life are rapidly increasing. The intensity of this religious effervescence is so great that surveys and reports have described the growth of Christianity with striking adjectives, such as "unprecedented," "astronomical," and "extraordinary." Even more remarkably, Christianity has only been present in some parts of Africa for a little over a century. Between 1900 and 2010, Christianity recorded a net increase of 57 percent. In particular, Catholicism grew from less than 1 percent of sub-Saharan Africa's population in 1910 to 16 percent in 2010.[1] Any visitor to towns and cities in sub-Saharan Africa can hardly miss the glaring public signs of intense religious activities.

Regrettably, accounts of this experience of religious growth and effervescence rarely pay attention to the particular needs of children or their role in the church. Children are almost invisible in the story of the church's growth in Africa, even though reports estimate that persons under fifteen make up 41 percent of the population.[2] Statistics of church growth often do not highlight the percentage of children and youth and tend to assume an adult demography. Consequently, statistics regarding children, such as the number admitted to the sacrament of baptism, consider them as adults in the making.

---

[1] These and other statistics are available through the Pew Research Center (pewforum.org). See, for example, "The Global Catholic Population," February 13, 2013. For the growth of Christianity in Africa, see Philip Jenkins, *The Next Christendom: The Coming of Global Christianity* (Oxford: Oxford University Press, 2002); and John L. Allen, Jr., *The Future Church: How Ten Trends Are Revolutionizing the Catholic Church* (New York: Doubleday, 2009).

[2] See various reports, including the "World Population Review," accessed October 5, 2020, https://worldpopulationreview.com/continents/africa-population.

Furthermore, even though reflection on the nature and mission of the church—ecclesiology—is an important theological category across global forms of Christianity, attention to children rarely plays a role in constructing theologies of the church, including in my own Roman Catholic tradition. Notwithstanding its tightly constructed doctrinal framework, Roman Catholic ecclesiology unfolds fairly oblivious to the needs and experiences of children. At best, these needs are presumed. However, they do not play a significant role in constructing the theological self-understanding of the church.

Unfortunately, lack of attention to children is detectable in my own writing on the church and its mission. In my previous theological research and scholarship dealing with the nature, mission, and function of the church in the context of social crises, I have presumed an adult subject, interlocutor, and audience. For example, in *From Crisis to Kairos,* my principal aim was to generate a framework for developing an ecclesiology that pays attention to social crises, not as extraneous factors or an afterthought, but as integral to the mission of the church and, therefore, constitutive of a holistic theology of the church in Africa and beyond.[3] Based on an empirical survey of the socioeconomic and political context of the mission of the church in Africa, I devised the categories of pilgrim, mother, and development as templates of a theological imagination of what church ought to be and do in times of displacement, HIV/AIDS, and poverty. These templates were founded on the assumption that the church could not stand on the sidelines of these crises as an indifferent observer. Viewing my previous work through a child-attentive lens, I realize now that, without exception, all agents discussed in *From Crisis to Kairos* were adults: women and men who were displaced, living with HIV/AIDS, or impoverished. The same was true of my theological reflections on the body of Christ; it was an adult body.[4]

As I reflect on the absence of attention to children in Roman Catholic doctrinal formulations of the church and in my own work, I must contend not only with the urgent needs of children in African society but also the crisis of child sexual abuse within the church. Pedophilia and child sexual abuse have convulsed the institutional edifice of the Roman Catholic Church worldwide. Children in the church have been harmed by perpetrators of abuse as well as church leaders who covered up crimes and enabled abuse to continue. Many individuals no longer consider the institutional church to be a safe place for

---

[3] Agbonkhianmeghe E. Orobator, *From Crisis to Kairos: A Theology of the Church in the Time of HIV/AIDS, Refugees, and Poverty* (Nairobi: Paulines Publications Africa, 2005).

[4] Agbonkhianmeghe E. Orobator, *The Church as Family: African Ecclesiology in Its Social Context* (Nairobi: Paulines Publications Africa, 2000); and *Reconciliation, Justice, and Peace: The Second African Synod*, ed. A. E. Orobator (Maryknoll, NY: Orbis Books, 2011).

children.⁵ How should the church respond? And how can anyone develop a credible theology and ethics within the church that pays attention to the voices and eyes of the child, when what the child hears and sees is laden with painful experiences of abuse and betrayal of trust?

Given the absence of attention to children in theological understandings of the church, the enormous needs of children, and child abuse in the Roman Catholic Church, this chapter seeks to reconceptualize the doctrine of the church and its ethical imperatives in the light of attention to children. I take an approach that is relatively new in my own work and in African Catholic theology. As in my previous work, this chapter places ethics at the heart of the church, and I draw on biblical and theological sources as well as insights from African literature, cultural anthropology, and the social sciences. However, here I articulate a stronger theology of the church by mining these sources for their insights about children and by attending more intentionally to the needs and agency of children and the church's ethical responsibilities to them. Any doctrine of the church that takes children seriously cannot be exhausted in an abstract or speculative theological exercise. Ethical questions and concerns regarding children must both shape the church's self-understanding and guide its action in the world.

Given my aim of placing both ethics and children at the heart of ecclesiology, this chapter is divided into three sections. After briefly clarifying the significance of my approach and its varied sources, I explore how children are perceived and treated in various African contexts, highlighting the many ways in which children's worth is undermined and their voices silenced in both church and society. I then draw insights from the Bible for taking children more seriously, particularly Jesus's treatment of children. Building on these sources, I critique some of the limitations of current African and Roman Catholic narratives of the church and offer a more robust theological understanding of the church shaped by and attentive to the needs and strengths of children. The chapter identifies three key duties and responsibilities to children: recognizing them as full members of and active participants in the body of Christ, seeking repentance for sins against them and caring for and protecting them, and defending the equality and dignity of all children. These ethical imperatives lead to a doctrine of the church that is radically inclusive and self-critical, and that honors the full humanity of children. Although the chapter focuses on

---

⁵ Over the past few years, the Roman Catholic Church has sought to respond to the scandal of pedophilia and child sexual abuse by clergy in a rash of policy statements, norms, and guidelines. See http://www.vatican.va/resources/index_en.htm. See also Agbonkhianmeghe E. Orobator, "Between Ecclesiology and Ethics: Promoting a Culture of Protection and Care in Church and Society," *Theological Studies* 80, no. 4 (2019): 897–915.

my own context in Africa and addresses ways to reformulate Roman Catholic understandings of the church, it provides a model for other Christian traditions around the world for rethinking ecclesiology and underscoring the church's responsibilities to children and youth.

Perceptions of Children in African Contexts

How does one begin the task of placing children and ethics at the heart of the church and its mission? What approach does one take, especially given the church's neglect of children both in its theological self-understanding and its action in the world? What sources does one use?

Before clarifying my general approach and sources, let me acknowledge that any answer to these questions carries the risk of appearing slightly contrived, because I write this chapter as an adult. Thus my approach is limited by my adult biases and prejudices. Yet the reality of unintended biases need not paralyze an honest and genuine attempt to rethink Christian doctrines and practices in the light of children and childhood. Furthermore, theological discourse attentive to children always involves an element of theological reconstruction and imagination. Accordingly, my approach calls for modesty, humility, and prudence in deference to the experiences and voices of children; the use of various sources; and contenting myself with the sincere admission that the child is not me.

Preliminary Clarifications

My own approach unfolds within two overlapping and overarching contexts: the Roman Catholic Church and African Indigenous traditions ("traditions" here used in the broad sense of beliefs, rituals, narratives, etc.). Students of African theology will recognize here that my approach is in line with the inculturation strand of theological reflection in Africa. In one of my previous works, *Theology Brewed in an African Pot,* I illustrated the meaning and practice of inculturation by using the imagery of two hands washing each other. Both "hands"—Christianity and African cultural and religious traditions—wash each other until both are clean. The process of inculturation is dynamic, dialogical, and relational, and both hands emerge from the process mutually enriched. Ensuring an ongoing interaction and conversation between Christian and African traditions has proven useful for generating new theological insight.[6]

As in my previous work, this chapter looks in two directions to find resources for its reflection on the church: biblical and Christian theological

---

[6] Agbonkhianmeghe E. Orobator, *Theology Brewed in an African Pot* (Maryknoll, NY: Orbis Books, 2008), 125–137.

sources as well as African literature and cultures. Here I gather theological insights primarily from the New Testament, African theologians, and Roman Catholic teachings. I also rely on studies of African cultures and on African oral traditions, narratives, and literature. The use of stories and literature as sources for theological reflection and analysis forms part of the broader methodological framework of African narrative theology.[7] It is commonly understood that, even in the contemporary context of a highly digitized information communication technology, the oral tradition retains a place of pride in African cultures. The body of narratives (stories, folktales, proverbs, legends, etc.) has been translated into written literature by past and present generations of African writers, several of them to international acclaim. Africa's rich narrative corpus remains the wellspring of African literature. Existing attempts to generate theological insight by drawing upon Africa's rich lore of narratives demonstrate how narratives offer a rich terrain upon which theology and African culture interact. The result is often a theological synthesis that portrays the African imagination, understanding, and experience of a distinctly African Christianity that could be designated, as I have done in my work, as Christianity brewed in an African pot.

While taking Christian and African sources seriously is crucial, the task of articulating a robust theology of the church that places children and ethics at its center must also adopt an approach that values the voices and experiences of children as well as the church's ethical responsibilities to children. This broader methodological framework critically retrieves insights from both Christian and African sources through a child-inclusive lens. Mining these sources with attention to children provides a useful methodological framework for negotiating the correlation between church as a community of believers and its ethical responsibility to the world, including children.

Children and Children's Voices in African Literature

I turn first to African literature for what it can tell us about African attitudes and behaviors toward children. Generally, African literature rarely, if ever, offers examples of tales told "out of the mouths of babes and infants" (Ps 8:2),[8] but there are some exceptions.

---

[7] Examples include Agbonkhianmeghe E. Orobator, *Religion and Faith in Africa: Confessions of an Animist* (Maryknoll, NY: Orbis Books, 2018); Emmanuel Katongole, *The Sacrifice of Africa: A Political Theology for Africa* (Grand Rapids: Eerdmans, 2010); and Joseph Healey and Donald Sybertz, *Toward an African Narrative Theology* (Maryknoll, NY: Orbis Books, 1996).

[8] Unless otherwise indicated, all biblical references come from *The New African Bible* (Nairobi: St. Paul Communications / Daughters of St. Paul, 2011).

Although the voices of children are not prominent, one genre that focuses on children's experience is African children's literature. Precolonial African literature prioritized oral narratives by adults targeted at children. In the twentieth century, a subtradition of writing known as "African children's literature" gained prominence. As literary scholars note, "At the heart of all such work lies the desire to provide African children with an Afrocentric view of the world, one that may balance and rectify the cultural, ideological, and other content of non-African text."[9] There are several illustrations of this repertoire of children's literature authored by some of Africa's most notable writers, including Nobel Laureate Wole Soyinka (*Aké: The Years of Childhood,* 1962), Chinua Achebe (*Chike and the River,* 1966), Onuora Nzekwu (*Eze Goes to School,* 1977), and Ngugi wa Thiong'o (*Nyamba Nene and the Flying Bus* and *Nyamba Nene's Pistol,* 1986). Although this canon of writing features experiences and challenges related to the transition from childhood to adulthood, it is written with a distinctively adult voice. The focus of authors of children's literature remains firmly fixed on children as objects and audience of a literary menu meticulously crafted and served up by grown-ups.

Some narratives addressed to adults adopt the perspective of the child. In biblical parlance, they are tales told out of the mouths of babes and infants rather than as adults *in fieri* (adults in the making).

For example, Guinean writer Camara Laye, loosely based his novel *The African Child* (1953) on his own childhood.[10] A classic in African literature, the novel details exquisitely the experience of growing up in an enchanted African village characterized by an extensive web of family ties, diverse occupations, religious practices, and cultural mores. Although the story is told by the adult Laye, the voice of the child rings loud and clear, and the novel lives up to its name by creating a unique portrait of an "African child" living in a world dominated by adults and defined by their needs. This child never "grows up" to be absorbed into an indistinct mass of adults and their preoccupation. In fact, *The African Child* reads like a window into the world of adults from a child's perspective.

Nigerian fiction writer Uwem Akpan's bestseller *Say You're One of Them* (2009) offers a second interesting example of stories that give children a voice. The book is a collection of short stories. In each one, a child narrates his or her experience of a variety of traumatizing events: war, child trafficking, reli-

---

[9] Douglas Killam and Ruth Rowe, eds., "Children's Literature," *The Companion to African Literatures* (Oxford: James Currey, 2000), 64.

[10] Originally written in French under the title, *L'enfant noir,* the book was translated into English and published under the titles *The Dark Child* (New York: Farrar Straus Giroux, 1954) and *The African Child* (London: Fontana Books, 1959).

gious fanaticism, poverty, and ethnic violence. Each narrative captures the gory and terrifying emotional details of growing up in an adult world that has lost its childhood innocence and purity. In this literary milieu, the child is not a distant, grown-up narrator; the children in the stories live every moment of each event or experience recounted. Each story gives a child a *voice*, and events that are perceived through and with the *eyes* of children are recounted in a manner that stretches across a literary spectrum of existential and moral challenges and spans time and space so that the reader cannot help but feel implicated and called to account by the child.

One of Akpan's short stories, "My Parents' Bedroom," recounts the Rwanda genocide of 1994 from the perspective of a child. The narrator is nine-year-old Monique. In the maddening frenzy of that time, she brings the story to a dramatic close with a blood-curdling eyewitness account of the night her father murdered her mother:

> As the mob closes in on our house, chanting, the ceiling people begin to pray. I recognize their voices as those of our Tutsi neighbor and fellow parishioners. They're silent as Papa opens the front door to the crowd, which is bigger than last night's and pushes into our home like floodwater.... Maman runs into her bedroom.... I run to Maman and sit with her on the bed. Soon, the mob enters the room too, bringing Papa. They give Papa a big machete. He begins to tremble, his eyes blinking. A man tears me away from Maman and pushes me toward Jean, who's in the corner. Papa is standing before Maman, his finger on the knife's handle.... Papa lands the machete on Maman's head. Her voice chokes and she falls off the bed and onto her back on the wooden floor. It's like a dream. The knife tumbles out of Papa's hand.... Maman straightens out on the floor as if she were yawning. Her feet kick, and her chest rises and locks as if she were holding her breath. There's blood everywhere—on everybody around her. It flows into Maman's eyes. She looks at us through the blood.... The blood overflows her eyelids, and Maman is weeping red tears. My bladder softens and pee flows down my legs toward the blood. The blood overpowers it, bathing my feet.[11]

Although fictional, Akpan's story is based on widely attested accounts of the horror that convulsed Rwanda in 1994. As witnesses, victims, and perpetrators, children were not spared.

---

[11] Uwem Akpan, *Say You're One of Them* (Boston: Little, Brown, 2008), 349–350.

Cultural Attitudes toward Children

The dearth of literary productions that adopt the voice, perspective, and insight of the child is rooted in a combination of other factors that are particular—though not exclusively confined—to the African context. Of these factors, the most significant one concerns cultural attitudes toward children.

Children are generally valued for what they represent for society rather than as persons and gifts in themselves.[12] Their worth appears to be relative to social expectations and cultural norms. This attitude has several implications. For example, in an African cultural, religious, and social worldview that prizes fertility as a guarantee of communal survival and a criterion for ascending to the rank of ancestors, childlessness counts as the African woman's worst nightmare. In this context, the biblical Hannah could have been an African woman, considering the derision and taunt she suffered at the hands of her "fruitful" co-wife (cf. 1 Sam 1:6) on account of her condition of childlessness.

Chinua Achebe's classic novel *Things Fall Apart* (1959) poignantly captures the dynamics of childlessness and its social, cultural, and personal implications.[13] While this novel can be interpreted in various ways, cultural anthropologists, philosophers, and theologians alike have used it as a ready inventory of constituent elements of African religion. Although I have not mined this novel for African perspectives on children and am not aware of any theologians who have, it provides a rich resource for theological reflection on children.[14]

The protagonist in Achebe's novel is the ambitious and bigoted megalomaniac Okonkwo. For him (and his community), not just having a child but having a male child is what ultimately validates a woman's identity. In this context, where the principal objective of marriage is to "produce sons," his second wife, Ekwefi, suffered the agonizing fate of African women: childlessness and infant mortality. As Achebe narrates,

> Ekwefi had suffered a good deal in her life. She had borne ten children and nine of them had died in infancy, usually before the age of three. As she buried one child after another her sorrow gave way to despair and then to grim resignation. The birth of her children, which should be a woman's crowning glory, became for Ekwefi mere physical

---

[12] *The New African Bible*'s commentary on Mark 10:6 reads, "Jesus' attitude towards children is a challenge to parents and society to regard them as children of God and respect them as human persons" (1765–1766).

[13] Chinua Achebe, *Things Fall Apart* (London: Penguin Books, 1994).

[14] Katongole has examined *Things Fall Apart* as a resource for political theology in Africa in *The Sacrifice of Africa*, 125–131, and I used it to explore African beliefs and practices in my *Theology Brewed in an African Pot*.

agony devoid of promise.... Her husband's first wife had already had three sons, all strong and healthy. When she had borne her third son in succession, Okonkwo had slaughtered a goat for her, as was the custom. Ekwefi had nothing but good wishes for her. But she had grown so bitter about her own *chi* that she could not rejoice with others over their good fortune.[15]

Ekwefi's agony reveals how, even though children occupy the center of life and are highly sought after, they are hardly prized for their intrinsic value as gifts of God but are instead the keys to a woman's identity, respect, and dignity in her community.

Oduyoye's Theological Analysis

Likewise, Africa theologian Mercy Amba Oduyoye (b. 1934) describes "the deep-seated antipathy and embarrassment related to childlessness in Africa."[16] She reflects on "the experience of women who belong to traditions where naming is according to fruitfulness in childbearing, but who for whatever reason do not join in 'increasing and multiplying' the human race."[17] In her analysis, Oduyoye demonstrates how the obsession with biological progeny or the "child factor" defines the worth of African women exclusively in terms of biological production and reproduction.[18] "The 'child factor' in Africa (and perhaps elsewhere) is complex, and its public faces are daunting; but nothing is more oppressive than the ordinary meanings imposed on the absence of children in a marriage. The silence that shrouds the issue compounds its potential for the disempowering of women."[19]

For Oduyoye, strands of biblical tradition and interpretation do not necessarily help overcome the burden of the child factor. "On the contrary, the Jewish and Christian traditions tell and retell stories of the Ruths and the Tamars of this world, who will pursue their men until they fulfill their cultural roles as wives and mothers. These are hailed as 'mothers' of Jesus."[20] Just as in Achebe's *Things Fall Apart*, overcoming biblical childlessness culminates in the birth of a male child destined for a prophetic, military, priestly, or leadership career.

---

[15] Achebe, *Things Fall Apart*, 77, 79.
[16] See Mercy Amba Oduyoye, "A Coming Home to Myself: The Childless Woman in the West African Space," in *Liberating Eschatology: Essays in Honor of Letty M. Russell*, ed. Margaret A. Farley and Serene Jones (Louisville, KY: Westminster John Knox Press, 1999).
[17] Oduyoye, "A Coming Home," 105, 117.
[18] Odoyoye, "A Coming Home," 107.
[19] Oduyoye, "A Coming Home," 119.
[20] Odoyoye, "A Coming Home," 115.

So prevalent is this gender bias that the denouement of biblical sagas of childlessness simply reinforces the regnant patriarchal cultural mindset and gender ideology.

More troubling is scripture's silence on perpetually barren women. If anything, Oduyoye contends, Christianity exacerbates the pain and shame of childlessness rather than offers resources for overcoming such negative labeling. As Oduyoye points out, there is "no empowering word and no ceremony to strengthen what may, for many reasons, turn out to be a childless marriage."[21] The implication is that cultural norms, religious rituals, and social expectations relating to childbearing and fertility place the child firmly at the center of the marital contract: its presence is prerequisite for validating this contract, just as its absence provides sufficient ground for nullifying it. "In Africa, lives and relationships are ruined daily because of the 'child factor,' especially by childlessness within a marriage."[22] Ultimately, in this context, the child is like a pawn in the unpredictable "adult" game of procreation, cultural expectations, and communal survival.

Oduyoye's personal journey doubles as a theological odyssey that culminates in her naming God as "the Mothering God," a concept grounded on the spiritual fecundity of the Divine, unfettered by biases and ideologies of biological procreativity or fruitfulness commonly invoked as yardsticks for defining and patrolling the borders of motherhood and the social and cultural worth of the child. "I emphasize 'mothering' as a quality of relating that which is found in God and is expected not only of women but of men and women because we are beings created in the image of God."[23] The Mothering God enthrones life and defeats death, which means transformation and liberation:

> African women who read the Bible with a critical eye discover in it the Triune God as liberator of the oppressed, the rescuer of the marginalized and all who live daily in the throes of pain, uncertainty and deprivation. Added to this is the fact that in African Religion, God is always present in human affairs, as in the rest of creation, as judge, healer and the one who takes the side of the weak and vulnerable.[24]

Although a powerful text, one theological and ethical task that Oduyoye does not undertake, although implies, is the possibility of valuing children not

---

[21] Odoyoye, "A Coming Home," 116.

[22] Oduyoye, "A Coming Home," 106.

[23] Mercy Amba Oduyoye, *Introducing African Women's Theology* (Cleveland: Pilgrim Press, 2001), 48.

[24] Oduyoye, *Introducing African Women's Theology*, 50.

as end results of a quest for biological fecundity but as life-giving gifts in themselves. Oduyoye's work and many other strands of African theology tend to overlook explicitly affirming that children are gifts of God and human beings made in the image of God. Yet this simple affirmation challenges our narrow views of them, regardless of our cultural contexts. As Bunge claims from a North American context, "Viewing children as gifts of God to the whole community radically challenges common assumptions of them as property of parents, as consumers, or as economic burdens to the community."[25] This insight has implications for the theology of church and its ethical praxis in many contexts, including Africa, a point to which I return later.

Narrow Perceptions and Children's Urgent Needs

Considering the foregoing analysis of African perceptions of children, it is clear that children are often valued for how they fulfill social expectations and validate cultural norms rather than as persons and gifts in themselves. Children also have little voice. They are seen but not heard in a society where age is revered and political systems prioritize gerontocratic privileges. Added to these narrow perceptions of children is a set of socioeconomic and political factors that make the continent a harsh environment for children: the high rates of infant mortality, disease, and poverty, and the dislocation of families as refugees and internally displaced persons. In particular, the unstable political history of some African countries has placed children at the receiving end of societal ills, and children are brutally used as child soldiers or trafficked for sex or labor.

The girl-child faces particular challenges in African societies and elsewhere in the world. From female genital mutilation to early and forced marriages and to the denial of educational opportunities, Africa is a tough place to be a girl-child. The status of the girl-child differs significantly from the status of the boy-child. The latter enjoys ascribed privileges on account of gender. In this sense, African societies do not necessarily differ from other societies, such as in Asia, where preference for the boy-child in some instances leads to widespread feticide.

Achebe's novel also illustrates the cultural gender-based bias against the girl-child. Okonkwo was blessed with a son, Nwoye, whom he considers effeminate and emasculated. His perpetual regret is that his eldest daughter, Ezinma, was not born a boy: "If Ezinma had been a boy I would have been happier. She has the right spirit."[26] When Nwoye later turned his back on his

---

[25] Marcia J. Bunge, "The Child, Religion, and the Academy: Developing Robust Theological and Religious Understandings of Children and Childhood," *Journal of Religion* 86, no. 4 (2006): 563.

[26] Achebe, *Things Fall Apart*, 66.

family and Indigenous religion to cast his lot with the Christian missionaries, Okonkwo summoned his five sons to his hut to deliver an admonition redolent of ingrained patriarchal bias and gender-based discrimination: "You have all seen the great abomination of your brother. Now he is no longer my son or your brother. I will only have a son who is a man, who will hold his head up among my people. If any one of you prefers to be a woman, let him follow Nwoye now while I am still alive so that I can curse him."[27] Achebe adds, Okonkwo "never stopped regretting that Ezinma was a girl."[28]

Biblical Insights

Given this brief analysis of African perceptions of children and their urgent needs, the task of revising our understanding of the church and its ethical imperatives becomes even more pressing. The Bible offers several clear mandates regarding the treatment of children, as biblical studies focusing on children remind us.[29] Children are gifts of God who are made in the image of God, and we are to value and respect them. They are our neighbors, and we are to love and care for them. Many biblical passages recognize the utter vulnerability of children and command that we seek justice for them, especially the orphan. Other passages tell stories of children and young people who answered God's call.

Our conceptions of children can also be informed by a closer examination of the teachings and example of Jesus. The subject of Jesus and children in the Gospels is not a new one. Many preachers and religious educators know about Jesus's encounters with and teachings about children. However, if we revisit these familiar passages with closer attention to what they might mean for developing more robust theologies of the church and its ethical responsibility, we gain fresh insights for theological reflection. I perceive at least three windows that the New Testament opens for the task of placing children and ethics at the heart of the church and its mission. All three windows underscore children's integrity, dignity, and agency.

John the Baptist and Jesus of Nazareth

The first window relates to the two central characters of the Gospels, whose infancy narratives are supplied by Matthew and Luke: John the Baptist and Jesus of Nazareth. Notwithstanding divergent—even conflicting—accounts,

---

[27] Achebe, *Things Fall Apart*, 172.
[28] Achebe, *Things Fall Apart*, 172.
[29] See, for example, Marcia J. Bunge, Terence Fretheim, and Beverly Roberts Gaventa, eds., *The Child in the Bible* (Grand Rapids: Eerdmans, 2008).

both men are cast in the mold of Old Testament figures, particularly regarding the circumstances surrounding their birth and early childhood as well as their biological parentage, social status, and career options. Their conception entails divine intervention, and the announcement of their birth fits a specific purpose.[30] In terms of their prophetic vocation and careers, John the Baptist and Jesus of Nazareth parallel Old Testament personalities such as Moses, Samuel, and Samson. In Matthew, especially, "When readers finish the infancy narrative, they have been given a whole OT background from the Law and the prophets."[31] After birth, certain ritual requirements shape their childhood—what they are allowed to consume and how they will be raised by their parents. They are the object of special care and responsibility by parents and extended family.

Children and the Kingdom of Heaven

A second window relates to how the adult Jesus welcomes children and connects them to the kingdom of heaven. His simple action of "placing a child among them" (cf. Matt 18:1–6; Mark 9:33–37; Luke 9:46–48) refocuses the direction of a badly conducted theological discourse. The effect of this action is not only to disrupt the dominant and regnant theological conception; more importantly, it generates new insight into how Jesus's followers are to understand "the kingdom of heaven." In this theological space, the powerful symbol and presence of the child alter and shape the way the discourse unfolds.[32] New hermeneutical possibilities emerge. For example, special privileges are attached to childhood: to them belongs the kingdom of heaven. They are exemplars of the kind of attitude (humility) required for accessing the kingdom of heaven. Besides, wisdom is no longer the preserve of adults. Any disregard for children or willful occasion of scandal provokes serious sanction and repercussion (cf. Matt 18:6). This is illustrated in the attempt by the disciples to deny children access to Jesus (cf. Mark 10:13–16). Reporting on Jesus's reaction, Mark portrays Jesus as indignant toward the disciples, reaching out to children, and lovingly embracing and blessing them. As in the case of Matthew 18:6, Mark stresses their unique status as privileged guests of the kingdom of God, almost on par with Jesus—for to receive a child openheartedly is as important as receiving the one sent by God (Mark 9:37).

---

[30] Raymond E. Brown, *The Birth of the Messiah: A Commentary on the Infancy Narratives in the Gospels of Matthew and Luke* (New York: Doubleday, 1993), 256–329.

[31] Raymond E. Brown, *An Introduction to the New Testament* (New York: Doubleday, 1997), 176.

[32] See Haddon Willmer, *Experimenting Together: One Way of Doing Child Theology* (South Woodford, UK: Child Theology Movement, 2007), 4–9.

Miracles Involving Children

A third and final window concerns miracles involving children (cf. Matt 15:21–28; 17:14–20; Mark 5:21–42). Miracles regarding the healing of children share some common traits. The accounts involve a mix of genders; boys and girls alike are the beneficiaries of Jesus's healing mission. Without exception, each request for healing elicits a response from Jesus. Furthermore, Jesus shows special care for the child before and after the miracle: he goes to the home of the child, touches the child, and makes provision for his or her care. Jesus shows genuine concern for the child's well-being and offers holistic care. Another miracle regarding children is found in the Gospel of John. In one of the greatest signs recorded in Johannine writings, a child offers the gifts for blessing and feeding the crowd (see John 6:1–14), itself a powerful Eucharistic event.

Although reference to Jesus's own childhood and his encounter with children is limited, all three windows expand and deepen our understanding of the integrity, dignity, and agency of children. Children deserve special care and attention, and they hold a privileged position in the kingdom of heaven. We are to welcome them, care for them, and learn from them.

Rethinking Ecclesiology

The limited yet privileged attention given to children in the New Testament as well as awareness of the urgent needs they face today prompts a closer examination of our notions of the church and its ethical responsibility to children. Given my own context as an African Roman Catholic, I introduce some of the strengths and weaknesses of the current Roman Catholic definition of the church, highlight two promising directions in African theology for expanding our view of the church, and offer a child-inclusive understanding of the church that honors children's agency and full humanity and emphasizes three particular ethical responsibilities of the church to children.

Church in the Roman Catholic Tradition

Within the broader scope of Roman Catholic theology, church has a fairly stable definition, both as an object of doctrinal formulation and as the privileged space for sacramental practice. Drawing on patristic and medieval sources, the Council of Trent (1545–1563), and subsequently the First Vatican Council (1869–1870), laid down a definition that described church as an institutional edifice circumscribed by complex theological issues of papal infallibility, clerical power, and sacramentality and understood to be the unchallenged recipient of tradition and possessor of truth handed down through an unbroken apostolic succession.

The classic expression of the ensuing model of church is found in the writings of Cardinal Robert Bellarmine (1542–1621). As Avery Dulles explains, for Bellarmine, "The one and true Church is the communion of men brought together by the profession of faith and conjoined in the communion of the same sacraments, under the government of the legitimate pastors and especially the one vicar of Christ on earth, the Roman pontiff."[33] Bellarmine also compares the church to a visible political society: "as visible and palpable as the community of the Roman people, or the Kingdom of France, or the Republic of Venice."[34] This understanding of church established a strict boundary of affiliation based on an unflinching allegiance to a set of creedal statements.

Although this approach gave visibility to the church as a recognizable institution that could claim separate existence and authority grounded on a divine mandate, it nevertheless contained some problematic characteristics that continue to define it, despite the emergence of other more pastoral and inclusive models of church.[35] These characteristics were embedded in a set of doctrinal markers: clericalism, juridicism, and triumphalism.[36] In this rigid doctrinal framework, church was understood to be the equivalent of a political society with a clearly delineated hierarchical structure for exercising authority and power over all things doctrinal, sacramental, liturgical, and ministerial. The top of this pyramid narrowed to one sole authority: the papacy. At the base, the lay faithful participated in worship and ministry to the extent that the clerical class permitted.

The Second Vatican Council and the Church as the People of God

While this hierarchal, clericalist definition of the church offered little space for taking children seriously, the Second Vatican Council (1962–1965) marked a watershed in the transition to a more pastoral understanding of church as the People of God. This council reopened the debate about the nature, theology, and mission of the church. While recognizing various ecclesiological symbols and models that have their roots in the Old and New Testaments, the council adopted a definition of church that understood it simply as the People of God. Even though it continued to maintain a hierarchical order of power and authority, this model offered a more inclusive approach based on shared communion in Christ.

Despite the fact that Vatican II's understanding of church created a more receptive space for paying attention to the voices and perspectives of children,

---

[33] Avery Dulles, *Models of the Church* (New York: Doubleday, 1987), 33.
[34] Dulles, *Models of the Church*, 26.
[35] See examples in Dulles, *Models of the Church*.
[36] Dulles, *Models of the Church*, 39.

contemporary Catholic documents rarely refer to children. Church documents typically conclude with exhortations or appeals addressed to different categories, including priests, religious, laypeople, professionals, men, women, and youth. Of course, the Catholic Church attends to children's needs in a variety of ways. In terms of care and protection, the church has established schools, hospitals, and agencies that serve children, regardless of religious affiliation, and has been an advocate for children's rights.

African Understandings of the Church and Its Mission

Although Vatican II articulated a more inclusive view of the church, since 1994, Catholic African theologians have been offering a particularly African twist to views of the church that makes room for stronger solidarity with and commitment to children. Prior to 1994, African theology in the Roman Catholic Church espoused a rather diffuse understanding of church that basically replicated the officially sanctioned Roman Catholic doctrine of church as a hierarchical institution. However, a new watershed occurred in African theology with two African Synods of Bishops held in Rome. At these consultations, serious attention was given to relations between the Roman Catholic Church and African religions. At the first African Synod in 1994, a specific option was allowed for an African model of church to be shaped by African religions and grounded in the notion of family. The second African Synod of 2009 reaffirmed this doctrine of the church and expanded its mission to include reconciliation, justice, and peace.[37]

The doctrine and theology of church as the family of God committed to reconciliation, justice, and peace offers a rich terrain for expanding the church's self-understanding and its ethical responsibilities. In reflecting on this doctrine and the main tenets of ethics and morality in the Roman Catholic Church from an African perspective, I have argued that the core of the church's ethical reflection and the foundation of moral principles is life.[38] Additionally, I have argued that we are to view life in an expansive manner, as a continuum. In this sense, the continuum of life is not confined to human life or even biological existence but rather extends to the natural world and even to the unborn and those who have died:

> The notion of expansiveness of life relates to the fact that life is not construed only as a reality constituted by the living; it also includes the ancestors and the yet-unborn. Furthermore, the category of life

---

[37] Pope Benedict XVI, *Africae Munus* (Ouidah, Benin: Post-Synodal Apostolic Exhortation, 2011); Orobator, *Reconciliation, Justice, and Peace*.

[38] Agbonkhianmeghe E. Orobator, "Ethics Brewed in an African Pot," *Journal of the Society of Christian Ethics* 31, no. 1 (2011): 3–16.

extends to and includes the natural universe. In this sense, therefore, from an African religio-cultural perspective, the moral imperative to protect human life also warrants the protection of sacred forests, trees, rivers, mountains, streams, and animals. This moral imperative, or duty, to protect the physical environment is founded on the vital link between the survival of human life and the environment. To protect the environment is to protect human life, since the survival of the latter ultimately depends on the survival of the former.[39]

From this perspective, the church can evaluate the ethical integrity of its actions on the basis of whether or not they enhance the quality of life as a communal experience.

Three Ethical Imperatives for the Church

Although my earlier work does not focus on children, my basic approach to ethics—"brewed in an African pot" with an expansive commitment to enhancing life—and the notion of the church as the family of God committed to reconciliation, justice, and peace both offer promising directions for reexamining a theology of the church with attention to children. Building on these promising directions, and considering the needs and strengths of children as well as Jesus's teaching and actions, how might we now strengthen our understanding of the church and its ethical imperatives? Although providing exhaustive answers exceeds the scope of this chapter, I identify three ethical imperatives that lead to a doctrine of the church that is radically inclusive and self-critical, and that honors the full humanity of children. These imperatives illustrate how rethinking the doctrine of the church in the light of attention to children yields insights both for ecclesiology and our treatment of children.

Defending Children as Full and Active Participants

Even though the Catholic Church in Africa understands the church as the family of God, offers a range of programs for children and youth, and supports an ethic of life, children are not always acknowledged as active agents or included as full members and active participants in the church. Certainly, the church has created spaces for children and young people in its congregations to grow spiritually. Many Catholic children have grown into the church, for example, via the weekly Sunday school that offers basic catechism, songs, games,

---

[39] Agbonkhianmeghe E. Orobator, "Ethics of HIV/AIDS Prevention: Paradigms of a New Discourse from an African Perspective," in *Applied Ethics in the World Church: The Padua Conference*, ed. Linda Hogan (Maryknoll, NY: Orbis Books, 2008), 149.

and didactic activities. Another typical Catholic Church experience for children is the Children's Mass. This practice varies from place to place and can be held weekly, monthly, or on special occasions. "Masses for Children" especially composed for the celebration comes with a complement of liturgical prayers. During such Masses, children routinely read from scripture, sing in a choir, and recite bidding prayers.

However, the matrix of debates regarding sacramental participation and ministerial leadership tends to follow a typically binary and polemical axis: man versus woman; male versus female. For some, this axis exhausts the debate about participation and inclusion. Amid discussions of seeking a dynamic and multivalent gender composition in church and society, the category of child is often left out. Without diminishing the importance of uplifting the leadership of women, the church must seek to broaden the scope of participation in leadership and ministry for both women and children.

The church can break free from the bonds of binary antagonism and be more inclusive by honoring the full humanity of children—their voices and their agency. Such an approach opens many possibilities for empowering children and enlivening the church. For example, recognizing that children have questions and ideas and that the Holy Spirit is already moving in their lives enriches faith formation programs and materials. Acknowledging that children are full members of the body of Christ with stories and voices of their own encourages the church to listen to their ideas and concerns. The church will not simply "pass on" knowledge to children and youth but rather engage and learn from them. Honoring their agency and leadership capacities also opens possibilities for enlivening worship and fostering meaningful intergenerational connections. Such an approach cultivates the growing intellectual, moral, spiritual, and leadership capacities of children.

Children are active agents who interact with the world from the beginning, and as they grow, they continue to learn from and contribute to relationships. As Haddon Willmer reminds us, although "agency" implies action, "agency" takes several forms and can apply to children and their interactions from the start. Agency does not always mean that "children must act or do something to impact the adults in contact with them."[40] Even infants and young children are agents "because their lives naturally make demands upon human society as a whole and upon adults in particular.... Through them changes take place in the adults who are in contact with them, as a helpless infant on arrival causes a household to change." Thus, children's agency is not always about abilities or virtues impacting adults but about "children as children encountering adults."[41]

---

[40] Sunny Tan, *Child Theology for the Churches of Asia: An Invitation* (South Woodford, UK: Child Theology Movement, 2007), 12–13.

[41] See Tan, *Child Theology for the Churches of Asia*, 12–13.

Seeking Repentance and Providing Genuine Care and Protection

Attention to children's needs and agency also prompts the church to repent, be more self-critical, and expand its understanding of the care and protection of children. The church already does care for children in a host of ways. In many places in Africa, church is synonymous with schools and hospitals, two key social structures that have contributed to the evolution of a more educated and healthier population of African children. This is a laudable achievement, and the issues advanced here do not seek to undermine the importance of the church's contribution to the education and health of African children.

However, given the urgent needs of children and the crisis of child sexual abuse in the church, the church must reflect more self-critically on its own maltreatment of children and repent for its failure to care for and protect children even within its own walls. The sexual abuse crisis has exposed more clearly than ever the church's lack of regard for the value and full humanity of children. Protecting the reputation of church leaders became more important than protecting children. Priests abused children, and fellow priests and church leaders covered up their crimes. The scandal of pedophilia exposes the hypocrisy and abuse of clerical and ecclesiastical power and, in many instances, renders the institutional church an unsafe space for children. The enormity of the physical, emotional, and spiritual harm done to children by spiritual leaders to whom they were entrusted is still emerging, and the full scale of damage may never be known, considering the sophistication of the cover-up and the psychological cost of retrieving painful memories and reliving the experience of abuse, itself an obstacle to telling one's story of abuse.

Considering this crisis, the church must readjust its self understanding, repent of its wrongdoing, and expand its concept of caring for and protecting children. "Care and protection" can no longer be equated simply with providing food, education, shelter, or health care for children. Genuine care and protection must also include providing care to victims of abuse and neglect and taking the legal and practical measures necessary to recognize and prevent child abuse and neglect—whether in homes, schools, sports facilities, detention centers, refugee camps, or the church itself. The church will only take up its full responsibility to care for and protect children when it recognizes its own wrongdoing and children's full humanity.

This calls for a repentant church that defines and judges its mission by the level of its commitment to the duties of caring for and protecting children. It is about developing a self-critical doctrine of the church: one that not only denounces the ills of society but focuses on where, as a Christian community, it might be failing to fulfill Jesus's command to honor, respect, and protect children as members of the church and honored guests of the kingdom of heaven. In other words, what is envisaged here is a church that can look honestly into its own history, practice, and institutions in light of whether or not they conform to the gospel truth that attributes to children ownership of and privileged access to the kingdom of heaven.

Defending the Dignity, Equality, and Rights of Children

A child-attentive understanding of the church will also promote stronger advocacy for all children. The Catholic Church already affirms an ethic of life, advocates strongly for the rights of all human beings, and supports the United Nations Convention on the Rights of the Child (CRC). However, Catholic statements related to children and children's rights are often focused more on abortion and adult rights and responsibilities. Despite the church's claims of a consistent ethic of life, its ethical statements on human rights rarely consider children or include them in their purview. If anything, they tend to presuppose an adult audience that seeks to act and make decisions with a well-(in)formed conscience. This is evident, for example, in the numerous church statements and discussions about matters of sexual ethics, such as marriage, contraception, abortion, and same-sex marriage or civil union. Here the category of "child" is best considered, if at all, as a vulnerable subject who counts in moral discourse to the extent that it is affected by the actions and decisions of adults. Ironically, in instances of controversy and disagreement over the precise nature and claims of sexual ethics, both sides of the ethical divide claim to be champions and advocates of the rights and well-being of the child.

Furthermore, the church has yet to speak out more forcefully and attend to the needs of girls. It is safe to assume that African societies have not always prioritized the protection of the rights of the child, particularly the girl-child.[42] In the context of the church, this situation defines a new domain of mission and ministry: defending the rights of the girl-child and affirming her dignity as a human being created in the image and likeness of God—*imago Dei*. This point calls for a doctrine and theology of church that challenge and overcome practices capable of reinforcing gender discrimination and affirm the equality and dignity of all. This task is better demonstrated and lived out rather than merely pronounced or expressed.

Despite the church's attention to the dignity of the human person, what remains to be seen is how this rhetoric effectively translates into ethical action

---

[42] Several African countries are signatories to the United Nations Convention on the Rights of the Child (1989). The Organization of Africa Unity, now the African Union, also has the African Charter on the Rights and Welfare of the Child (1999). The level of adherence of individual countries to these articles and protocols varies.

on behalf of children, specifically the girl-child. In the Roman Catholic Church, where roles are gender-specific, with priority accorded to men/male clerical and ecclesiastical functionaries, it becomes easy for the girl-child to lower her expectations because she lacks visible female role models who not only model leadership, authority, and participation but are also empowered to act and lead the community of worship *in persona Christi*. For the Roman Catholic Church steeped in a tradition of patriarchal and hierarchical leadership, this proposition raises the ethical stakes significantly. Perhaps more importantly, it demonstrates how theology—in this case, ecclesiology—could benefit from a radical reformulation of its assumptions about children as a matter of ethical imperative.

Conclusion

In this chapter, I have argued that placing children and ethics at the heart of the church has positive implications for the community of the disciples of Jesus. Attending to the needs and strengths of children in our midst enlivens the church and helps to correct the illusion that ethics and ecclesiology run on parallel tracks. Understanding our ethical obligations to children also leads to a doctrine of the church that is radically inclusive and self-critical, and that honors the full humanity of all people, including children. It is a church that celebrates the dignity and intrinsic value of all of God's children without discrimination, as proclaimed in the Gospel. This inclusive, life-affirming notion of the body of Christ empowers all those who assemble around the crucified and risen Christ to proclaim the good news and to promote the flourishing of God's creation and people of all ages.

9

Reclaiming the Virtue of Humility through a Child-Inclusive Lens

Perry T. Hamalis

Among the world's religious traditions, the theme of humility is not exclusive to Christianity, but it is basic to it. Some scholars, like Kari Konkola, have boldly claimed that "humility was a quintessentially Christian discovery,"[1] and have credited Jesus and the early Christian movement with introducing the concept of humility as a virtue. Others have contested this claim by locating and analyzing appeals to humility in sources that predate Jesus and his followers.[2] Regardless of where and when the virtue of humility originated, its significance, historically, within Christianity concerns both ethics and theology—proper human living and the nature or character of God. In the New Testament, for example, Christians are exhorted to humble themselves before God (cf. Jas 4:10; 1 Pet 5:6), a teaching embraced by other religious traditions; yet Christians also proclaim a God who is radically humble and whose example of extreme humility, in the person of Jesus Christ, becomes the model for Christians' own lives (see Phil 2:5–11).[3]

---

[1] Kari Konkola, "Have We Lost Humility?" *Humanitas* 18 (2005): 182. See also the discussion in Frank Pakenham, *Humility* (London: Fontana Books, 1969), 50–55.

[2] Stephen Dawes examines the Hebrew word 'anāwâ, which is typically translated as "humility," and argues that Jewish sources like Ben Sira, the 'Qumran literature, and Proverbs articulate a developed account of humility as a virtue. See his "anāwâ in Translation and Tradition," *Vetus Testamentum* 41 (1991): 38–48. For a Hindu perspective, see Graham M. Schweig, "Humility and Passion: A Caitanyite Vaishnava Ethic of Devotion," *Journal of Religious Ethics* 30 (2002): 421–444.

[3] I do not mean to suggest that *only* Christians connect humility to both ethics and theology. Ronald Green, for example, has argued compellingly that humility is both a "genuine constitutive virtue for Jewish ethical thought" and that "God's holiness must be interpreted to include as its central feature His humility." See his, "Jewish Ethics and the Virtue of Humility," *Journal of Religious Ethics* 1 (1973): 53–63.

Despite humility's prominent place within Christian theology and ethics from the early Church to the Reformation, scholars have noted a major shift in attitudes toward humility in the West from the early modern period to the present.[4] Influential Western philosophers, including Machiavelli, Spinoza, Hume, and Nietzsche, critiqued traditional Christian teachings on humility with such effectiveness that many Christian thinkers and communities (either consciously or unconsciously) distanced themselves from traditional views.

Among most Christians today, humility is still regarded as a virtue rather than a vice, as it is among several critics of Christian morality.[5] However, positive and constructive treatments of humility as a moral virtue have become rare within Christian scholarly discourse. Even a renewed interest in the virtues and in virtue ethics over the past four decades has yielded relatively few academic studies centered on the virtue of humility.[6] And while attention to humility has declined, scholarly interest in the importance of "self-love" and "self-esteem" for Christians has increased.[7] One important reason for this shift among Christians is that several recent feminist and liberation theologians have argued that humility, as it is now understood and practiced in many churches, (1) promotes the passive acceptance of gender, race, class, and other inequalities; (2) undermines efforts to affirm and protect the inherent dignity of all human persons, especially vulnerable populations, like women and children; (3) weakens the drive to pursue excellence; and perhaps most importantly (4) too often becomes

---

[4] See the account of this shift in Mark Button, "'A Monkish Kind of Virtue'? For and against Humility," *Political Theory* 33 (2005): 840–868. Kari Konkola provides an insightful quantitative analysis of humility's disappearance from modern Western Christianity in "Have We Lost Humility?" See also Kari Konkola, "Meek Imperialists: Humility in 17th-Century England," *Trinity Journal* 28 (2007): 3–35.

[5] Solomon Schimmel summarizes the point well: "Devotional works provide antidotes to pride and try to cultivate humility. Psychologists offer workshops on overcoming inferiority complexes and building self-esteem. Indeed the very connotation of 'pride' has been reversed from a reprehensible to an admirable trait in the transition from traditional religion to contemporary secularism." See his *The Seven Deadly Sins: Jewish, Christian, and Classical Reflections on Human Psychology* (New York: Oxford University Press, 1997), 36–54.

[6] Some noteworthy exceptions include James L. Heft, Reuven Firestone, and Omid Safi, eds., *Learned Ignorance: Intellectual Humility among Jews, Christians, and Muslims* (New York: Oxford University Press, 2011); André Louf, *The Way of Humility*, trans. Lawrence Cunningham (Kalamazoo, MI: Cistercian Publications, 2007); and Archimandrite Chrysostomos, ed., *Themes in Orthodox Patristic Psychology*, vol. 1, *Humility* (Etna, CA: Center for Traditionalist Orthodox Studies, 1983).

[7] To be sure, recent scholarship on self-love in Christian ethics has made an important and much-needed contribution to the field. See, for example, Darlene Fozard Weaver's superb study, *Self-Love and Christian Ethics* (Cambridge: Cambridge University Press, 2002).

humiliation—not a state of character developed through the repeated voluntary decisions of the humble person, but rather a state imposed upon the weak and enforced by the powerful.[8]

These are valid concerns grounded in an abundance of heartbreaking historical evidence across all denominational boundaries. Since "humility" has often been misused within churches by those in positions of power, it cannot simply be endorsed uncritically. Only two paths, it seems, remain open to the leaders and members of today's Christian communities. The first is to continue to critique or deemphasize humility as a Christian moral virtue, with the hope of eroding its potential for abuse. The second is to rethink, reinterpret, or reevaluate humility in ways that restore its authentic Christian meaning and practice, and delegitimize its inauthentic, abusive, and exclusionary forms.

My aim here is to contribute positively to the second path noted above by reflecting on humility through a child-attentive and Eastern Orthodox lens. As a proponent of restoring humility's vital role, I stand with colleagues like Caryn Riswold and Elizabeth Hinson-Hasty, who argue for recovering "genuine humility" within normative Christian thought,[9] as well as with Sarah Coakley and Aristotle Papanikolaou, who reinterpret and recapture the concept of *kenosis* amid sharp criticisms from some Christian feminists.[10] However, unlike my colleagues, I prioritize the significance of children in understanding humility's meaning in both its proper and improper applications in the lives of Christians.

I first consider an overview of the two basic meanings of humility within the New Testament and early Christian sources—humility as "voluntary lowliness" and humility as "awareness of sin"—being mindful of their propensity for misuse by those in power. I then employ a child-attentive lens to the passages on humility in Matthew 18:1–5, showing how "placing the child in the midst"

---

[8] For a helpful overview of feminist Christian critiques of humility, see Elizabeth L. Hinson-Hasty, "Revisiting Feminist Discussions of Sin and Genuine Humility," *Journal of Feminist Studies in Religion* 28, no. 1 (2012): 108–114. Two of the seminal works advancing this argument are Valerie Saiving Goldberg, "The Human Situation: A Feminine View," *Journal of Religion* 40, no. 2 (1960): 100–112, and Mary Daly, *Beyond God the Father* (Boston: Beacon Press, 1985).

[9] See Caryn D. Riswold, "Inhabiting Paradox: God and Feminist Theology for the Third Wave," in *Transformative Lutheran Theologies: Feminist, Womanist, and Mujerista Perspectives*, ed. Mary J. Streufert (Minneapolis: Fortress Press, 2010), 45–56, and Hinson-Hasty, "Revisiting Feminist Discussions of Sin and Genuine Humility."

[10] See Sarah Coakley, "Kenosis and Subversion: On the Repression of 'Vulnerability' in Christian Feminist Writing," in *Swallowing a Fishbone? Feminist Theologians Debate Christianity*, ed. Margaret Daphne Hampson (London: SPCK, 1996), 82–111, and Aristotle Papanikolaou, "Person, Kenosis and Abuse: Hans Urs von Balthasar and Feminist Theologies in Conversation," *Modern Theology* 19, no. 1 (2003): 41–65.

challenges the sufficiency of humility's two basic meanings and reveals an often-overlooked third understanding of humility: "acknowledging one's need for others." Third, I explore selected insights from the Eastern Orthodox iconographic and spiritual tradition pertaining to humility, highlighting the integral place that humility holds and the prevalence of all three stipulated meanings of humility. Finally, I consider the implications of a robust and child-attentive understanding of humility for both Orthodox and non-Orthodox Christians. Specifically, I explore the significance of humility for defending the dignity of children, the benefit of expanding our understanding of Christ, and the need to cultivate humility in ways that are age-appropriate, context-specific, and life-giving. This full-bodied and child-inclusive view of humility exposes the pitfalls of either dismissing humility or using it in ways that harm and humiliate children, thereby helping to recapture the vital role of humility in Christian thought and practice.

An Overview of "Humility" in Early Christian Sources

"Humility," which derives etymologically from the Latin *humus*, signifying "earth," "ground," or "soil," has a range of definitions within Christian thought and practice.[11] First, stemming from the foundational theological belief that Jesus is the incarnate Word—fully God and fully human—and based on the witness of the early church recorded in the New Testament, few Christians would deny that God expresses and exemplifies humility in the person of Jesus Christ. Frank Pakenham states it well: "There is hardly a passage in the Gospel story which does not throw some light, directly or indirectly, on humility as divinely interpreted."[12] Jesus is born in a manger (Luke 2), lives among society's most marginalized persons, washes his disciples' feet (John 13), and suffers a brutal and utterly humiliating death.[13] There are also several explicit biblical references to Jesus as "humble." Most significant, perhaps, is the Philippian hymn (Phil 2:5–11), which describes Jesus's incarnation and crucifixion as

---

[11] Space limitations here preclude a focused analysis of humility as an intellectual virtue. For those interested in this topic, I recommend Heft, Firestone, and Safi, *Learned Ignorance*. For a study of this theme in a Greek patristic source, see Steven Pardue, "On Faithfully Knowing an Infinite God: Humility as an Intellectual Virtue in Gregory of Nyssa's *Congra Eunomium* II," *International Journal of Systematic Theology* 13, no. 1 (2011): 62–76. For an analysis of humility and epistemology in Thomas Aquinas's work, see Lisa Fullam, "Humility and Its Moral Epistemological Implications," in *Virtue*, ed. Charles E. Curran and Lisa A Fullam (New York: Paulist Press, 2011), 250–274.

[12] Pakenham, *Humility*, 59.

[13] For a developed analysis of this theme, see John Macquarrie, *The Humility of God* (Philadelphia: Westminster Press, 1978).

acts of "emptying himself" (Phil 2:7) and "humbling himself" (Phil 2:8). In the Gospel of Matthew, Jesus's entry into Jerusalem on a donkey relates to the Jewish prophecy of a "humble king" (Matt 21:5, cf. Zech 9:9)—and in the same Gospel, Jesus describes himself as "'gentle and humble in heart'" (Matt 11:29) when offering rest to those who are weary and carrying heavy burdens.

From these passages, an initial understanding of humility emerges as "voluntary lowliness" or "willing acceptance of a low position." The connection to *humus*, here, is evident. For Christians, God's own humility is affirmed at the most fundamental level through the voluntary *lowliness* and *earthiness* of Jesus Christ. This is communicated not only in the account of God's movement from heaven to *earth*—from being fully and eternally God to becoming incarnate and fully human in history—but also in the manner of Jesus's life—from the gritty conditions of his birth, to the status of his family, friends, and interlocutors, to the subservient stance he takes in relation to others, to the form of his death. Yet the *voluntary* quality of humility within this context is equally important. Just as God was not compelled either to create the world or to care for it, God was not compelled to become incarnate or to live in the humble manner that Jesus did. Divine humility lies in God's *willingness to embrace lowliness*, not merely *in being low*. Clement of Rome articulates this core conviction when he writes (ca. 95 CE), "The coming of our Lord Jesus Christ, the Sceptre of God's Majesty, was in no pomp of pride and haughtiness—as it could so well have been—but in self-abasement."[14]

Furthermore, God's voluntary self-abasement is not an end in itself; its aim is love, reconciliation, and salvation. The Logos's descent, or *katabasis*—both from heaven to earth and from incarnate life to death on the cross—leads ultimately to his ascent, or *anabasis*, both in his victorious resurrection and in his glorious ascension.[15] Christ's voluntary lowliness points beyond itself and signals humility as the way to exaltation. In short, from an early Christian perspective, humility is fundamental to the incarnation, life, and death of the Lord Jesus Christ, as well as to his resurrection from the dead and ascension into heaven. And all of these are, of course, expressions of God's ultimate love for creation (see John 3:16).

Humility as a theological (divine) theme reinforces and elevates humility as an ethical (human) theme within early Christianity. Jesus proclaims, "'Blessed are the poor in spirit,'" in the first of his Beatitudes (Matt 5:3), and he praises

---

[14] *The First Epistle of Clement to the Corinthians* 16, in Andrew Louth, trans. and ed., *Early Christian Writings: The Apostolic Fathers* (New York: Penguin Books, 1987), 29.

[15] For a discussion of the *katabasis-anabasis* theme in early Christian literature, see Richard N. Longenecker, *Studies in Hermeneutics, Christology, and Discipleship* (Sheffield: Sheffield Phoenix Press, 2004), 169–171.

the humble tax collector over the self-righteous Pharisee (Luke 18:9–14). St. Paul uses the term "humility" to describe the proper way of ministering to and serving others (2 Cor 10:1; cf. Acts 20:19). Followers of Jesus are reminded repeatedly that "those who exalt themselves will be humbled, and those who humble themselves will be exalted" (Matt 23:12; Luke 14:11; 18:14; 2 Cor 11:7; Jas 4:10; 1 Pet 5:6), a clear repetition of the *katabasis-anabasis* theme. And the Philippian hymn noted earlier not only describes Jesus's self-emptying humility, it also exhorts readers to "let the same mind be in you that was in Christ Jesus" (Phil 2: 5).

These more ethical passages extend the first meaning of humility, "willing acceptance of a low position," from the context of describing the character of Jesus Christ to the context of calling Jesus's followers toward a similar mode of existence. Hence Christians are taught to embrace lowliness in their relationships to God and to other human beings. In relating to God, the ethical call to humility is an exhortation to acknowledge one's identity as a *human* person, as one formed by *humus* and gifted with the breath of life (cf. Gen 2:7). Here, humility is knowing and accepting one's "creatureliness."[16] Complementarily, in relating to one's neighbors, the ethical call to humility implies a willingness to subordinate oneself to others in a spirit of service and philanthropy. Here, the emphasis is on *voluntarily* following a mode of existence that helps prevent factions within the community, thus promoting peace, cooperation, and mutual growth in holiness (cf. Eph 4; Phil 2; 1 Pet 2–5).

Alongside these and other ethical passages, a second understanding of humility emerges that can be described as *pursuing and sustaining an awareness of one's moral failures or sinfulness* when measured against the standards of God's law and Christ's perfection. The early church's account of God's holiness convicts all believers—who can possibly "'be perfect, just as your Father in heaven is perfect'" (Matt 5:48)?—even as it communicates God's mercy. As the psalmist beckons, "Hear my prayer, O LORD, give ear to my supplications. . . . Do not enter into judgment with your servant, for no one living is righteous before you" (Ps 143:1–2). St. Paul, of course, develops this core theological-ethical claim in his teachings on law and justification by faith (cf. Rom 3:9–23; Gal 3). Humility, in this second sense, is the proper response to God when people of faith engage in self-assessment with moral depth and honesty. Humility is knowing not only one's creatureliness but also one's moral brokenness and sinfulness.

In the New Testament and early Christian context, the normative force of this second understanding of humility extends to relationships with one's

---

[16] For a superb analysis of this theme, see Norman Wirzba, "The Touch of Humility: An Invitation to Creatureliness," *Modern Theology* 24, no. 2 (2008): 225–244.

fellow human beings. Christians are taught to sustain a humble mindfulness of their own sinfulness rather than a prideful mind-set that judges and condemns others (cf. Matt 7:1–29; Luke 6:37–42; Jas 4:11–12). The parable of the Publican and the Pharisee (Luke 18:10–14)—with its dual focus on the lowly and marginalized status of the publican within society and the publican's honest acknowledgment of his sinfulness—provides a striking account of humility's multiple ethical meanings within the context of early Christianity.[17] It underscores humility's connection to freedom (*voluntary* lowliness) and truth (*accurate* self-assessment). Similarly, the often-cited biblical passage "Toward the scorners he is scornful, but to the humble he shows favor" (Prov 3:34; cf. 1 Pet 5:5; Jas 4:6) encompasses humility as both "willing acceptance of a subordinate position in relation to God/neighbor" and "awareness of one's sinfulness in relation to God/neighbor."

These two basic scriptural meanings of humility have formed Christian theology and ethics for centuries; however, they are also the reason that many modern philosophers, psychologists, and recent theologians have criticized Christian humility. When interpreted and applied in certain ways, these two meanings of humility have justified the exclusion, neglect, and exploitation of children and vulnerable adults; fostered abuses of power (men over women, adults over children, whites over persons of color, etc.); undercut Christians' efforts to advocate for themselves and critique immoral practices; and led some believers to self-hatred and despair. While many applications of these two understandings of humility are not exploitative, one wonders if there is another way for us to think about it. A child-attentive approach can help us to identify a way that is genuinely Christian, but less likely to be twisted or applied unjustly.

A Child-Attentive Approach to Humility

Simply stated, child-attentive theology (or Child Theology) is a contextual theology in which ethical claims and doctrines within Christianity are reexamined from a standpoint that pays attention to the experiences of children and affirms their full dignity and humanity.[18] Child Theology "places a child in the midst" (Matt 18:2) of Christian teachings to provide a critical and vital perspective that is too often neglected, leading both to misinterpretations of the gospel and mistreatment of children. How, then, might a child-attentive approach shape—or reshape—our understanding of Christian humility? Two ways seem

---

[17] Within the Eastern Orthodox liturgical cycle, the parable of the Publican and the Pharisee is read annually on the first Sunday of the Triodion, the three-week period of preparation prior to the start of Great Lent. In this way, humility inaugurates and sets the tone for the most significant season of the ecclesiastical year.

[18] For an overview of Child Theology, see the works of Marcia J. Bunge.

especially salient. First, a child-attentive approach reveals a third meaning of the term "humility," which complements the first two meanings, and second, it deepens our prior analysis of humility's first and second meanings and decenters them within Christian thought.

The opening verses of Matthew 18 are the biblical locus of a child-attentive understanding of humility. There, Jesus is presented as responding to his disciples' query about hierarchy in the kingdom by placing a child among them and saying, "'Whoever becomes humble like this child is the greatest in the kingdom of heaven'" (Matt 18:4). In what way, we might ask, is this child manifesting humility? Consider the two basic meanings of humility delineated earlier. There is no evidence in these verses, contextual or otherwise, that Jesus intends the second meaning of humility: "sustaining an awareness of one's sinfulness." The child to whom Jesus refers is not presented in the text as exemplifying either a self-condemnatory disposition vis-à-vis God's righteousness or a strong resistance to judging others. Instead, the context suggests that this child represents all young children insofar as they, unlike Jesus's disciples (Matt 18:1–3), lack concern for superior status or reputation. Children—especially the very young—are humble because they are not interested in "who is the greatest in the kingdom of heaven."[19] A connection here appears to our first meaning of humility, "willing acceptance of a low position." The child whom Jesus places "among them" (18:2) seems content with her or his low status; the child is unambitious, and disinclined to imagine holding a place of higher honor.

Yet there seems to be something more in Jesus's appeal to a child in Matthew 18, something that transcends the narrative's immediate context. Insofar as representing children more broadly, this child communicates a quality of *dependence*, a fragility and vulnerability. Awareness of such characteristics in oneself makes it difficult for someone to forget his or her need for others. As Pakenham writes, "The humility of a child does seem to contain two elements less likely to be found in adults: one, a sense of one's own weakness; the other, a dependence on the strength of others."[20] Children, especially in their earliest years, cannot survive without others—without the sustenance and attention that their parents or caregivers provide. On some level, they seem to know this; they cry, reach out, and cling to others. Furthermore, while children test this conviction as they mature, they maintain a general awareness and acceptance of their dependent state during their childhood.[21] By connecting humility to the

---

[19] I am indebted here to Keith J. White's essay, "'He Placed a Little Child in the Midst': Jesus, the Kingdom, and Children," in *The Child in the Bible*, ed. Marcia J. Bunge (Grand Rapids: Eerdmans, 2008), 353–374.

[20] Pakenham, *Humility*, 60.

[21] For an extended theological analysis of this theme, see David Jensen, *Graced Vulnerability: A Theology of Childhood* (Cleveland: Pilgrim Press, 2005).

child, Jesus reveals a third understanding of humility as "acknowledging one's need for others." To be humble is to be childlike in the sense of being aware of oneself (and accepting oneself) as a creature whose existence depends on sustaining relationships with others. In other words, Jesus's claim, "'Unless you change and become like children, you will never enter the kingdom of heaven'" (Matt 18:3), can be rephrased as "unless you change your mind-set of self-sufficiency and acknowledge your need for God and neighbor, you will never enter the kingdom of heaven." This understanding of humility presents a sharp critique of both Jesus's society and our own.[22]

In addition to this third understanding of humility and revealing the inappropriateness of the second meaning in this context, Jesus's teachings on children enhance our first understanding of humility as the willing acceptance of a subordinate position in relation to God/neighbor. Historians and biblical scholars have noted that children typically held a marginal, vulnerable, and devalued position in the first-century Near East.[23] Children were regarded as lowly, weak, and fragile, and caring for children was a low-status activity relegated to the domain of marginalized women.[24] When the Gospels report that Jesus "received" the children (cf. Matt 19:13–15; Mark 10:13–16; Luke 18:15–17), and that he taught, "'Whoever welcomes one such child in my name welcomes me'" (Matt 18:5; Mark 9:37; Luke 9:48), he communicates a twofold message. First, Jesus's own radical humility is manifested in his welcoming and embracing of children and, even more, in his self-identification with the child. Keith White notes that "children, Jesus, and the kingdom of heaven in Matthew's Gospel inform one another and are congruent to such an extent that they might be said to be inseparable."[25] Second, while Jesus willingly lowers himself to a role that was typically fulfilled by marginalized women, he also teaches others to follow his humble lead, to see his humble face in the humble faces of children, and to understand humility as constitutive of the path to the kingdom by welcoming and fully including children within the community.

---

[22] Cf. White, "He Placed a Little Child in the Midst," 371.

[23] Joachim Jeremias, for example, notes that children were often categorized with slaves and disabled adults in first-century texts. See Joachim Jeremias, *New Testament Theology: The Proclamation of Jesus* (New York: Scribner's, 1971), 227.

[24] See the helpful discussion in Judith M. Gundry-Volf, "The Least and the Greatest: Children in the New Testament," in *The Child in Christian Thought*, ed. Marcia J. Bunge (Grand Rapids: Eerdmans, 2001), 42–44.

[25] White, "He Placed a Little Child in the Midst," 372. White goes on to make the insightful connection between Jesus's self-identification with the child and his self-identification with marginalized adults in the last judgment teaching of Matthew 25:31–46.

Selected Insights from Orthodox Christian Thought

Like the historical Roman Catholic and Protestant Christian communities, the historical Orthodox Church affirmed the fundamental importance of humility for Christian thought and life. Yet unlike some Christian communities, and notwithstanding interpretations and applications that have sometimes been deeply unjust, the Orthodox Church has maintained from ancient times its normative emphasis on humility. Humility's central significance emerges in multiple layers of the Orthodox tradition—from the popularization of the "humiliated Christ" by Russian thinkers and artists,[26] to the identification of "apophaticism" (or negative theology) as Orthodoxy's distinctive approach to theology within epistemological limits,[27] to humility's repeated identification within Orthodoxy's liturgical and spiritual texts as the "mother of all virtues" and therapeutic corrective to pride's poison. Several elements of Orthodox praxis also highlight the theme of humility, including a long and flourishing tradition of monasticism, the ongoing practice of face-to-face confession to a spiritual father, the use of the body in prayer, and even the style of Orthodox art and music.[28] As one scholar notes, "At the heart of Orthodox spirituality, indeed at the core of Orthodox theology is an understanding of humility. All theological thought, all virtues, and all spiritual pursuits collapse like a house built on sand, if they are not rooted in humility."[29] For the Orthodox, deemphasizing humility would be a fundamental betrayal of their understanding of the gospel. The only option is to recapture authentic humility and reject its distorted expressions.

In this section, I explore insights gained through a child-attentive approach by considering three sets of humility-related resources from the Orthodox tradition: (1) the Extreme Humility and Nativity icons of Jesus Christ, (2) the writings of Saints Anthony the Great and Dorotheos of Gaza, and (3) the sacramental practices and teachings on the value of cultivating humility in children.

---

[26] See, for example, Nadejda Gorodetzky, *The Humiliated Christ in Modern Russian Thought* (New York: AMS Press, 1973). For a more focused study on Sergius Bulgakov, see Paul Gavrilyuk, "The Kenotic Theology of Sergius Bulgakov," *Scottish Journal of Theology* 58 (2005): 251–269.

[27] Apophaticism is a theology that deliberately speaks about what God is not, rather than what God is. For a thorough study, see Aristotle Papanikolaou, *Being with God: Trinity, Apophaticism, and Divine-Human Communion* (Notre Dame, IN: University of Notre Dame Press, 2006).

[28] The connection between humility and both Byzantine chant and iconography is discussed extensively, for example, in Constantine Cavarnos, *Byzantine Sacred Art*, 2nd ed. (Belmont, MA: Institute for Byzantine and Modern Greek Studies, 1992).

[29] Archimandrite Chrysostomos, "Humility and Orthodox Spirituality," in Chrysostomos, *Orthodox Patristic Psychology*, 1:17.

The Icons of Christ's Extreme Humility and Nativity

Commenting on the significance of the Philippian hymn (Phil 2:5–11) within Orthodoxy, Fr. Nicholas Sakharov writes, "This drama of Christ's *kenosis* (self-emptying), depicted in the Pauline words, is abundantly featured throughout the whole of Eastern Orthodox tradition—in the patristic writings in general and in the liturgy in particular."[30] Recall the two moments in Christ's life that St. Paul references explicitly in these verses: Christ's incarnation ("he emptied himself, taking the form of a slave, being born in human likeness" [2:7]) and his crucifixion ("he humbled himself and became obedient to the point of death—even death on a cross" [2:8]). Christ's earthly life begins and ends in radical, kenotic humility. While other moments also exemplify his profound humility, Christ's incarnation and crucifixion hold particular significance for illuminating humility's theological meaning for Orthodox Christians, a point expressed well not only in the patristic and liturgical texts but also in Orthodox iconography.

Figure 1. Traditional Icon of "Extreme Humility"

---

[30] *I Love Therefore I Am: The Theological Legacy of Archimandrite Sophrony* (Crestwood, NY: St. Vladimir's Seminary Press, 2002), 93.

One Orthodox icon known as Extreme Humility or in Greek, "ἡ ἄκρα ταπείνωσις" (see Figure 1), depicts Christ upright and naked from the waist up with his cross behind him, his head bowed to the side, his right ribs with a pierce mark, and his hands crossed in front of his waist bearing the marks of nails. Around his waist is a boxlike tomb. Liturgically, this icon is featured on Good Friday in commemoration of Christ's death and burial. It epitomizes the ethos of Holy Week and focuses the faithful on Christ's death and on the humble disposition he maintains throughout his life and passion. The image teaches that the deepest expression of humility or, more accurate to the Greek, *"akra"*—the *height* of humility—is to *submit* oneself wholly to God and neighbor, even unto the point of crucifixion. Humility's first meaning as willing acceptance of a low position is thus underscored. The icon also conveys God's humble descent, or *katabasis*, as a triple movement down: (1) from eternity into human nature and history, (2) from earthly life to the humiliation of the cross, and (3) from the cross to the tomb and down to Hades. The first point is conveyed in the halo over Jesus's head reading "Ο ΩΝ," the Septuagint Greek term for "I AM" (Exod 3:14); the second point is clear from the cross and from Christ's nakedness and wounds; and the third point is depicted by Jesus's body as "floating" or even "sinking down" into the tomb's darkness. Through Jesus's peaceful expression, the icon further suggests that he willingly accepts all three of these downward movements as the way to salvation, as the inevitable path for the one who seeks the *anabasis* of all creation. This *katabasis-anabasis* paradox is articulated in the icon by the cross's inscription, "The King of Glory."

What one does not see in the Orthodox christological tradition, including in this icon, is an effort to communicate Christ's humility through the use of gory realism. In the Extreme Humility icon, Christ's side and hands are wounded, but the horrific details of humiliation and crucifixion are omitted. Furthermore, while Christ is portrayed as dead and already within the tomb, Christ's facial expression is more suggestive of sleep than of death.[31] Within the Orthodox tradition, this stylistic practice protects the full divinity of Christ, even as it communicates one of his most vulnerable, humble, and characteristically "human" moments. Viewers are reminded that the Crucified One never stops being the Logos—the second person of the Trinity—who deserves our ultimate respect. Importantly, the icon also communicates a critique of inauthentic, exploitative humility and seeks to protect children and other members of the church from being exposed unnecessarily to graphic images that may be psychologically damaging. Humility here eschews sensationalism, preserves dignity, and guards against despair and trauma.

---

[31] See Hans Belting, "An Image and Its Function in the Liturgy: The Man of Sorrows in Byzantium," *Dumbarton Oaks Papers* 34/35 (1980/1981): 1–16.

Figure 2. Icon of the "Nativity of Christ"

Shifting attention to the other pole of humility within Christ's earthly life, consider selected features of the Byzantine "Nativity of Christ" icon (see Figure 2). Like the preceding image of Christ's death, this icon communicates the willing acceptance of a low position through multiple details. The cave setting and manger indicate the Holy Family's rejection from the inn (Luke 2:7). Mary, the Mother of God, is the one upon whose "lowliness" God looked with favor (Luke 1:48) and whose obedience to God even went to the point of accepting an otherwise humiliating status (unwed mother).[32] In the bottom left corner sits Joseph, literally and figuratively "below" Mary, humbly contemplating the meaning of these miraculous events for himself, his family, and his people. The angels at the top of the scene have *descended* to sing praise (Luke 2:13–14). A dynamic of voluntary lowliness—a dance of humility—energizes this icon.

While the image's other details are pulled mainly from the Gospel narratives of Matthew and Luke, the iconic depiction of Christ seems especially

---

[32] In the Orthodox tradition, Mary is referred to as the *Theotokos*, the "bearer of God," a term defended on Christological grounds at the Council of Ephesus in 431. She is venerated as the greatest of all saints and is regarded as a model of Christian life and humility. See Kyriaki K. FitzGerald, "A Person in Communion: The Witness of Mary, the Mother of God," *Greek Orthodox Theological Review* 46, no. 3–4 (2001): 229–253.

Johannine. The eternal Logos, through whom all creation was made (John 1:3), has wondrously and willingly been made flesh and now dwells among the earthly creatures (John 1:14). Furthermore, he has done so not because a lowly state is good in itself or out of compulsion, but voluntarily and out of love, so that the world might be saved through him (John 3:16–17).

The iconographer communicates these theological claims through lines and colors, using artistic techniques and details consistent with those in the Extreme Humility icon. Notice, first, that the cloth bands used to wrap the infant Jesus resemble burial cloths, and that the manger parallels the tomb that surrounds him in the Extreme Humility icon. Again, the point of Christ's *katabasis* is the *anabasis* of all creation through his death and resurrection. The Nativity icon expresses this theme and Orthodox teaching with clarity—Jesus is born to die for the salvation of all. Notice also in the enlarged image that the expression of the infant Jesus is mature and serious (see Figure 3). There are no chubby cheeks or curly locks of hair. Instead, Jesus's face resembles that of an adult man more than that of a newborn.

Figure 3. Nativity of Christ (detail)

As was the case with communicating sleep more than death in the Extreme Humility icon, the tradition of giving an adult face to the Christ child in this icon serves to express and protect the full divinity of Christ during a radically human moment. Orthodox Christology confesses, "One Lord Jesus Christ," who unites his fully human nature with his fully divine nature within the single divine Hypostasis of the Son. As John McGuckin states,

What this means simply is that Jesus, and the Lord, and the Christ, are one and the same person. He who was the humble Son of Man, who suffered and died, is the self-same subject who was "with God in the beginning" as Word and Wisdom of the Father. It is this simple axiom that marks the heart of Orthodox Christology.[33]

The iconic *kenosis* of Christ signals a trajectory within Orthodox theology that proclaims God's radical humility in a distinctive way—one that emphasizes the first meaning of humility as voluntary lowliness even as it staunchly resists any suggestion of a loss or compromise of Christ's divinity. At the same time, however, the third meaning of humility is communicated. The Christ child *needs* his earthly mother even as the entire creation—including Mary and Joseph, the animals, and the angels—*need* Christ. For Orthodox Christianity, humility lies not only in creation's need for our Creator, but also in the Creator's need for creation.

Saints Anthony the Great and Dorotheos of Gaza

A short anecdote from *Sayings of the Desert Fathers*, attributed to St. Anthony the Great, summarizes the significance of humility within Eastern Orthodoxy's spiritual and ascetical tradition:

> Abba Anthony said, "Once I had a vision, in which I saw all the snares that the enemy [Satan] spreads out over the world and I said, groaning, 'What can possibly deliver a person from such snares?!' Then I heard a voice saying to me, 'Humility.'"[34]

Three noteworthy teachings can be gleaned from this text. First, Anthony's vision depicts a world that is broken, spiritually dangerous, and saturated with traps and temptations that can prevent a person's progress in holiness. Both the landscape of society and the landscape of one's own heart are treacherous due to the fallen condition. Spiritual advancement, thus, is neither easy nor pleasant; it requires sweat and tears and entails bumps and bruises. *Askesis*, or spiritual struggle, is necessary for progress toward holiness, just as physical exercise is necessary for progress toward athletic excellence.[35]

---

[33] John A. McGuckin, "Christ," in *The Encyclopedia of Eastern Orthodox Christianity*, vol. I, ed. John A. McGuckin (Malden and Oxford: Wiley-Blackwell, 2011), 120.

[34] Anthony #7, translation mine. Cf. Benedicta Ward, trans. *The Sayings of the Desert Fathers*, rev. ed. (Kalamazoo, MI: Cistercian Publications, 1984), 2.

[35] See John Chryssavgis, "The Spiritual Way," in *The Cambridge Companion to*

Second, humility is a virtue of fundamental importance. It is the one-word answer and singular focus in St. Anthony's anecdote, not because other virtues are irrelevant, but because, from an Orthodox perspective, humility fortifies and holds together so many vital elements for growth in Christian life. In the sixth century, St. Dorotheos of Gaza expresses this teaching through the use of an extended metaphor:

> First, [one] must lay the foundation, which is faith. Without faith, as the Apostle says, it is impossible to please God (Heb 11:6).... [Now] the builder must set his stones in mortar. If he piles up his stones without mortar, the stones come apart and the house falls down. The mortar is humility, which is comprised from the earth and lies under the feet of all. Any virtue existing without humility is no virtue at all, as it says in the saying of the elders: "As it is impossible to construct a ship without nails, so there is no hope of being saved without humility."[36]

Anthony's anecdote and Dorotheos's words both reiterate the pervasive significance of humility for spiritual progress and salvation. Without humility, there is no hope. Humility, within their ethical visions, is the condition for the possibility of fulfilling one's potential as a human person called to holiness and communion with God. Humility is the gritty mortar preventing the collapse of all that is built; it is the nails holding together the ship, the ark of the church, amid the chaotic waters of each age.

Finally, St. Anthony's anecdote suggests that humility constitutes the very method for spiritual development itself, a claim also found in the broader Orthodox ethical tradition.[37] A method guides us through a world and, according to St. Anthony, is an endeavor that demands and consists in humility.

Within Orthodoxy more broadly, humility as method relates to two underlying convictions. First is that pride, egoism, and individualism are the governing characteristics of the fallen human condition. Humility, as the antithesis of these, serves as the healing method or effective treatment for this root cause of corruption, sin, and spiritual illness. Turning again to St. Dorotheos, we read,

> What then is the medicine and what the cause of our contempt [for God's commandments]? Listen to what the Lord himself tells us:

Orthodox Christian Theology, ed. Mary B. Cunningham and Elizabeth Theokritoff (Cambridge: Cambridge University Press, 2008), 150–163.

[36] Dorotheos of Gaza, *Discourses and Sayings*, trans. Eric P. Wheeler (Kalamazoo, MI: Cistercian Publications, 1977), 202–203.

[37] See Perry T. Hamalis, "Ethics," in *The Orthodox Christian World*, ed. Augustine Casiday (London and New York: Routledge, 2012), 419-431.

"Learn of me, for I am meek and humble of heart and you shall find rest for your souls" (Matt 11:29). There you have it in a nutshell: Christ has taught us the root and cause of all evils and also the remedy for it, leading to all good. He shows us that pretentions to superiority [pride] cast us down and that it is impossible to obtain mercy except by the contrary, that is to say, by humility.[38]

In ways similar to St. Augustine, Reinhold Niebuhr, and others, the Orthodox tradition generally regards pride as the root of sin and spiritual sickness. To eliminate or even deemphasize humility would be to shun the cure of humanity's predicament.

Second, Orthodoxy stresses a communal approach to the spiritual life. Alone, one cannot travel safely across a world covered with spiritual traps; however, *with others*, with God's grace, with an experienced spiritual guide, with virtuous friends, with a worshiping community, and with the examples of Christ and the saints in front of us always, all things are possible. In other words, the third meaning of humility, acknowledging our need for others, becoming childlike, and being willing to learn from the wisdom and experience of others is the method—the way—across the treacherous landscapes around and within us.

Orthodox Sacramental Practices and Teachings

A third set of resources from the Orthodox tradition relates more directly to children and the practical questions that must be considered in our present-day context: Should Christian parents strive to cultivate humility or self-esteem in their children? Is there a way to encourage both character traits in a manner that respects and enhances children's lives? The Orthodox Church affirms the full humanity and dignity of children in a variety of ways. Indeed, Orthodox Christians are distinct in their practice of inviting children to participate from their infancy in the sacraments; baptism, chrismation/confirmation, and Eucharist / Holy Communion are all offered to children who are as young as forty days old.[39] Such full inclusion of children in the life of the Orthodox Church is a bold affirmation of the full humanity and dignity of children, despite their immaturity. It is a practice reminiscent of Jesus's radical inclusion of the child among the disciples (Matt 18:2). Yet the Orthodox Church couples this affir-

---

[38] Dorotheos of Gaza, *Discourses and Sayings*, 81.
[39] A few exceptions to children's full participation exist, however, since the Orthodox Church maintains a minimum age for marriage, monastic tonsure, and ordination. Yet in these three contexts the rationale seems to be more for protecting children than for excluding them from participation. One should also note that these three sacraments are distinct because, unlike the others, not all adult members of the church participate in them.

mation of dignity with an unapologetic effort to cultivate authentic humility in children. Consider this advice from another Orthodox theologian, Sr. Magdalen of Essex:

> We must not try to overcome insecurity or inferiority complexes by inculcating vanity. Pride in oneself is even more dangerous than an inferiority complex. Thinking one is worth nothing is not an obstacle to salvation unless it leads to despair about God. I am not suggesting we force children to a degree of self-condemnation which is beyond them at present; but humility is the only basis of mental and emotional health. What the child needs is hope based on living faith, in God and in the love of those around him/her, whatever his/her lack of abilities or qualities.[40]

Notice how Sr. Magdalen's words focus on children's spiritual well-being by recommending authentic humility without compromising dignity. In a world where children are often either caressed as mini-gods who can do no wrong or crushed as insignificant, worthless, and stupid, the approach to humility suggested here is a healthy and much-needed middle way.

Implications

In this final part, I shift from a more interpretive to a more constructive purpose, synthesizing the implications for Christian thought and practice of the various dimensions of humility already outlined. More specifically, I suggest that a robust, child-inclusive concept of humility can help promote the dignity of children, expand our understanding of Christ, and cultivate humility in life-giving ways.

Defending Humility Is Defending Children

A child-attentive approach to humility highlights a serious danger that comes with the shift away from humility within Christian theology and ethics. The above analysis has shown that within the biblical tradition, "children/the child" is the only *category* of persons identified as "humble" (Matt 18:4). In other references to humility, a particular person models the virtue—Jesus (Matt 11:29; 21:5; Phil 2:8), a specific publican (Luke 18:14), the Apostle Paul (2 Cor 10:1)—or, alternatively, humility is prescribed for all members of the faith community (Jas 4:10; 1 Pet 3:8; Col 3:12). If it is true that children represent humility like

---

[40] Sister Magdalen, *Conversations with Children* (Essex, UK: Stavropegic Monastery of St. John the Baptist, 2001), 117.

no other category of persons, then from a biblical perspective, relentless critiques of humility cannot help but undermine the integrity and dignity of children. When we devalue all forms of humility, the vulnerable and dependent child is either overlooked as lacking value or pressured to be something she or he is not (independent, self-sufficient, etc.) in order to be seen as valuable. Thus, defending the value of genuine humility means defending the value of children, and vice versa. Yet defending the value of genuine humility also means rejecting all acts of humiliation, exploitation, or exclusion leveled against a child.

Through its continued emphasis on the value of humility, Orthodox Christianity can make an important contribution to protecting the dignity of children and preventing their further marginalization in society. Orthodox practice already honors children in noteworthy ways (e.g., infant/child participation in the church's full sacramental life), and further reflection on children and childhood in Orthodox theology promises hearty yields. We can sense this by considering the effects of placing the child in the midst of one fundamental Orthodox theological teaching, the iconic *kenosis* of Christ, and one fundamental ethical teaching, the role of humility in spiritual development.

Expanding Our Understanding of Christ

In discussing the Extreme Humility and Nativity icons, it is evident that the Orthodox way of visually communicating God's humility is an important corrective to the tendency among some Christian communities to focus upon the gory details of Jesus's torture and crucifixion. Children can be turned away from the faith if not psychologically harmed by such graphically violent imagery, from which many Christians would censor their children were the subject matter something other than the life and death of Jesus. Commenting on Mel Gibson's blockbuster *The Passion of the Christ*, Björn Krondorfer asks, "Why does the depiction of a religious founder being ripped apart with graphic realism attract such widespread popularity? What does it tell us about the present cultural moment that brings forth such a movie?"[41] Orthodoxy's sensitive use of Byzantine icons critiques such cultural trends and provides teaching resources for children that avoid sensationalizing violence without devolving into shallow cartoons like the (comparatively profitable) *Veggie Tales* series. A child-inclusive perspective on humility emphasizes this dimension of Orthodoxy and points to new ways of teaching and presenting the gospel message.[42]

---

[41] See his "Mel Gibson's Alter Ego: A Male Passion for Violence," *Cross Currents* 54, no. 1 (2004): 16–21.

[42] Denny Weaver's work holds particular promise for constructive thinking about

Orthodoxy, however, sometimes has the opposite tendency: to forget the full humanity of Jesus Christ—at least in practice. A child-inclusive theological lens may help correct this equally risky Christology by affirming Jesus's real childhood—his infancy, fragility, vulnerability, and so on—as well as his unequivocal endorsement of children and "childlikeness." Increased attention to Jesus as "child" (cf. Matt 18:5; Mark 9:37; Luke 9:48) may help Orthodox Christians relate with Christ in a more personal manner. Placing the child in the midst of Orthodox Christology could thus serve a similar role today as the one that the "humiliated Christ" theme played in a previous generation within Russia. As Nadejda Gorodetzky (1901–1985) writes:

> None of the Russian writers on kenosis had questioned the divinity of Christ. There was in the country an opposite tendency of falling into other-worldliness in doctrine and in everyday life. If in the sixteenth century the foolishness of Basil the innocent counterbalanced the future growth of the idea of "the third Rome," it was important that in the nineteenth century the thought of the self-emptying and humiliation of Christ should emphasize Christ's true humanity and bring closer to us the reality of the Gospels and of the Creed.[43]

Today, with an excess of icons of Christ in imperial dress and a tendency among Orthodox theologians to discuss Christ in obfuscating language, Child Theology can restore a balance, reminding the faithful that Christ is both fully divine *and* fully human.

Cultivating Spiritual Growth

I noted earlier that Orthodoxy's emphasis on the value of humility can ground an emphasis on the value of children. Notwithstanding this claim, a Child Theology approach to Orthodox ethics also reminds us that an overemphasis on humility—especially on humility's first and second meanings—can slip dangerously into the abusive humiliation of children. While Orthodox theology tends to avoid images and detailed accounts of Christ's extreme humiliation, we sometimes use extreme images when striving to induce or deepen humility in ourselves and others. Consider, for example, the following passage from the fourteenth-century Orthodox saint, Theognostos:

---

violence, children, and Orthodox iconography. See *The Nonviolent Atonement*, 2nd ed. (Grand Rapids: Eerdmans, 2011).

[43] Gorodetzky, *Humiliated Christ in Modern Russian Thought*, 126.

> Consciously look on yourself as an ant or a worm, so that you can become a man formed by God. If you fail to do the first, the second cannot happen. The lower you descend, the higher you ascend; and when, like the psalmist, you regard yourself as nothing before the Lord (cf. Ps 39:5), then imperceptibly you will grow great. And when you begin to realize that you have nothing and know nothing, then you will become rich in the Lord through practice of the virtues and spiritual knowledge.[44]

Such teachings have their place in many contexts and cultures, and with spiritually mature adults; however, they may be harmful in other cultures, with less spiritually mature adults, and with children. In theory, Orthodoxy articulates the vital role of discernment, especially for those giving spiritual counsel (priests, elders, teachers, parents, etc.); yet in practice, the necessary effort is not always made, or the wisdom is lacking to "translate" such texts for vulnerable audiences. Here is where the critiques of humility by contextual theologies advanced from the perspective of women, racial minorities, citizens of developing nations, *and children* must be taken seriously.

As noted in the teaching from Sr. Magdalen of Essex, humility needs to be cultivated so that it is age-appropriate, context-specific, and life-giving. Children, as well as some adults, may need the virtue of humility to be communicated and prescribed differently than spiritually mature adults or those in highly developed, individualistic, and materialistic cultures. Informed by this richer notion of humility, adults can cultivate humility in children in life-giving and appropriate ways that encourage and honor children and avoid the pitfalls of either rejecting attention to humility in spiritual transformation altogether or using distorted and even abusive notions of humility that harm and humiliate children. Therefore, placing the child in the midst of Christian teachings on humility offers many practical implications for upholding the spiritual lives and dignity of children in the church and the home.

Conclusion

Biblical scholar Craig Evans (b. 1952) has written,

> Standing at the very heart of Jesus' kingdom summons was his demand that people humble themselves. Apart from such humbling, exaltation will be impossible. Christology in particular and Christian theology in

---

[44] St. Theognostos, "On the Practice of the Virtues, Contemplation, and the Priesthood," in *The Philokalia: Volume Two*, trans. and ed. G. E. H. Palmer, Philip Sherrard, and Kallistos Ware (London: Faber and Faber, 1981), 359.

general must work through the implications of this ethic, not simply for a better and more accurate "orthodoxy," but for a more effective and life-changing "orthopraxy."[45]

This chapter responds to Evans's challenge and critiques a dominant trend by examining an approach to humility that takes into account children and uses resources of early Christianity and Eastern Orthodoxy. By placing the child in the midst of traditional Christian teachings on humility, theoretical as well as practical insights have emerged. This approach shows that the meaning of humility is multilayered and reveals an important child-grounded understanding of humility as "acknowledging our need for others" that complements and contrasts with the predominant meanings of humility as "voluntary lowliness" and "awareness of sin." While this additional meaning of humility does not prevent misunderstanding or misuse of the term, it decenters the two dominant meanings of humility so that it is Christ-endorsed and child-inclusive.

For Christology, this robust notion of humility reminds us that Christ is fully divine and fully human, a point that can become lost within Orthodoxy's traditionally high Christology. Recapturing a fuller understanding of Christ's humility can also correct tendencies in various Christian traditions and cultural contexts to sensationalize Christ's crucifixion or to teach children about Jesus by relying on either violent images of his death or shallow cartoons about his life.

For ethics, increased attention to children reveals a more refined understanding of the meaning of humility for Christians and its role in spiritual growth. An Orthodox child-attentive theology also critiques normative accounts of humility at two extremes—those that reject humility in the name of protecting self-esteem and those that prescribe an inappropriate humility for children. In these and other ways, reflecting on humility with attention to children enriches theological understandings of humility, Christ's humanity, and children's dignity, highlighting the significance of cultivating humility in ways that are age-appropriate, context-specific, and life-giving.

---

[45] Craig A. Evans, "Jesus' Ethic of Humility," *Trinity Journal* 13 (1992): 138.

10

A Decolonial Approach to Formation and Discipleship

Valerie Michaelson

Decolonial scholars across disciplines examine the history and enduring impact of colonialism. They call for justice through the overturning of violent, oppressive, and overarching colonial structures that continue to threaten and marginalize Indigenous peoples.[1] Their scholarship has exposed the often complicit role of churches as animating partners in the harms caused by colonization. In fact, in reevaluating the church's record over the past five hundred years, scholars are observing that Christians repeatedly provided the ideological pretext and justification for atrocities against Indigenous peoples around the globe.[2] Because of the fundamentally destructive role that Christian church leaders played within Indigenous communities and nations, decolonial scholarship often presumes a non-Christian framework.[3] Yet a growing number of theologians worldwide are informed by and contributing to the emerging interdisciplinary field of decolonial studies.

---

[1] Waziyatawin Angela Wilson and Michael Yellow Bird, eds., *For Indigenous Eyes Only: A Decolonization Handboook* (Santa Fe: School for Advanced Research, 2005); Marie Battiste, Lynne Bell, and Len M. Findlay, "Decolonizing Education in Canadian Universities: An Interdisciplinary, International, Indigenous Research Project," *Canadian Journal of Native Education* 26, no. 2 (2002): 82; Sarah de Leeuw and Margo Greenwood, "Turning a New Page: Cultural Safety, Critical Creative Literary Interventions, Truth and Reconciliation, and the Crisis of Child Welfare," *AlterNative: An International Journal of Indigenous Peoples* 13, no. 3 (2017): 142–151.

[2] Mark MacDonald, "A Prophetic Call to Churches in Canada," in *Decolonizing Discipline: Children, Corporal Punishment, Christian Theologies, and Reconciliation*, vol. 3, ed. Valerie Michaelson and Joan E. Durrant (Winnipeg: University of Manitoba Press, 2020), 17–22.

[3] Andrea Smith, "Decolonization in Unexpected Places: Native Evangelicalism and the Rearticulation of Mission," *American Quarterly* 62, no. 3 (2010): 569–590.

By engaging with decolonial scholarship, Christian theologians are probing the "diversity, complexity, and promise"[4] of combining decolonial thinking with Christian theologies. They aim to discern and dismantle colonial ideologies, which have caused violence and corrupted the gospel message, and thereby also strengthen the church's commitment to seek justice.

For decades, theologians in Canada have collaborated under the umbrella of the Canadian Decolonial Theology Project. Led by Michel Andraos, Lee Cormie, Néstor Medina, and Becca Whitla, they "unsanitize and dismantle" the myth of Canada as a "benign, welcoming, generous, peace-keeping, multicultural nation and society."[5] Rooted in their shared commitments to "liberation struggles, practices and activism,"[6] they call on Christian leaders in Canada to rethink key areas of church life. These and other theologians recognize that colonial systems and structures are fundamentally in conflict with the biblical teachings of love, justice, and liberation.

Through my engagement with decolonial studies, I have realized that, when applied to Christian theology, decolonial approaches offer a way forward in many areas of theology for realigning Christian thought and practice with the message and example of Jesus. This thereby challenges the church to create societies in which all people are valued, protected, and have equitable opportunities to flourish. Specifically, in my work, I have used a decolonial approach to theology to rethink the discipline of children.[7] Although decolonial theologians globally have explored a range of issues, little attention has been given to children and childhood. In our Canadian context, this holds a certain irony because some of the worst instances of colonial violence in Canada have been directed at First Nations, Inuit, and Métis children.[8] My work has included attention to the abuse of Indigenous children in the residential school system as well as the ways that normative Western European interpretations of Christian texts, especially verses in Proverbs regarding the "rod," have been used to justify and propagate violence toward children.

I have worked particularly with scholars across disciplines in understanding the harms caused by corporal punishment. The testimony of abused children

---

[4] Michel Andraos, Lee Cormie, Néstor Medina, and Becca Whitla, "Decolonial Theological Encounters: An Introduction," *Toronto Journal of Theology* 33, no. 2 (2017): 259–60, 259.

[5] Néstor Medina and Becca Whitla, "(An) Other Canada Is Possible: Rethinking Canada's Colonial Legacy," *Horizontes Decoloniales / Decolonial Horizons* 5 (2019): 13–42.

[6] Andraos et al., "Decolonial Theological Encounters," 260.

[7] See Michaelson and Durrant, eds., *Decolonizing Discipline*.

[8] This point was raised when I presented my work and spent time with members of the Canadian Decolonial Theology Project at the American Academy of Religion conference in Denver, Colorado, in November 2018.

as well as scientific research over the past thirty years is clear and consistent: at best, corporal punishment does nothing to promote the behavioral changes that parents might hope for and has no positive impact on children's development; at worst, it places children's developmental health at risk and impairs their capacities for empathy, nonviolent conflict resolution, and resilience.[9] Yet even when all this evidence is readily available, parents and church leaders continue to use selected biblical texts to rationalize and normalize corporal punishment against children. Churches and faith-based groups need to ask uncomfortable questions about the communal social norms that condone violence as an acceptable way to resolve conflicts and regulate behaviors. Furthermore, churches have the opportunity—and moral responsibility—to take an active stance against all forms of violence toward children.

My research around the value of decolonial approaches to issues related to corporal punishment, children, and discipline has raised many questions about how the church approaches faith formation and discipleship, two key themes in Christian faith and life. Jesus came to offer life abundant and commanded his followers to love God and love the neighbor. Thus, according to the biblical witness, the church is called to pass down this message to young people through its teachings, spiritual practices, and compassionate and just actions in the world. In the church, formation and discipleship are part of a lifelong process of growing in faith, loving others, and seeking justice.

Although some churches in Canada have indicated their commitment to move forward in the spirit of reconciliation with the Original Peoples, there are disturbing signs in the very understanding of and approaches to formation and discipleship that are undermining these efforts. Some churches have certainly been engaged in the truth and reconciliation efforts and given many public apologies for the roles that individual leaders and the overarching structures and theologies of the churches have played. However, in many ways, the church continues to perpetuate the same colonial narratives, attitudes, and behaviors that have caused so much harm.

Attention to the formation of children in Christian churches may well appear inconsequential to the broader issues at stake, especially when the larger goal is self-determination and "the return of enough land and power for Indigenous nations to be self-sufficient."[10] Yet as long as churches approach

---

[9] Michaelson and Durrant, *Decolonizing Discipline*. See also Joan Durrant and Ron Ensom, "Physical Punishment of Children: Lessons from 20 Years of Research," *CMAJ* 184, no. 12 (2012): 1373–1377; Elizabeth T. Gershoff and Andrew Grogan-Kaylor, "Spanking and Child Outcomes: Old Controversies and New Meta-Analyses," *Journal of Family Psychology* 30, no. 4 (2016): 453.

[10] Alfred Taiaiake, *Wasase: Indigenous Pathways of Action and Freedom* (Toronto:

faith formation in ways that continue to spread the same harmful colonial narratives and attitudes, rather than equipping both children and adults to be active participants in the creation of a more just future, we are simply reinforcing the status quo in yet another generation.

In this chapter, I therefore draw on decolonial theological approaches to rethink Christian understandings of and approaches to faith formation and discipleship. First, I consider the historical context in Canada, identifying and giving examples where these same colonial narratives continue to guide policy and practice while fueling continued harm—narratives that require our attention and deconstruction. Second, I draw attention to some of the approaches to faith formation in Canadian churches that actually reinforce and even expand the same harmful colonial ideologies and attitudes of domination and control. Finally, I consider ways that decolonial theological approaches can aid us, not only in Canada but in all places around the globe tainted by colonialism, in rethinking how the formation of both children and adults in church contexts might address profound injustices, overturn oppressive structures, and lead to the flourishing of all people and the planet. By reexamining our approaches to faith formation and discipleship through a decolonial lens and with attention to children, we can begin to replace harmful attitudes and practices with a renewed commitment to those who are under threat from the colonial system that shapes Canadian society.

My own commitment to strengthening the church's approach to faith formation and engaging with the decolonial struggle in Canada is interconnected with, and inseparable from my own faith and personal experiences.[11] As a student of Christian theology in the 1990s, I was not exposed to decolonial theological voices, nor was I aware of Canadian decolonial writers from other disciplines such as education[12] and the health sciences.[13] Later, when I worked in parish ministry and was tasked with shaping children's formation, I propagated the same Eurocentric and colonial theological messages that had shaped me thus far. I was oblivious to the radical personal transformation that reconciliation

---

University of Toronto Press, 2005), quoted in Jeffrey S. Denis and Kerry A. Bailey, "'You Can't Have Reconciliation without Justice': How Non-Indigenous Participants in Canada's Truth and Reconciliation Process Understand Their Roles and Goals," in *The Limits of Settler Colonial Reconciliation* (Singapore: Singer, 2016), 137.

[11] Michel Andraos, "Doing Theology after the TRC," *Toronto Journal of Theology* 32, no. 3 (2017): 295–301.

[12] Marie Battiste, "You Can't Be the Global Doctor If You're the Colonial Disease," *Teaching as Activism* (2005): 121–133.

[13] Carrie Bourassa, Kim McKay-McNabb, and Mary Hampton, "Racism, Sexism and Colonialism: The Impact on the Health of Aboriginal Women in Canada," *Canadian Woman Studies* 24, no. 1 (2004): 2.

required, and also to my complicit role in the system in which I was operating. I hope that my reflections here can provide a springboard for theologians in other contexts to understand the benefits—and moral imperative—of engaging and rethinking other doctrines and practices in the light of attention both to children and colonial oppressions.

Historical Context

In Canada, the harms of colonization have been well documented. Through targeted colonial government policies such as the 1876 Indian Act, Indigenous peoples have been violently displaced and systematically marginalized over centuries.[14] One of the worst implementations of colonial violence occurred between the 1870s and the early 1990s through the church- and government-run residential schools. Over 150,000 Inuit, Métis, and First Nations children between the ages of four and sixteen were forcefully removed from their homes and placed in residential schools with the goal of "separating Aboriginal children from their families, in order to minimize and weaken family ties and cultural linkages, and to indoctrinate children into a new culture—the culture of the legally dominant Euro-Christian Canadian society."[15] The sobering direct testimony of survivors to the treatment they endured is documented through initiatives such as the website *Where Are the Children?*[16] and volumes such as *The Survivors Speak: A Report of the Truth and Reconciliation Commission*[17] and *A Knock on the Door: The Essential History of Residential Schools from the Truth and Reconciliation Commission of Canada*.[18] The churches in Canada were primary animators of this colonial system and ran many of these schools. Their broader systemwide participation—combined with acts of sexual, physical, emotional, spiritual, and cultural abuses by individuals (often condoned by

---

[14] Truth and Reconciliation Commission of Canada (TRC), *Canada's Residential Schools: The History,* Part 1: *Origins to 1939,* vol. 1 of *The Final Report of the Truth and Reconciliation Commission of Canada* (Kingston: McGill-Queen's University Press, 2015).

[15] Truth and Reconciliation Commission of Canada, *Honouring the Truth, Reconciling for the Future: Summary of the Final Report of the Truth and Reconciliation Commission of Canada* (Library and Archives Canada Cataloguing in Publication, 2015), v.

[16] "Where Are the Children? Healing the Legacy of the Residential Schools," Legacy of Hope Foundation, 2020, http://legacyofhope.ca/wherearethechildren/.

[17] Truth and Reconciliation Commission of Canada, *The Survivors Speak: A Report of the Truth and Reconciliation Commission of Canada* (Winnipeg: Truth and Reconciliation Commission of Canada, 2015).

[18] Phil Fontaine and Aimée Craft, *A Knock on the Door: The Essential History of Residential Schools from the Truth and Reconciliation Commission of Canada,* vol. 1 (Winnipeg: University of Manitoba Press, 2015).

church leaders)—has been well documented by Canada's Truth and Reconciliation Commission, active between 2008 and 2015.[19]

While many arguments have been used to rationalize the racist roots and practices of colonization,[20] the Western European Doctrine of Discovery merits particular scrutiny. Robert J. Miller, an enrolled citizen of the Eastern Shawnee Tribe and a professor of law at the Sandra Day O'Connor College of Law, references this doctrine as "the international law of colonialism."[21] Rooted in the papal bull *Inter Caetera*, it has been widely recognized as the "driving force behind some of the church's worst abuses of Indigenous peoples,"[22] not only in Canada but worldwide. According to the Assembly of First Nations, the Doctrine of Discovery was "used to dehumanize, exploit and subjugate Indigenous Peoples and dispossess [them] of [their] most basic rights. This was the very foundation of genocide."[23] By promoting the ideology that Christians should enjoy a moral and legal right to dominate Indigenous peoples and invade and seize any of the "undiscovered lands" populated by non-Christians, this doctrine "codified racial hierarchies in the law, placing European, Christian nations in the position of power."[24] The ideological justification provided by the Doctrine of Discovery was pervasive and far reaching. It led to the suppression and disruption of many Indigenous languages, cultures, ceremonies, environmental preservation practices, and traditions. It further fostered attitudes and

---

[19] Truth and Reconciliation Commission of Canada, *Canada's Residential Schools*.

[20] Truth and Reconciliation Commission of Canada, *Honouring the Truth*, 1.

[21] Robert J. Miller, "The Doctrine of Discovery: The International Law of Colonialism," *Indigenous Peoples' Journal of Law, Culture and Resistance* 5 (2019): 35–42, 35.

[22] Bishop Mark MacDonald, quoted by André Forget in "Church's Knowledge of Doctrine of Discovery 'Woefully Inadequate,'" *Anglican Journal*, August 28, 2015. For more on the damage incurred through the Doctrine of Discovery, see WCC Executive Committee, "Statement on the Doctrine of Discovery and Its Enduring Impact on Indigenous Peoples," World Council of Churches, February 17, 2012, https://www.oikoumene.org.

[23] UN Economic and Social Council, *Thirteenth Session: Permanent Forum on Indigenous Issues, Study on the Impacts of the Doctrine of Discovery on Indigenous Peoples, Including Mechanisms, Processes and Instruments of Redress* [study by forum member Edward John] (New York: United Nations, 2014), Doc. E/C.19/2014/3.

[24] Doctrine of Discovery Task Force, "Creating a New Family: A Circle of Conversation on the Doctrine of Christian Discovery," Christian Reformed Church in North America, 6, accessed November 24, 2020, https://www.crcna.org/sites/default/files/doctrine_of_discovery.pdf. Much decolonial thinking reminds us that antiracism is not decolonization: Decolonization is fundamentally about land, and is not (as Eve Tuck writes) a metaphor for other things we want to do to improve our societies and schools. But equally, racism against Indigenous peoples is a barrier to bringing about the repatriation of Indigenous land and life.

relationships of power and privilege that continue to impact directly the health and well-being of Indigenous peoples in Canada today, including children.

In 2007, as one of the conditions of the Indian Residential Schools Settlement Agreement, the Truth and Reconciliation Commission (TRC) of Canada was established to initiate a "truth telling and reconciliation process" with the overarching goal of working toward a "stronger and healthier future."[25] Canada's truth and reconciliation process was a catalyst by which some churches began to recognize the harms in which they had participated.

To date, the United Church of Canada (1986), the Anglican Church (1993), the Presbyterian Church of Canada (1994), and the Missionary Oblates of Mary Immaculate (2001) have all issued formal apologies for their roles in these residential schools.[26] Beyond apologies, other reconciliation initiatives include the repudiation of the Doctrine of Discovery by many Christian churches in Canada.[27] Another initiative was launched in 2019 by the United Church. This involved a national call for church members to write to senators in support of Bill C-262, an act to ensure that the laws of Canada are in harmony with the United Nations Declaration on the Rights of Indigenous Peoples (UNDRIP).[28]

An important further step forward for some First Nations, Inuit, and Métis peoples in Canada who self-identify as Christian was taken in July 2019: the establishment of a fully self-determining Indigenous church within the Anglican Church of Canada. More ecumenically, KAIROS, an organization

---

[25] Truth and Reconciliation Commission of Canada, Schedule "N," Mandate for the Truth and Reconciliation Commission, accessed December 6, 2020, http://www.residentialschoolsettlement.ca/SCHEDULE_N.pdf.

[26] The delivery of a papal apology was number 58 of the TRC Calls to Action. See Truth and Reconciliation Commission of Canada, *The Truth and Reconciliation Commission of Canada: Calls to Action 58* (Winnipeg: Truth and Reconciliation Commission of Canada, 2015), 5. Yet up to the time of this writing, the request for Pope Francis, head of the Catholic Church, to apologize to residential school survivors and their families for the role of Roman Catholic churches in the abuses has been declined. See Mia Rabson, "Pope Won't Personally Apologize for Catholic Church's Role in Residential Schools," *Globe and Mail*, March 27, 2018.

[27] The TRC's Call to Action 49 is a direct charge for the church bodies that have not yet repudiated the Doctrine of Discovery to do so. See Truth and Reconciliation Commission of Canada, *The Truth and Reconciliation Commission of Canada: Calls to Action 49* (Winnipeg: Truth and Reconciliation Commission of Canada, 2015), 5.

[28] United Church of Canada, "Church Leaders: Make C-262 Unanimous," United Church of Canada, accessed August 28, 2019, https://www.united-church.ca/news/church-leaders-make-c-262-vote-unanimous; UN General Assembly, United Nations Declaration on the Rights of Indigenous Peoples, Resolution adopted by the General Assembly, October 2, 2007.

that unites Canadian churches and other religious bodies to advocate for social change, has made decolonization and reconciliation initiatives clear priorities. Their popular blanket exercise has become a powerful tool for helping people understand the harms caused by colonization, the significance of the TRC, and the complexity and importance of reconciliation. Created in 1997, the blanket exercise is an experiential history lesson in which participants hear the story of settlement while standing on blankets that are continuously folded and removed to represent the loss of land that took place between the arrival of Europeans and the present day. It is being used across Canada and around the world.[29]

On a national level, an important output of Canada's truth and reconciliation process was the 2015 release of 94 Calls to Action, which are sometimes framed as a starting place for reconciliation. In my own work, I have tried to address the sixth of these Calls to Action: a call for the Government of Canada to remove the law that allows for the corporal punishment of children (as sixty-one countries around the world have done and dozens more have made a full commitment to do).[30] In Canada, interpretations of scripture are one of the reasons corporal punishment has been normalized in the parenting toolbox. Concepts such as "spare the rod; spoil the child" (based on Prov 13:24) have been widely used to justify corporal punishment. One of the most egregious examples of this was the use of corporal punishment (along with other forms of physical, sexual, cultural, and spiritual violence) against Indigenous children in the residential schools. In 2017, our research team responded to this Call to Action by forming a multidisciplinary group of stakeholders to write a theological statement calling on Christians across Canada to support Call to Action 6 as an act of reconciliation and to work together to stop the normalization and justification of violence against children through the use of Christian theological texts (or by any other means). Along with the statement, we also produced the 2020 edited volume *Decolonizing Discipline: Children, Corporal Punishment, Christian Theologies, and Reconciliation*. Here, theologians addressed the inadequate and shallow theologies that were initially used to justify and normalize corporal punishment. In other chapters, First Nations, Inuit, and Métis scholars and leaders share their wisdom on how traditional knowledges that were disrupted and shamed as "uncivilized" by colonial leaders

---

[29] KAIROS, "History of the Blanket Exercise," KAIROS Canada 2019, accessed November 30, 2020, https://www.kairosblanketexercise.org/about/#history.

[30] Elizabeth R. Gershoff and Joan E. Durrant, "Legal Prohibitions of Physical Punishment," in *Ending the Physical Punishment of Children: A Guide for Clinicians and Practitioners*, ed. E. T. Gershoff and S. J. Lee (Washington, DC: American Psychological Association, 2020), 155–163.

have, in reality, supported parents in important ways from time immemorial and continue to do so.

While there are hopeful signs, there is debate in Canada as to how useful frameworks such as our Truth and Reconciliation Commission or even the United Nations Declaration on the Rights of Indigenous Peoples are in terms of meaningful decolonization and reconciliation, and whether, indeed, they can lead to the necessary "radical transformation of society, based on respect for Indigenous self-determination and nation-to-nation treaties."[31]

The Formation of Children and Colonial Attitudes and Behaviors

Colonial oppressions in Canada are shaped by interrelated issues that include broken treaties, systemic and structural racism, stolen land, the normalization of violence, and cheaply bought innocence. Because I am limited by space, in this next section, I draw attention to just two issues: Eurocentrism and racism. I hope that readers will find constructive ways of moving this dialogue about decolonizing formation forward that draw attention to different issues. Oppressions do not work in isolation, and there are many more interrelated strands to be explored.

Eurocentrism

In Canada, programs and resources targeting the formation of children are often shaped by the dominant European culture. Consequently, we are left with what Latino Canadian theologian Néstor Medina describes as "the inadequacy of pervasive Eurocentric expressions of theology and the exclusive character of its intellectual baggage."[32] One example of what this looks like is in the ways that biblical stories, which are often foundational to child formation initiatives, are interpreted and thus told. Take, for example, the exodus narrative. Culminating with the story of the triumphant entry of Joshua leading the Israelites across the Jordan River and into the promised land, children from a young age are often taught to identify with the Israelites. They begin as oppressed slaves in Egypt, are dramatically rescued through God's miraculous parting of the Red Sea, and then are prepared for forty years for a new life in the promised land that is ultimately given to them by God in order to build and establish their lives.[33] For those of

---

[31] Denis and Bailey, "'You Can't Have Reconciliation without Justice,'" 137–158.

[32] Here, Medina is writing specifically about how Latina/o theologies deploy the notion of *mestizaje* as a framework for doing theology. See Néstor Medina, "A Decolonial Primer," *Toronto Journal of Theology* 33, no. 2 (2017): 279–287, 284.

[33] This is pointed out by Joëlle Morgan, "Restorying Indigenous-Settler Relations in

us who identify with the dominant culture, the unsettling yet salient parallel between the entry of the Israelites into the promised land to the attempted annihilation of the First Peoples on Turtle Island, and the change in role from oppressed to oppressor that such a reading requires, is rarely considered.

Decolonial thinking demands more of us than protecting our own comfort and indoctrinating our children to do the same. Decentering privileged Western European ways of interpreting Christian sacred texts to make room for decolonial theological voices, as told by Indigenous peoples—globally and in Canada—can open space not only for a counternarrative, but for a protest "against the claims of political and religious empires over land, people, earth, minds, and the future."[34] Certainly, many such voices exist.[35] In his edited volume *Buffalo Shout, Salmon Cry: Conversations on Creation, Land Justice, and Life Together*, Steve Heinrichs invites a diverse array of scholars, artists, and others to explore the historic wounds created by stolen land, exploitation, racism, and the place of Christian theologies.[36] Such a theological approach is critical, because even while the Doctrine of Discovery has been repudiated by many Christian churches in Canada, when an interpretation that normalizes and even glorifies the domination of land that is already somebody's home is part of our children's formation, we are at one and the same time refuting the colonial narrative while also expanding it. Likely well-meaning leaders, who operate within a culture that has established this kind of behavior as normative, are effectively using Eurocentric interpretations of this narrative to position children as "the good guys" while simultaneously normalizing and reinforcing the same oppressive colonial attitudes for yet another generation.

Racism

Racism is another pernicious fruit of colonization, and it is not usually as distant as we think or hope. Bishop Mark MacDonald, primate of the Self-Determining Anglican Church in Canada, writes that "for significant parts of Canadian society . . . outright prejudice against Indigenous people is no longer accepted in

---

Canada: Taking a Decolonial Turn toward a Settler Theology of Liberation," PhD diss., Université Saint-Paul/Saint Paul University, 2018, 298.

[34] Jione Havea, *People and Land: Decolonizing Theologies* (Lanham, MD: Rowman and Littlefield, 2020).

[35] Illustratively, see Chammah J. Kaunda and Mutale M. Kaunda, "Jubilee as Restoration of Eco-Relationality: A Decolonial Theological Critique of 'Land Expropriation without Compensation' in South Africa," *Transformation* 36, no. 2 (2019): 89–99; Havea, *People and Land*.

[36] Steve Heinrichs, ed., *Buffalo Shout, Salmon Cry: Conversations on Creation, Land Justice, and Life Together* (Harrisonburg, VA: Herald Press, 2013).

polite conversation and behaviour." But as MacDonald continues, "The systemic nature of racism is revealed in that long after direct statements of prejudice are rejected, bias and fear of 'the other' are still embedded in all the various structures and institutions of our society—including the institution of the church."[37]

MacDonald's claim that racism is present structurally and implicitly in many areas of church life should give church leaders pause to rethink all areas of church life through an antiracist lens. In child formation, children's Bibles provide a salient example of racism through white centering. Here, more often than not, we find white-skinned, blond-haired angels; a fair-skinned depiction of Mary (if not blonde herself); and even a light-skinned baby/man Jesus.[38] When whiteness is centered in children's Bibles and other like resources—and it is possibly most damaging through pictures of a white Jesus and a white Mary, biblical characters whom many young children strive to emulate—it fuels the often unconscious racial assumption that whatever else a "good Christian" looks like, they are white or fair-skinned.[39] Certainly, an emerging genre (easily searchable through "racially diverse children's Bibles") is to be celebrated. Yet children who are Black, Indigenous, and other people of color need more than the chance to be some "shining example of diversity."[40] What is needed is for children who self-identify as Black, Indigenous, or a person of color to see themselves represented as "an integral and valued part of the mosaic"[41] that is the Christian life. This is a small but necessary early step in the deep, disruptive, and sustained antiracist work that needs to follow.

---

[37] Mark MacDonald, "Spiritual Struggle, Systemic Evil," *Anglican Journal*, February 26, 2018.

[38] Jeremy Punt, "The Other in South African Children's Bibles: Politics and (Biblical) Systems of Othering," in *Text, Image, and Otherness in Children's Bibles: What Is in the Picture?*, ed. Caroline Vander Stichele and Hugh S Pyper (Atlanta: Society of Biblical Literature, 2012), 73; Susanne Scholz, "Veggies, Women, and Other Strangers in Children's Bible DVDs: Toward the Creation of Feminist Bible Films," in *Text, Image, and Otherness in Children's Bibles*, 118; Walter Dean Myers, "Where Are the People of Color in Children's Books?," *New York Times*, Sunday Review, March 15.

[39] This problem of implicit white centering, of course, is not unique to children's Bibles. In Philip Nel's book *Was the Cat in the Hat Black?: The Hidden Racism of Children's Literature*, he draws attention to the culture of "color-blind racism" that is so persistent in children's literature. His concerns about "the efficiency of structural racism" in children's literature can equally be applied to children's Bibles. What Nel argues is that the implicit racist ideologies that are unconsciously present "tend to do [their] dirty work beyond public view, fueled as much by unconscious racial assumptions as by conscious ones." The same, I argue, is true for children's Bibles that center whiteness as normative in the Christian life. See Philip Nel, *Was the Cat in the Hat Black?: The Hidden Racism of Children's Literature, and the Need for Diverse Books* (New York: Oxford University Press, 2017).

[40] Myers, "Where Are the People of Color in Children's Books?"

[41] Myers, "Where Are the People of Color in Children's Books?"

Both of our examples—Eurocentrism and racism—reinforce each other and lead to interrelated oppressive messages, attitudes, and behaviors. There are many other examples that I have not had space to discuss, including the normalization of violence against children through the use of corporal punishment that I noted earlier. However, one shared feature between Eurocentrism, racism, and indeed, the normalization of violence is their shared roots with the Doctrine of Discovery. "How much longer," writes Miller, "can modern-day societies and churches continue to tolerate the kind of ignorance, and non-Christian principles of death, domination, prejudice, inequity, and violation of sovereign and human rights that the Doctrine of Discovery represents?"[42] He continues, "All settler societies need to learn how to repudiate and repeal this Doctrine because it is based on ethnocentric, racist, religious, and feudal ideas that have no place in the modern-day world."[43]

Therefore, despite the commitments of many churches to move forward in the spirit of reconciliation, many common approaches to the formation of children serve to replicate colonization all over again. In this way, we remain deeply embedded in what Sarah de Leeuw, Margo Greenwood, and Nicole Lindsay have described as a relationship "in which non-Indigenous subjects, and by extension the institutions they/we inhabit, are making efforts to decolonize, to refute colonialism while still existing within and expanding it."[44]

Decolonial Approaches to Formation

Colonial powers need far more than a superficial makeover or facelift to render them less oppressive and more appealing. In the church and elsewhere, they need to be dismantled altogether. Decolonial theological approaches can guide us in this task and help us to disrupt our repetition of historic harms and strengthen our commitment to all children. In churches in Canada and globally, we have the capacity to provide critical leadership in decolonizing the faith formation of children and adults. We have the opportunity to dismantle the narratives that have grown from our own tradition and have sustained Eurocentrism, racism, and other harms, and replace them with a new theological imagining of what formation and discipleship for the whole church mean. This final section presents some ideas that are rooted in the ways that decolonial thinking has shaped my own ideas about formation and discipleship for the whole church.

---

[42] Miller, "Doctrine of Discovery," 42.
[43] Miller, "Doctrine of Discovery," 42.
[44] Sarah de Leeuw, Margo Greenwood, and Nicole Lindsay, "Troubling Good Intentions," *Settler Colonial Studies* 3, no. 3/4 (2013): 385.

Educational Materials

Decolonial approaches to the formation of children in church contexts compel us to reconsider how deeply Western European theological interpretations continue to regulate the worldview that we teach our children. These new approaches challenge the transmission of narratives in which stolen land is celebrated, white skin is implicitly at the top of a racial hierarchy, and cheap innocence is attained. Decolonial theological approaches engage honestly with the complicit role of churches in perpetuating racist systems around the globe and call us all to move forward to a more just future.

While these new approaches are rarely integrated into resources that are used with children, they are available. See, for example, "Reconciliation Activities for Children" developed by the Presbyterian Church of Canada in 2017.[45] I commend the people who have developed this resource as trailblazers in an underresourced area of church life. I am cautious to put too much stock in proposing education as a way forward because, as important as it is, the reality remains that unless education happens at the same time that structural inequities and implicit biases are also addressed, these efforts mean little.

Reevaluating Service Projects and Advocacy

Fostering a love of neighbor in our children is often a foundational tenet of formation and discipleship. Regrettably, it is common to involve children in charity projects that provide a simplistic response to marginalization and privilege that take into account individual circumstances but not wider systemic and structural injustices.[46] Rather than address inequities through deep justice, we teach our children simply to address guilt with charity. Consequently, good intentions to foster a love of neighbor map readily onto what Eve Tuck and K. Wayne Yang describe as "settler moves to innocence."[47] These are the "strategies or positionings that attempt to relieve the settler of feelings of guilt or responsibility without giving up land or power or privilege, without having to change much at all."[48] If this is indeed our approach, we reveal the truth of any apologies that churches may have offered. Our words are empty: *we continue to worship an empire that has no clothes.*

---

[45] The Presbyterian Church in Canada, "Reconciliation Activities for Children, Justice Ministries," accessed November 24, 2020, https://presbyterian.ca/wp-content/uploads/Reconciliation_Activities_for_Children.pdf.

[46] An example of such a project would be Operation Christmas Child by Samaritan's Purse. See https://www.samaritanspurse.ca/what-we-do/operation-christmas-child/.

[47] Eve Tuck and K. Wayne Yang, "Decolonization Is Not a Metaphor." *Decolonization: Indigeneity, Education and Society* 1, no. 1 (2012): 1–40, 10.

[48] Tuck and Yang, "Decolonization Is Not Metaphor," 10.

Efforts to teach our children love of neighbor are far better spent in laying the foundations for the long-term, slow, and generally unrewarded work of advocating for justice. For example, in developmentally appropriate ways, we can help children and adults to understand the underlying structural dynamics of power and advantage that leave First Nations, Inuit, and Métis children at a higher risk for disparities in education, health, and infrastructure than any other population of children in Canada,[49] and tangibly work together (involving our children) in Indigenous-led partnerships in local communities to address these disparities. How do these issues relate to formation and discipleship? Because the formation efforts of those in churches are to benefit all children, not only the children of the dominant culture within Canadian churches. Unless *all* children are given equitable opportunities to flourish, efforts by churches fall short of the biblical vision. Furthermore, when we teach any child to be a "good person" in a way that offers a façade of innocence without the hard work of justice and the redistribution of power, we do them a profound disservice for their long-term journey of discipleship.

Implementing an Antiracist Approach

Earlier in this chapter, I used the example of the implicit hierarchy of whiteness in children's Bibles and other resources that guide the formation of children, and noted how this can cause an implicit, tacit, yet viscerally present hierarchy of whiteness for what it means to be a good Christian. Ultimately, if we are to address the systemic and structural racism that is experienced by many First Nations, Inuit, and Métis peoples in Canada, diversifying these resources is scarcely even the tip of the iceberg. Even today, outrageous stories dominate the news in Canada as to the racist treatment of Indigenous peoples such as Joyce Echaquan[50] in Canada's health care system. Racism is a problem on a systemic public level in Canada, and it is also a problem in churches.

As many have noted, it is not possible to engage meaningfully in antiracism work without also examining white privilege and "the unearned power

---

[49] Assembly of First Nations Environmental Stewardship Unit, *The Health of First Nations Children and the Environment: Discussion Paper* (Ottawa: Assembly of First Nations), March 2008, https://www.afn.ca/uploads/files/rp-discussion_paper_re_childrens_health_and_the_environment.pdf.

[50] Morgan Lowrie and Kelly Geraldine Malone, "Joyce Echaquan's Death Highlights Systemic Racism in Health Care, Experts Say," *Global News*, October 4, 2020, https://globalnews.ca; Marie-Claude Tremblay, "Joyce Echaquan's Death: How a Decolonizing Approach Could Help Tackle Racism in Health Care," *The Conversation*, October 22, 2020, https://theconversation.com. [Image: Demonstrators hold a vigil marking the death of Joyce Echaquan, who recorded insults hurled at her by staff at the Joliette, Quebec, hospital while she was there for treatment. The Canadian Press/Paul Chiasson.]

and privilege that [flow] from that identity."[51] In my own work, I have found the scholarship of Layla Saad,[52] Peggy McIntosh,[53] and Robin DiAngelo[54] to be extremely helpful. Though not without criticism, their work offers practical ways to address racism at individual and system levels and can readily facilitate discussions in church contexts. Antiracism resources, such "Undoing Racism" developed by the Canadian Council of Churches, exist specifically for use with adults in church contexts. Robust, developmentally appropriate resources for addressing racism with children in secular contexts also exist[55] yet, to my knowledge, have rarely (if ever) been a sustained priority for use in the formation of children or been adapted for use in intergenerational church contexts. This needs to change.

Beyond resources, adults need to model how they are being intentionally antiracist in their own everyday lives and contexts, because children learn from what they see, hear, and experience. Layla Saad, for example, focuses on behaviors and attitudes such as white apathy, white centering, white saviorism, tokenism, and what she calls "optical allyship," and provides concrete ways that white people can do the hard and intentional work of facing their own deeply embedded—often invisible even to them—racism and become intentionally antiracist. Decision-makers and those in positions of power in Canadian churches have the opportunity to draw on the work of Saad and other scholars, to assist in their own inner work of identifying, understanding, and disrupting these attitudes and behaviors in their own lives.[56] When leaders have done that inner work, they are much better equipped to engage in the outerwork of becoming antiracist and dismantling racism in their own domain of influence. All of this, then, necessarily needs to influence our approaches to the formation and discipleship of children. Unless we can find tangible ways to address explicit and implicit, individual and structural racism, any efforts at decolonizing are empty.

---

[51] The Canadian Council of Churches, "Undoing Racism," 2020, https://www.councilofchurches.ca/social-justice/undoing-racism/.

[52] Layla F. Saad, *Me and White Supremacy: Combat Racism, Change the World, and Become a Good Ancestor* (Naperville, IL: Sourcebooks, 2020), 156.

[53] Peggy McIntosh, "Unpacking the Knapsack of White Privilege," *Independent School* 49, no. 2 (1990): 31–36; Peggy McIntosh, "White Privilege and Male Privilege," *Race, Ethnicity and Gender: Selected Readings* (2007): 377–385.

[54] Robin DiAngelo, *White Fragility: Why It's So Hard for White People to Talk about Racism* (New York: Beacon Press, 2018).

[55] Anastasia Higginbotham, *Not My Idea: A Book about Whiteness* (New York: Dotir Press, 2018).

[56] Note that none of the three scholars mentioned in this section position themselves as decolonial in their work on race. My reasoning for including them is that since racism is such a core colonial oppression, and so deeply entwined with the Doctrine of Discovery, their work is helpful.

Eliminating Violence against Children

At the beginning of this chapter, I described my own work related to the violence against children in the form of corporal punishment. Here, I agree that leaders in Christian churches have an opportunity and responsibility to challenge colonial theologies that use Christian doctrine and biblical texts to justify violence and work for an end to punitive violence against children. Despite our team's 2017 theological statement that called on Christians to petition the Canadian government to ensure the full protection of children, uptake by churches has been underwhelming. Yet a full reading of scripture is incompatible with physical punishment,[57] and with the liberating biblical vision of children and childhood.[58] If church leaders had the will, they could work together to increase awareness in our communities of the impact of violence, including physical punishment, in homes, families, institutions, and communities; to be active in the protection of children; and to develop healthy, effective, and nonviolent approaches to discipline in raising children and youth. A decolonial theological approach demands action and tangible responses from all those in power, to work toward creating a world in which children are not only protected from all forms of violence but have the opportunity to flourish as whole human beings.

It is much more convenient to keep colonization at arm's length: something that happened "out there," away from our own civilized lives. In churches, even post-TRC, *we are naive if we think that churches operate outside these larger forces.* As a white, settler Christian, I find no comfort in the arguments presented in this chapter. I have had no success in reconciling my personal participation in a system that has benefited me, and marginalized so many, and that is not my goal. One of my personal aims in engaging in this work is simply to be aware of the truth of how my own history and leadership in the Christian church intersects with the broader, global story of colonization, and to be able to move forward from that awareness.[59] Almost certainly, there are uncomfortable

---

[57] Marcia Bunge, "The Significance of Robust Theologies of Childhood for Honouring Children's Full Humanity and Rejecting Corporal Punishment," in Michaekon and Dorrant, *Decolonizing Discipline*, 108–124.

[58] Marcia J. Bunge, "The Child, Religion, and the Academy: Developing Robust Theological and Religious Understandings of Children and Childhood," *Journal of Religion* 86, no. 4 (2006): 549–579.

[59] I am grateful to Laura Murray, whose articulation of her own position as a historian who recognizes the complexity of her own participation in colonization has shaped my own thinking. This section paraphrases some of her ideas for my own context and discipline. See L. J. Murray, "Settler and Indigenous Stories of Kingston/Ka'tarohkwi: A Case Study in Critical Heritage Pedagogy," *Journal of Canadian Studies* 52, no. 1 (2018): 249–279, 265.

realities that we as settlers need to lean into rather than resist. Yet in the long term, guilt just "draws energy away from shared decolonizing thinking and action,"[60] whereas honest reflection on the truth of the situation we are in, and on how we got here, helps us to move forward in courage. We are not locked into some perverse historical chain that is preprogrammed for oppression; we have choices about our action and inaction that we will accept, and about the church that we will create together. An important piece of this work that to date has been left out of this dialogue relates to the formation and discipleship of children.

If we choose to engage in this work, we can anticipate that it will be heart-wrenching, uncomfortable, and resisted. It must involve a concrete transfer of power from those in the dominant culture to those who have been marginalized and oppressed; authentic partnerships with Elders, Knowledge Keepers, and Survivors; and deep and sustained listening. It requires those in the dominant culture to be guided by those who have been colonized. For church leaders and community members who want to undertake the substantive and sustained work required in decolonization, no reward should be expected. Saad cites Chimamanda Ngozi Adichie, who writes, "Racism should never have happened and so you don't get a cookie for reducing it."[61] This is equally true for reducing the harms caused by colonization.

This work is our responsibility and our privilege. The decolonial theological thinking that decenters Western European theological interpretations opens up many new and rich avenues not only for inviting children to understand the disturbing reality of Christianity's presence on Turtle Island, but also for enlarging children's understanding of the Christian life.[62] Consequently, it provides a way forward that is more in keeping with the substantial, uncomfortable, and costly work of true reconciliation. All children will then be better prepared to participate in shaping a shared future that is just, and that honors the dignity and goodness of all peoples and creation.

Conclusion

There is much more to be said about the potential of decolonial thinking to provide insights and advances for the theologies and practices that not only guide child formation in Canadian church contexts but that have relevance for

---

[60] Murray, "Settler and Indigenous Stories of Kingston/Ka'tarohkwi," 265.

[61] Saad, *Me and White Supremacy,* 156.

[62] Ray Aldred, "An Indigenous Reinterpretation of Repentance: A Step on the Journey to Reconciliation," in *So Great a Salvation: Soteriology in the Majority World* (Carlisle, UK: Langham Global Library, 2017), 116; Terry Leblanc and Jennifer Leblanc, "NAIITS: Contextual Mission, Indigenous Context," *Missiology* 39, no. 1 (2011): 87–100.

the whole church body. I am deeply aware of the incompleteness and tentative nature of my work. I hope that others pick up the various strands of dialogue and move them forward in challenging, productive, and ever unsettling ways. Marie Battiste writes poignantly about her hope that educational contexts can move from being sites of reproduction to being sites of change,[63] and I share her hope for church contexts as well.

The grim realization of how much harm has been caused through Western European approaches to faith formation and discipleship in the name of Christianity is sobering. The global church needs to account for much. Yet, as my colleagues in the Canadian Decolonial Theology Project remind me, "Another world is possible."[64] Decolonial theologies help those who are engaging with colonization and reconciliation from a position of Christian faith to do so in a way that aligns more closely with the radical and liberating teachings of Jesus.

---

[63] Marie Battiste, *Decolonizing Education: Nourishing the Learning Spirit* (Saskatoon: Purich Publishing, 2017).

[64] Andraos et al., "Decolonial Theological Encounters," 260.

11

Reforming Mission with Child-Attentive Theology

D. J. Konz

Mission is a historically important area of Christian thought and practice that has recently become increasingly controversial. Jesus called his followers to love their neighbors as themselves and sent them into all the world to make disciples, teach, and baptize (cf. Matt 22:38; 28:19). For some followers of Jesus today, combining these two commands seems complex and challenging, particularly in culturally and religiously diverse contexts. Furthermore, the history of the church is littered with haunting chapters when conversion was coerced and mission was accompanied by colonialization, dispossession, cultural disenfranchisement, and even abuse or violence. In some parts of the church, such challenges have caused growing hesitancy about the validity of mission today. In other churches and parachurch organizations, enthusiasm for mission remains strong, but continued theological circumspection about how that mission is conducted in a healthy and not harmful manner is urgently needed.

Challenges regarding mission are especially acute when it comes to mission with and among children. Given children's impressionability, particular vulnerabilities, and the heartbreaking recent accounts of child abuse and maltreatment in the church, some churches are shying away from mission to and ministry with children.[1] With growing pluralism and the need for religious tolerance, some Christian parents are even hesitant to take their children to church, choosing to wait for their children to decide for themselves when or if they would like to participate in any religious traditions at all. Other parents and church leaders, liberal and conservative, worry that children and young people are being disregarded or neglected in the church's mission. Church leaders see

---

[1] Many churches are finding ways to minister to children by introducing strict child protection measures; safe and appropriate ministry to younger generations is both a moral imperative and essential to the future of the church.

children continually bombarded by messages from social media, which impact their sense of identity and affect their mental and spiritual well-being, and are searching for positive ways to pass along the life-giving message of the gospel.

How, then, is the church to navigate these challenging problems and sometimes polar positions? How might children be engaged in mission in a careful but faithful and legitimate way? And—for the purpose of this volume—in what ways can responding to the particular challenges of mission with children improve good mission theology and practice more broadly? In other words, how might a child-attentive theological reflection on mission bring fresh insights on how the church conceives and conducts mission with all human beings?

This chapter addresses these questions by examining some of the particular challenges of engaging in mission with and to children and by proposing ways of responding to these challenges with the aim of strengthening mission theology and practice in general. Christian mission is understood here as the sending of the church in gospel witness, by its presence, words, and works in the world, to the redemptive presence, Word, and works of God in Jesus Christ and the Spirit.[2] The chapter begins by outlining some of the key pitfalls and challenges of mission with children, including the problems of their objectification and instrumentalization. The chapter then draws on three aspects of the theology of twentieth-century theologian Karl Barth to propose some theological means of addressing some of these challenges, examines the relevance and interplay of these aspects of Barth's theology for a healthy practice of mission with children, and concludes with observations about how our child-attentive discussion can inform Christian mission practice more broadly. The key argument, therefore, is that considering mission in a child-attentive manner brings into sharp relief some of the challenging questions of mission as a human enterprise in general, and that carefully addressing questions raised by child-attentiveness may, in turn, lead to a richer mission theology and practice, which may correspond more closely to the divine mission itself.

Key Challenges

The church has engaged in mission with children since its earliest days.[3] In many such instances, the church has done so with love and compassion, providing children with a place of safety and welcome, education, Christian teaching and

---

[2] This sending of the church in the leading of the Spirit is a subsequent and subservient sending to the divine *missions* of Son and Spirit from the Father (see John 20:21–22).

[3] For more on the history of the church's mission with children, see D. J. Konz, "The Many and the One: Theology, Mission, and Child in Historical Perspective," in *Theology, Mission, and Child: Global Perspectives*, ed. Bill Prevette et al. (Oxford: Regnum Books International, 2014), 23–46.

ethical formation, and a place to encounter, observe, and enter into a living Christian faith. Nevertheless, despite these many commendable episodes, the church has an ambivalent record with children. Often, the church has ignored, patronized, or belittled children by failing to acknowledge their full humanity and developing agency.[4] At its worst—all too often—the church has caused direct harm through physical, psycho-emotional, spiritual, or sexual violence.[5]

Even today, Christian mission with children is plagued with pitfalls, including more subtle forms of ill treatment. Some of these challenges are well acknowledged, such as the objectification and instrumentalization of children (especially vulnerable children) for the purposes of mission marketing and fundraising.[6] Many of the challenges are not unique to children, but the relative cognitive, social, theological, and personal development of children, along with their particular physical, social, emotional, and perhaps spiritual vulnerabilities, make them particularly susceptible to risks and problematic practice. As such, children are a litmus test of mission theology and practice more broadly. Some of these risks include subtle or overt coercion, emotional manipulation, and misuse of power imbalances or enticements that, unintentionally or otherwise, take advantage of a child's limited capacities and personal agency in the attempt to "convert" them to Christ. Some child evangelism practices, resting on theologically problematic underlying notions that the eternal fate of the child rests in the evangelist's hands, have been explicitly fear-inducing and forceful.[7]

In recent years, children have sometimes been considered soft targets by mission groups, a receptive "unreached people group" that should be evangelized before age has hardened children's attitudes, worldviews, or resistance to the Christian gospel.[8] In these instances, children risk being reduced to a

---

[4] Historical studies of childhood are exposing both positive and negative chapters in the church's treatment of children. Burgeoning work in the history of childhood was sparked by the work Philippe Ariès. See Philippe Ariès, *Centuries of Childhood: A Social History of Family Life*, trans. Robert Baldick (London: Jonathan Cape, 1962).

[5] For just one of many examples, see the personal experiences described in Wess Stafford, *Too Small to Ignore: Why Children Are the Next Big Thing* (Colorado Springs, CO: Waterbrook Press, 2005).

[6] See Dan Brewster, *Future Impact: Connecting Child, Church, and Mission* (Colorado Springs, CO: Compassion International, 2010); and Ruth Padilla de Borst, "Children in Mission: A Challenge to Christian Movements and Organisations," in *Now and Next: A Compendium of Papers Presented at the Now and Next Theological Conference on Children, Nairobi, Kenya, March 9–12, 2011*, ed. Siga Arles et al. (Colorado Springs, CO: Compassion International, 2011), 173–182.

[7] See examples cited in John McNeill, *Children before God: Biblical Themes in the Works of John Calvin and Jonathan Edwards* (Eugene, OR: Pickwick Publications, 2017), 4–6.

[8] See Dan Brewster, "The 4/14 Window: Child Ministries and Mission Strategy,"

strategy whether it be giving the mission greater "success," reaching the children's families and communities, or even achieving the lofty goal of global Christianization and "transformation."[9] Consequently, children have been subtly objectified—that is, treated more as strategic objects, rather than living human subjects—and instrumentalized,[10] a particular form of objectification that sees children as a means to other ends.[11]

Further potential or actual harm can be caused when children are evangelized without the consent of their parents. This can lead to parental hostility toward and punishment of the child, and even domestic violence, or outright alienation of the child from its family (sometimes in communities where such alienation can have severe consequences). Similarly problematic is the evangelization of children from non-Christian religious backgrounds, where not only families but the wider community may reject a child who begins to identify with the Christian faith; such children may not have the internal or external resources needed to endure such isolation or social and cultural rejection.[12] As indicated earlier, in the worst instances, children have experienced actual physical, sexual, and emotional abuse in churches, monasteries, mission schools, and institutions, or any number of ecclesial and mission-related settings.

While it is vital to acknowledge and prevent such harms, advocates of mission have also rightly observed that the church too frequently disregards or neglects children in its mission. Sometimes this is because of concern for dangers raised above; other times it is because of adult-normative attitudes and

---

Transformation 14, no. 2 (1997): 18–21. Much of the resurgence of interest in mission with children over the past two decades stems from North American research which concluded that if a person does not follow Jesus Christ before or during their teenage years, she or he most likely never will. George Barna, *Transforming Children into Spiritual Champions* (Ventura, CA: Regal Books, 2003). This research is sometimes extrapolated as representing a universal reality, despite the particularity of the North American context of the research.

[9] See Luis Bush, *The 4/14 Window: Raising Up a New Generation to Transform the World* (Colorado Springs, CO: Compassion International, 2009).

[10] See Padilla de Borst, "Children in Mission," 180–181.

[11] For a longer response to the objectification, adultification, and instrumentalization of children in mission, see D. J. Konz, "Karl Barth's Theological Anthropology as a Resource for Overcoming the Objectification of Children in Mission," in *Conversion and Transformation: Children and Youth in Mission Contexts*, ed. Valentin Kozhuharov and Johannes J. Knoetze (Wellington, South Africa: Christian Literature Fund, 2017), 136–150; and, previously, D. J. Konz, "Response 1," in *Now and Next: A Compendium of Papers Presented at the Now and Next Theological Conference on Children, Nairobi, Kenya, March 9–12, 2011*, ed. Siga Arles et al. (Colorado Springs, CO: Compassion International, 2011), 183–190.

[12] Some advocates of child evangelism are commendably sensitive to such issues and offer guidance on navigating them carefully. See, for example, Brewster, *Future Impact*, 227–235.

marginalization of children in the church, where, for cultural or other reasons, children are seen as having no consequence or importance—social, cultural, spiritual, or otherwise.[13] At times, the church in its mission endeavors has not even recognized children as being fully human.[14] In some contemporary societies, excluding children from mission may be due to an uncritical internalization of the secularism view that even the children of Christian parents should not have religious commitment thrust upon them; rather, children in pluralistic or secular settings should be "free" to follow their own faith journey and find their "authentic self," without any explicit guidance from their parents or local faith communities. This overlooking of children in relation to mission—intentional or unintentional—can downplay not only the children's developing agency, but also their rightful place in the church and its mission. Furthermore, it is difficult to see how children will explore the Christian faith if it is not presented to them in a living way through the witness of Christian parents and Christian faith communities.

While children should legitimately be encouraged to be engaged in the church's mission of witness, the critical question is how the church navigates these challenging problems and sometimes polar positions morally, ethically, and with integrity.

Addressing the Challenges

The theology of Karl Barth—the twentieth-century Swiss theologian whose profound contribution to theology is pervaded by a concern for mission—offers valuable resources for addressing these challenges. While Barth's theology, particularly in his monumental *Church Dogmatics*, does not often have the child specifically in mind,[15] his theological ideas can be profitably applied to the challenges posed by mission with children outlined above.

In particular, three aspects of Barth's theology offer helpful applications to a theology and practice of mission with children and mission more broadly. These three aspects are (1) Barth's anthropological emphasis on humanity as "co-humanity," and his related insights for treating each person as a subject

---

[13] For a biblical example, see Matthew 19:13–15 // Mark 10:13–16, where Jesus strongly rebukes his disciples for turning children away from him (cf. Mark 10:14). Instead, Jesus blesses the children, and uses the moment to teach his disciples about the nature of God and God's kingdom.

[14] Konz, "The Many and the One."

[15] Karl Barth, *Church Dogmatics: The Doctrine of Creation*, ed. G. W. Bromiley and T. F. Torrance, trans. H. Knight et al. (Edinburgh: T & T Clark, 1960) (henceforth *CD*). Two exceptions are an extended passage titled "Parents and Children" in *CD* III/4 (§54.2), and in Barth's treatment of the doctrine of baptism in the *CD* IV/4 fragment.

(not an object); (2) Barth's conception of the proper relation of divine action and human activity in mission; and (3) his prioritization of the language of witness—through words and works—to the divine Word and works, over terms like evangelism, proselytism, and conversion, which arguably can be more readily associated with manipulation, coercion, or other problematic mission practices.

Emphasizing Our Co-Humanity

First, Barth's anthropology, especially his rendering of the intersubjective *I-Thou* relation, can assist in overcoming the objectification and instrumentalization of children in mission and help to restore their full subjectivity.[16]

For Barth, Jesus Christ is the *true* human being, that is, the one who is archetypically and ontologically determinative of true humanity, and the true divine image bearer.[17] As the true human being, Jesus Christ demonstrates and thus reveals that humanity is relationally constituted—specifically, to be truly human is to be with and for God,[18] and with and for other human beings.[19] Barth writes, "When we think of the humanity of Jesus, humanity is to be described unequivocally as fellow-humanity. In the light of the man Jesus, [the human being] is the cosmic being which exists absolutely for its fellows."[20] Humanity is, therefore, not a substantial, universal quality, of which Jesus, or any individual, is a particular expression. No individual human can be truly human in isolation or abstraction from other human beings;[21] there is no self-sufficient, autonomous human being—an "I," alone—but rather only an "I" in encounter with a "Thou."[22] According to Barth's relational ontology, humanity occurs in the dynamic encounter between subjects: humanity in encounter with God, and in encounter with other human beings. Humanity is thus co-humanity, and

---

[16] This point is examined in greater detail in Konz, "Karl Barth's Theological Anthropology."

[17] *CD* III/2, 132–133, 219.

[18] Barth's Christology is highly Chalcedonian; see George Hunsinger, *How to Read Karl Barth: The Shape of His Theology* (Oxford: Oxford University Press, 1991), 185–224. In the person of Jesus Christ the divine and human coexist. Hence, as well as being the true or real human being, Jesus Christ is also the divine Counterpart with whom each human being is confronted. *CD* III/2, 134–136.

[19] *CD* III/2, 203ff.

[20] *CD* III/2, 208.

[21] *CD* III/2, 226–231.

[22] *CD* III/2, 244–249. Barth uses various phrases to describe how this encounter constitutes our own human existence: "I am as I am in relation"; "I am in encounter"; "I am as Thou art"; "I am only as Thou art." *CD* III/2, 246, 247, 248, 249.

anything less, for Barth, is inhumanity.[23] To objectify another—that is, to regard them as an It, not a Thou, to my "I"—is to dehumanize both the Other and the Self (i.e., the one who objectifies).[24] Similarly, to view or use the Other for the Self's purposes dehumanizes both parties, but particularly contradicts the humanity of the "I." Christian mission risks dehumanizing both itself and those it engages when it objectifies or attempts to use children as a means to its own ends, whether for marketing and fundraising purposes, missional goals, or purely for the purpose of global evangelization, as outlined above.

Barth proposes four criteria or "marks" of the *I-Thou* encounter in which humanity consists: mutual openness to the "other" (looking the other person in the eye), mutual speech and hearing, the rendering of mutual assistance, and pursuing all such things gladly.[25] While these criteria might be critiqued, they represent Barth's emphasis on the depth of encounter in which each regards the other person as essential to their own being, and constitutive of their shared humanity. That depth of encounter challenges the Christian community to remain intensely and concretely committed to the full subjectivity and humanity of the others it encounters in its witness to Christ—including children. In such an authentically loving and genuine encounter, an individual becomes, like Christ, the image of God by authentically reflecting the cares, concerns, love, and intersubjectivity of God's own Self, revealed in Jesus Christ.

Children are treated as human subjects when we are for *them and their best interests*, not our own—including our mission aspirations. Furthermore, they are treated as human subjects when we genuinely and deeply see, listen to, welcome, serve, and allow ourselves to be humanized in an authentic encounter with each one as a unique Thou. With each child we encounter, our own humanity is tested, and either constituted or shown to be inhumanity masquerading as humanity. Only in genuine intersubjective encounter does the church genuinely witness to the One who was with and for God, and with and for all humanity, and who defined both human being and the divine mission—including to children.

Balancing Divine and Human Agency

As well as addressing the objectification, instrumentalization, and thus dehumanization of children, the church can mitigate some of the risks inherent in mission with and to children by properly ordering its understanding of divine

---

[23] *CD* III/2, 228.

[24] This risk of objectification is in part why Barth rejects Martin Buber's category of "I-It" relations.

[25] *CD* III/2, 250–265.

and human agency, that is, the relationship between God's own missional action and human/ecclesial mission activity. Indeed, some of the issues identified earlier in this chapter may arise from considering mission as first and foremost a human work, albeit performed in faithfulness to a divine "commission" or "command" (cf. Matt 28:18–19).[26] The danger of an imbalanced understanding of divine activity and human action may be especially heightened when working with children. A sense of divine "mandate" to "preach the gospel" to all creatures and to the ends of the earth may act as a strong driver to evangelize or "convert" children, with all the attendant issues already noted.[27]

The great achievement of *missio Dei* theology of the past century was to theologically relocate mission fundamentally in the being and action of God.[28] The corollary of this move was that human mission came to be seen as subsidiary to, or participatory in, the divine mission.[29] Although Barth himself does not seem to have used the term "*missio Dei*," the concept likely has its genesis in the resurgent Trinitarianism of twentieth-century theology, led by Barth,[30] and perhaps in his emphasis at a 1932 mission conference that *missions* classically referred to the sending of the divine Self in the Son and Spirit, from the Father.[31] Accordingly, for Barth, mission can only be what it should be, and not

---

[26] I have written elsewhere on the imbalance in understanding between divine and human agency that can occur when mission is predicated primarily on the so-called Great Commission, without such a "co-mission" being clearly located within the broader context of the work of the triune God—Father sending Son and Spirit. See D. J. Konz, "The Even Greater Commission: Relating the Great Commission to the *Missio Dei*, and Human Agency to Divine Activity, in Mission," *Missiology* 46, no. 4 (2018): 333–349.

[27] Overemphasizing human agency can lead to the presumption that human missional activity can bring about "salvation," "conversion," and reconciliation with God, and, therefore, to ill-conceived efforts to effect these outcomes. Such possibilities are only properly attributed to the divine work in Christ and Spirit. See Konz, "The Even Greater Commission," 335.

[28] For a short history of the development of *missio Dei* as a missiological concept, see David Bosch, *Transforming Mission: Paradigm Shifts in Theology of Mission* (Maryknoll, NY: Orbis Books, 1991), 389–393.

[29] More radical proponents sought to divorce the *missio Dei* from ecclesial action and locate it in human political revolutions, and the like; however, this position is difficult to support with scriptural data.

[30] Here I am in general agreement with Flett, who finds no trace of the term "*missio Dei*" in Barth's work; I differ in holding that the genealogy of the *idea*, if not the term, may be traced to Barth's influence on the theology of early proponents. See John G. Flett, *The Witness of God: The Trinity, Missio Dei, Karl Barth, and the Nature of Christian Community* (Grand Rapids: Eerdmans, 2010); Konz, "The Even Greater Commission."

[31] Karl Barth, "Die Theologie und die Mission in der Gegenwart: Vortrag, gehalten an der Brandenburgischen Missionskonferenz in Berlin am 11. April 1932," in *Theologische Fragen und Antworten: Gesammelte Vorträge* (Zollikon: Evangelischer Verlag, 1957),

some reality forsaken by God, by divine grace.[32] However, while Barth underscores the absolute necessity of divine action and grace to the church's mission, in the leading of Spirit, nevertheless he does affirm the place of human activity and agency.

In his doctrine of reconciliation, Barth provides an asymmetrical but cooperative understanding of divine/human agency: God's reconciling and redemptive works remain the actions of God in the Christ event, and by the Spirit. For Barth, following the death, resurrection, and ascension of Christ, the Spirit continues the presence and work of Christ in the world by gathering, building up, and sending out the church in unity with the Spirit to witness to the divine work. In its act of service to the prior and precedent Word and work of God, the church may, by grace, actively cooperate in the divine mission. Consequently, there occurs "a differentiated fellowship of action in which Christ is always superior and the Christian subordinate."[33] Thus the Spirit continues the *missio Dei* by acting in concert with the church, which in turn witnesses *to* the world concerning what God has done in Christ *for* the world.[34]

For Barth, the church "transgresses the limits of its mission and tasks" if it arrogates to itself what only God can do: speak the divine Word and see that Word come to effect in human beings.[35] The Spirit is the divine agent who, in Barth's language, remains Lord of the divine work. The church *serves* the divine mission, and precisely in this way participates in it.[36] While God in divine freedom can operate *extra muros ecclesiae* (outside the preaching and ministry of the church),[37] the indwelling Spirit empowers Christians "to become with Him proclaimers of the reconciliation of the world accomplished in Him, heralds of His person and work."[38]

100–126; for excerpts in English, see Karl Barth, "A Matter of Divine Purpose," in *Classic Texts in Mission and World Christianity*, ed. Norman E. Thomas, American Society of Missiology Series 20 (Maryknoll, NY: Orbis Books, 1995), 104–106.

[32] Barth, "Matter of Divine Purpose," 105.

[33] *CD* IV/3, 598. Indeed, for Barth, Christ "does not will to be alone in this action of His for the world and [humanity], but to call certain [people] to His side, to invite and summon them to participate in what He does" (*CD* IV/3, 598).

[34] For Barth, Christ and the Spirit are closely identified: the Holy Spirit is not "a relatively or absolutely . . . independently operative force" mediating between Jesus Christ and human beings, but rather the Spirit is "the power of His [Christ's] presence, work and Word, as the shining of the life of which He is the fullness" (*CD* IV/3, 503).

[35] *CD* IV/3, 833.

[36] As Barth insists, "The honor of [mission's] success is not [its] own, but always God's" (Barth, "Matter of Divine Purpose," 105).

[37] *CD* IV/3, 516.

[38] *CD* IV/3, 606.

Such an understanding of a proper ordering of divine activity and human action in mission can both reduce the temptation to coercively proselytize children vulnerable to manipulative techniques, power imbalances, or enticements, and affirm the vital role of the church in bearing witness to Christ in the power of the Spirit. There is thus cause in Barth's double-agency theology to neither neglect mission, including with children, nor to overstate its own power and agency in the task: not everything the church thinks is mission is the work of God the Spirit, and only by grace is its work ever actually mission.

Mission as Human Witness to the Divine Word and Works

Building on this theological basis, it is helpful to consider how the category of "witness" provides an alternative but multifaceted primary frame for approaching mission with and among children. Barth's preferencing of the notion of witness, through word and works, over terms like evangelism, proselytism, conversion, and the like, may further help avoid the pitfalls in mission and ministry with children already outlined.

While Barth conceives of the proclamation of the gospel—God's *Yes!* to the world in Jesus Christ—as the church's imperative task,[39] he theologically frames this task in terms of "witness."[40] Indeed, for Barth, the essence of the Christian's calling is to bear witness;[41] it is the raison d'être of the Christian life.[42] While Christ alone remains "the Speaker of the Word of God, as well as the Doer of His work,"[43] and Christians may "actually do more to compromise, disrupt and hinder the prophetic action of Christ than to further it,"[44] by God's grace, Christ permits and commands the Christian community's "ministering co-operation" in Christ's own Word and work.[45] The content of Christian witness is "the self-witness of

---

[39] This theme permeates *Church Dogmatics* from *CD* I/1 onward. Indeed, the entire purpose of theology as a discipline and task, in Barth's view, is to continually conform church proclamation to the divine Word itself; see *CD* I/1, §3, 47–88.

[40] "Witness" is not a novel category in relation to mission. However, for Barth it becomes an increasingly dominant notion in *Church Dogmatics*, to the point where he regards it as "the controlling principle of the structure of Christian existence" (*CD* IV/3, 571). For Barth, the Christian is a twofold witness to Christ: first, the Christian is one who "has seen and heard the acts of God," and subsequently, therefore, "is called to the work of declaration to others that which [the Christian] has seen as God's act and heard as [God's] Word" (*CD* IV/3, 593).

[41] *CD* IV/3, 575.
[42] *CD* IV/3, 576.
[43] *CD* IV/3, 606.
[44] *CD* IV/3, 607.
[45] *CD* IV/3, 608. Barth's theology of witness reflects his concern, examined earlier, to order and articulate properly the relationship of divine and human action in human

Jesus Christ, the Gospel of the act and revelation of God accomplished in Him as the good, the unambiguously glad and gladdening news of God's omnipotent and merciful *Yes!* to His creation."[46]

Not only the individual Christian but the Christian community—which is called, gathered, and built up by Christ through the Spirit—exists so as to be sent into the world in the Spirit,[47] as "the society which exists for the world."[48] The content of the church's witness is, at its irreducible core, the declaration of the gospel, which is to proclaim "the existence of the living Jesus Christ yesterday, to-day and to-morrow."[49]

Although the church must witness to Christ if it is to be the church and discharge its vital ministry, its witness to God's reconciliation in Christ is not reducible to certain acts of "evangelism" or "proselytizing." Rather, for Barth, it can occur in many forms, "directly or indirectly, explicitly or implicitly, in some kind of human speech or in eloquent silence, in specific acts and modes of conduct or in intentional and well-considered abstentions from action."[50] While the efficacy of the church's witness rests solely in God's gracious action by the Spirit, the church's witness to the Gospel strives within its human limits to address its audience in a manner that is explicable and applicable to that audience. Furthermore, there is no uniform means for witness, but a manifold multiplicity.[51]

Within this multiplicity and differentiation, however, Barth discerns a basic twofold form: "speech which is also action on the one side, and action which is also speech on the other."[52] Put another way, some witness predomi-

---

proclamation. As Nimmo summarizes, commenting on *CD* I/2, "Where proclamation truly occurs, there takes place a divine event in which God overcomes the attendant human incapacity to speak and to hear the Word of God, as the human words of proclamation are inspired and used by the Spirit.... Yet in the light of the reality of this event, the church cannot fall into arrogant complacency; instead it must devote itself to the task of preaching in humility and prayer" (Paul T. Nimmo, *Barth: A Guide for the Perplexed*, Guides for the Perplexed [London: Bloomsbury T & T Clark, 2017], 45). The same can be echoed in relation to Barth's idea of "witness."

[46] *CD* IV/3, 660.

[47] *CD* IV/3, 763.

[48] *CD* IV/3, 784. Barth writes, "Firstly and supremely it is God who exists for the world. And since the community of Jesus Christ exists first and foremost for God, it has no option but in its own manner and place to exist for the world" (*CD* IV/3, 762). Thus, it is with the task of confessing Jesus Christ "that the community is sent into the world and exists for it" (*CD* IV/3, 795).

[49] *CD* IV/3, 845. For Barth the gospel includes, in longer form, the declaration of "the grace of God addressed to [the human being] as His creature, the covenant concluded and sealed between Him and [humanity], the act of God in which it took place that He reconciled an opposing and gainsaying world to Himself" (*CD* IV/3, 845).

[50] *CD* IV/3, 845.

[51] *CD* IV/3, 854.

[52] *CD* IV/3, 862.

nantly takes the form of words, and some predominantly takes the form of works, while each is also a form of the other. Among the works that witness to Christ, in Barth's view, are those of diaconal service, which includes bringing material relief to those in need. In particular, for Barth, "caring for the sick, the feeble, and the mentally confused and threatened, looking after orphans, helping prisoners, finding new homes for refugees, stretching out a hand to stranded and shattered fellow [human beings] of all kinds," represent for the church "a unique chance to unequivocally accomplish and manifest its witness as a ministry of witness."[53] While both word and works go hand in hand in the church's witness to its Lord, at times it is necessary and appropriate to engage primarily in a witness of words, accompanied by works. At other times, witness is primarily through works, accompanied by words.[54]

Barth's notion of witness has significant implications for our understanding of mission to children. Witness better captures the agential distinction between the divine Word and works, and corresponding human action in service of that Word and works.[55] Furthermore, "witness" recognizes and respects the developing agency of children, their location in families and communities, their vulnerability, and their full human subjectivity—by not seeking to force, coerce, or manipulate children, recognizing instead that while the church witnesses to the Word and work of God in Christ, it is God's own prerogative to make Godself known to the child in a divine encounter between God's "I" and the child's "Thou."

Relevance to a Healthy Mission with Children

These three areas of Barth's theology—his anthropological proposal that humanity is actualized in the shared intersubjective encounter, the proper ordering of the relationship between divine and human agency in mission, and

---

[53] *CD* IV/3, 891. In Barth's view, it is vital to the witness of the church that it stands in solidarity with the least, and last, for "without this active solidarity with the least of little ones, without this concrete witness to Jesus the Crucified, who as such is the Neighbour of the lost, its witness may be ever so pure and full at other points, but it is all futile" (*CD* IV/3, 891).

[54] Both correspond to the divine reality that God's work of reconciliation is also a revelation of God, and his revelation itself an act of reconciliation.

[55] As noted above, while it is legitimate to acknowledge "the true and concrete participation of the Christian in the great context of the history of God with the world, and therefore of salvation history," nevertheless "we must not say anything which would even in the slightest degree equate the Christian with God and thus declare him [or her] to be . . . the reconciler or co-reconciler of the world" (*CD* II/2, 599). For Barth, there remains an "indestructible differentiation and irreversible order" in the relation between divine works and human cooperation therein.

the prioritization of the category of witness—converge to help mitigate some of the risks and issues outlined in the chapter's first section. This next section examines further the relevance and synergy of these emphases to a child-attentive mission.

While children are no more or less human than their adult counterparts, they are often more vulnerable human beings than many adults.[56] Because of their various vulnerabilities, it is particularly incumbent on the church to recognize children as subjects, so as to strive continually to avoid attitudes and actions, intentional or unintentional, that hurt, harm, objectify, or dehumanize children. Resisting the objectification of children means regarding each child as an individual being of great particularity and full personhood, and engaging each child according to her or his own specific development, needs, and being. To paraphrase Barth, each child is a whole world, and the request that each child makes of others is not merely to know this or that about her or him, but to know the child him- or herself, and therefore their whole world of being.[57]

Nevertheless, a proper understanding of the double agency of divine and human word and works can help put into proper perspective the church's role in the faith journey of a child. Recognizing the limits and possibilities of human action in mission can help the church resist the temptation or compulsion to feel it needs to "save" children in the soteriological sense through whatever methods of proselytism seem effective in evoking a response. This is not at all to downplay the importance of the church being faithful to its vocation to witness by its words and works to Christ—in fact, in Barth's account, such witness is constitutive of the church and fundamental to the Christian life. To avoid engaging with children because of the risks introduces other risks. Even if one does not follow Barth entirely on the primacy of the Christian calling to witness, avoiding cooperating with the Spirit in the self-attestation of Christ risks contradicting one of the church's key vocations and tasks. Furthermore, the children of Christian families who do not encounter God's great *Yes!* in Jesus Christ in the words and works of their family and faith community risk, at minimum, a missed opportunity to hear and explore the gospel, the Christian faith, and the Christian life. At a time when children from Christian families are turning away from the faith in significant numbers, a deficient understanding of the gospel—and a lack of living witness to Christ in their lives—may be a contributor.

Barth's employment here of the category of witness, however, affords the church a way of conceiving of its missional relationship and responsibility to

---

[56] Not all adults are less vulnerable than all children; for example, very elderly, infirm, or disabled adults may be equally or more vulnerable than some—especially older—children.

[57] *CD* III/2, 258.

children—inside and outside of the church—without resorting to coercive or problematic practices. The church's role is to witness by word and works, recognizing that an authentic response by the child is contingent on the work of the Holy Spirit in concert with the child's developing spiritual agency. The church cannot bring about faith, especially not forcefully, though by God's grace it can cooperate in a child's faith journey and help provide children with the theological language and tools to articulate their faith in age-appropriate ways. Furthermore, Barth's affirmation of works alongside words emphasizes the missional validity and necessity of acting to meet the needs of "the least of little ones."[58] Witness by works (which, for Barth, is not a wordless witness) may be a particularly pertinent form of witness in communities where evangelism or conversion of children puts them at risk. In such settings, the witness of works echoes and corresponds in its own limited human manner to the reconciliatory and redemptive work of God, and God may speak God's own Word in and through that human witness. In settings where such sensitivities are not at issue—for example, with the children of Christian parents, or parents who are open to Christian education or teaching—a witness of words (which should never be a workless witness) may be far more appropriate, and Barth would have us speak in accordance with the divine Word in such settings.

Understanding and respecting each child as a unique human subject are reflected when works and words are attenuated to the child's capacity to understand, receive, and benefit from those words and works. Hence, human witness should be not only age-appropriate but also responsive to the particularity of the one who is addressed or served, such that their individual subjectivity is embraced, their existence enhanced, and their humanity affirmed. Doing so also affirms and actualizes the humanity of the one who speaks with and serves the child, and the church itself, in its mission. In such moments of genuine co-humanity and encounter, a correspondence occurs between the witness and the One to whom the church witnesses, who loves the child in its uniqueness and particularity, and who effected the divine reconciliation inclusive of that particular, individual child. By grace, that correspondence is not only a moment of authentic witness but potentially a moment of genuine cooperation between human mission and the divine mission in the Spirit of Christ.

Conclusion

As well as improving mission practice with children, this child-attentive theological reflection on mission also provides fresh perspectives on how the church conceives and conducts mission with all peoples.

---

[58] *CD* IV/3, 891.

This is so, first, because the church is continually at risk of objectifying not only children but any and all others in its mission. Objectification can occur if the church overemphasizes the distinction between members of the Christian community and those with whom it engages outside that community,[59] and if it views those people as targets of mission or their conversion as a means by which the Christian community can maintain its social, political, and cultural power in a post-Christendom world.[60] The challenge to regard our fellow human beings not just as missional "others" but as intersubjectively necessary to the realization of our own and shared humanity is true of children and all human beings. Children simply underscore the sinful tendency to objectify others, including in mission. Second, while children may be particularly vulnerable to power imbalances, or coercive or manipulative practices, they are not alone. Wrestling with the challenge of engaging children with a fundamentally respectful regard for their particularity and personhood reminds us to do so with each person, especially in an era of corporatized mission agencies, strategies, targets, and similar objectifying tendencies.

Barth's caution against overstating the human role in the divine mission, coupled with more consciously employing the category of witness, may help the church maintain a more balanced posture in its missiology and praxis. However, while Barth exhorts the church to recognize that Jesus Christ remains both the Lord and primary active agent, through the Spirit, of the divine mission, Barth also reminds the church that it cannot grow lax in its vital calling to serve the divine mission through its own corresponding words and works. As Barth's deeply missional theology reiterates again and again, God has said a great and overwhelming *Yes!* to his human creatures in Jesus Christ, and by grace invites those who have already heard and embraced this *Yes!* to cooperate with the Spirit by bearing witness to the world of this inestimably good news. A nonwitnessing church, for Barth, is not the church of Jesus Christ.

In these and other ways, a child-attentive theological reflection on Barth's theology may potentially help reform the mission theology and practices of the church—a church that must rise to the challenge of faithful service to the self-witness of God in Christ in its own particular era. If children present some of the most acute challenges to mission, responding effectively to those challenges will likely make mission more sensitive to the humanity and dignity of all to

---

[59] Barth helps here also by taking seriously but relativizing the distinction between the Christian and the non-Christian. For Barth, both stand under the determination of Christ's death and resurrection (*CD* III/2, 493–494). The Christian is sent as a witness to their fellow human beings of that shared determination in Jesus Christ.

[60] See J. C. Hoekendijk, *The Church Inside Out*, ed. L A. Hoedemaker, Pieter Tijmes, and Isaac C. Rottenberg (London: SCM, 1967), 13–17.

whom the church bears witness. In doing so, it may help the church to correspond more faithfully to the sending God, who, in the love of the Father, by the Spirit of Christ, sends the church into the world with words and works that testify to God's own great redemptive *Yes!* to people not only of all nations—but also of all ages.

12

Reimagining Hope *with* and *like* Children

Dirk J. Smit

Many biblical texts and Christian theologians have connected children with hope. Several biblical passages refer to children in visions of peace and a promising future. In Isaiah's vision of the peaceful kingdom, for example, the wolf lives with the lamb, the calf and the lion lie down together, and a little child leads them (Isa 11:6–9). Theologians have also spoken of children as metaphors of hope. In the words of the well-known theologian of hope Jürgen Moltmann (b. 1926), in many ways children can be "a metaphor of the hope to rise from the ruins, a symbol of life's future over against the powers of origin and over against violent suffering and death inflicted by the mighty."[1] He relates this idea to Hannah Arendt's notion of "natality" as the new beginning that comes into the world with every birth.[2]

As a Reformed theologian from South Africa who lived through the apartheid era, I have reflected on and been challenged by a host of meaningful and multifaceted relationships between children and hope. One important yet less cited biblical passage that inspires me and other theologians to reflect on hope and children is from Hebrews 11. This chapter focuses on faith "as the assurance of things hoped for, the convictions of things *not* seen" (Heb 11:1, emphasis added) and refers to the baby Moses as "beautiful"—"By faith Moses was hidden by his parents for three months after his birth, because they saw that the child was beautiful; and they were not afraid of the king's edict" (Heb 11:23). Theologians have wondered what the parents of Moses really saw in the child to say he was "beautiful" and to let go of their fears. It was not simply that the

---

[1] Jürgen Moltmann, "Child and Childhood as Metaphors of Hope," *Theology Today* 56, no. 4 (2000): 592–603.
[2] Hannah Arendt, *The Human Condition* (Chicago: University of Chicago Press, 1958); see also Elisabeth Moltmann-Wendel, "Natalität und die Liebe zur Welt," *Evangelische Theologie* 48 (1998): 283–294.

parents thought he was a beautiful baby in a physical sense, since the author's primary point in the chapter is that faith is the ability to see what *cannot* be seen with the natural eye.

It was this description of Moses and the witnesses in Hebrews 11–12 that led Martin Luther and other Reformers to describe faith as seeing what we do *not* see and *not* seeing what we do see (*haec enim est fidei natura . . . videre, quod non videt, et non videre quod videt*). This is how the readers know that what is seen was made from what is not seen (11:3); how Enoch was taken away as to not see death (11:5); how Noah, when warned about events yet unseen, respected the warning and acted on it (11:7); how Abraham looked forward to the city of God (11:10); how, in summary, all these witnesses died without having received the promises, but from a distance saw and greeted them (11:13); and how Moses himself looked ahead to the reward (11:26) and persevered as though he saw him who is invisible (11:27).

John Calvin saw this ambiguity in Hebrews 11:23 clearly. As he wrote in his *Commentary on Hebrews*, the words about Moses's parents could not mean that they were induced to hide the child "by the beauty of the child," since that would be "contrary to the character of faith" and contrary to what the author argues in this chapter using the examples of witnesses. No, Calvin explained, "The parents of Moses were not charmed with his beauty, so as to be induced by pity to save him, as the case commonly is with human beings; but there was some mark, as it were, of future excellency imprinted on the child, which gave promise of something extraordinary. . . . They were inspired with the hope of an approaching deliverance; for they considered that the child was destined for the performance of great things."[3]

In short, Moses's parents imagined something in the child that the human eye could not see—a mark of future excellence, a destiny for the performance of great things, the hope of an approaching deliverance. Thus, they were willing to act on their imagination by hiding the child despite the threats of the powers and authorities of their day. With this description, the author is doing something remarkable—for who here really is the witness of hope? Who is the subject, the author's example of faith? Certainly, the child Moses bears the mark of future excellence, the promise of great things, and the hope of an approaching deliverance. The child therefore becomes the carrier, symbol, and metaphor of hope. At the same time, the parents are the witnesses—those embodying the faith for which the author calls. They are the ones who actually hope, who imagine, and who dream. In doing so, are they not in a way becoming like children? Are they not performing the hope they imagine in the child? Are they

---

[3] John Calvin, *Commentary on Hebrews* (Grand Rapids: Christian Classics Ethereal Library), 256.

not trusting the future they see as promise in the face of the child? Are they not themselves performing what the child represents through knowing and hoping like children?

For many historical and contextual reasons, many South African theologians—and many theologians across Africa—have utilized this form of imagination during years of struggle and suffering and dreamed of promises of approaching deliverance. Their names, lives, and contributions could perhaps be added to the long list of witnesses in Hebrews 11. Many of them often worked with and alongside children and young people. They spoke and wrote both directly to children and adults and about the children of our country and continent. Many of them imagined beautiful futures for the children and acted upon promises of great things, often despite the threats of realities and powers. They also reimagined the future, inspired and moved by the courageousness and hopefulness of children.

The aim of this chapter is to rethink the nature of hope by highlighting some of the ways that prominent South African theologians honored, engaged, and listened to children as well as incorporated childlike knowing and hoping into their works and actions as they imagined and worked toward a better tomorrow. The chapter has three sections. First, we discuss how David Bosch, Denise Ackermann, and Desmond Tutu infused into their lives and works a childlike capacity to act through hoping against hope and to lament what is happening while also rejoicing in what was promised and what is surely coming. We then consider ways in which Willie Jonker, Beyers Naudé, and Jaap Durand embraced a childlike ability to know through their willingness to live, reconfigure, and reimagine without full knowledge and certainties. Finally, we examine how Russel Botman, Hennie Rossouw, and Allan Boesak utilized childlike practices of imagining, playing, and dreaming in order to remain hopeful for radically new tomorrows during the dark days of the past. These examples invite all readers to honor children and to act, know, and hope as children so that we may join the long cloud of witnesses who saw what the eye cannot see, dreamed of different worlds, and acted out these imaginations.

Acting Like Children?

What do children do? Children cry and laugh easily—and it is possible to imagine both weeping and laughing as expressions of the same ability to hope. This means to imagine something different; and either to laugh, submit to, and therefore rejoice in these alternative realities, or to cry, resist, and therefore refuse to accept their present situation and express longing for things that could and should be different. It is therefore not surprising that all three of these themes—hoping against all hope, weeping and lamenting what is but should not be happening, and laughing and rejoicing in what was promised and what is surely coming—are dominant in the life and work of many South African theologians during the dark years of struggle and of many African theological students and church leaders today. Examples could be multiplied, but the three well-known voices of David Bosch, Denise Ackermann, and Desmond Tutu are insightful representatives of both weeping and laughing, thus doing with their lives and thoughts what children often seem to do so naturally.

Hoping against Hope

The year 1976 marked the beginning of the uprising of school children in the township of Soweto, South Africa, against the oppressive system of apartheid. This movement—led by children, students, and youth—catalyzed rolling resistance throughout the country, especially after the death of thirteen-year-old Hector Pieterson. After years of struggle, suppression, and increased counter-resistance, the face of the nation was changed.

Two years later, South African missiologist David Bosch (1929–1992) was invited to address the pupils of one of the famous English private schools for boys in the country.[4] The theme of his address was "Prisoners of History or Prisoners of Hope?" Throughout, Bosch claimed that we are all "prisoners of history," and in many complex ways the products of our past—or rather, in apartheid South Africa, our deeply divisive pasts. About his own childhood, he said that South Africans thought about one another not as people but as categories. South Africans grew up with constructions and images of the enemy. Across the many divisions keeping them apart—as if in prisons—South African children hardly met one another, knew one another, experienced a common life, or shared a future.

Bosch addresses the differences between the prison of history and the prison of hope. "Prisoners of history look back to the past," he said, "to the events of the past, to the conflicts and misunderstandings of the past, and make these absolutely normative for today. Their past governs their today and also their tomorrow. Prisoners of hope, however, are oriented toward the future. They believe that history need not repeat itself. They believe that something new is possible."[5]

---

[4] For background on Bosch, see the essays honoring him in J. N. J. Kritzinger and Willem A. Saayman, eds., *Mission in Creative Tension: A Dialogue with David Bosch* (Pretoria, South Africa: Missiological Society, 1990), and Saayman and Kritzinger, eds., *Mission in Bold Humility: David Bosch's Work Considered* (Maryknoll, NY: Orbis Books, 1996).

[5] David Bosch, "Prisoners of History or Prisoners of Hope?," *The Hiltonian* 114 (March 1979), 14–15.

He then told stories from his own childhood experiences about how South Africans could not see one another clearly, "because of the high walls of the different prisons [of history] in which we were" and because they "looked at one another [only] through key-holes." However, he also told stories from his own experiences and from the Bible about being prisoners of hope, such as the prophet Zechariah's description of the exiles as still prisoners in Babylon (Zech 9:12), because "they are moving forward into a future which is different from the past, which is something new, coming from the hand of God."[6] His address inspired hope within the children—conveying the conviction that history need not repeat itself, that something new was possible, that the future could be different from the past.

In the following years, Bosch developed these fundamental convictions in papers, publications, and books, and demonstrated them in his activities in church and public life. In a well-known journal article titled "Paul on Human Hopes," Bosch suggests that the New Testament gives us reason to hope and, in particular, that Paul be read as a "biblical spokesperson on the subject of hope for justice and peace in the world." After all, in liberation theology circles, as well as in world mission and evangelism, he said, Paul was regarded very differently—namely, uninterested in what could be called human or historical hopes. Some saw Paul's assumed disinterest in historical hopes as negative; others as positive. Indeed, Bosch noted that a superficial reading of Paul's letters did not suggest that the poor and oppressed should hope for any improvement in their situation. Among other references, Bosch also specifically referenced "the form of this world [which] is passing away" (1 Cor 7:31). A first reading could indeed suggest that Paul had little interest in worldly affairs and secular hopes.

However, Bosch offered his own reading of Paul "about this-worldly realities and hopes," and painted a radically different picture. Paul's language about the dawning of a new age and a period of active waiting between resurrection and completion calls for Christian ethics in light of the Easter morning and the presence of the Spirit, and is, therefore, "full of signs of hope and calls for hope-full involvement in the historical here and now." The ethic that baptized believers practice is an ethic of hope, anticipation, and reckoning with God's possibilities. For Paul, the church as community is the foundation for a sociopolitical ethic, powerfully demonstrated in his political views about the new unity between Jews and Gentiles and also about slaves and free persons. Together, the church "constitutes a community of hope which groans and labors for the redemption of the entire world." For Paul, it is unwarranted to separate theology from ethics, because faith is made effective through love. Consequently, working for justice is an expression of justification, loving fellow human beings is a mani-

---

[6] Bosch, "Prisoners of History or Prisoners of Hope?"

festation of faith, and exerting ourselves for the liberation of the oppressed brings salvation. For Paul, therefore, the calling of Christians is a calling to serve our neighbors, communities, and societies throughout the world.

All of these claims ended in Bosch's final observation: "hoping against hope." He asked what we should do in situations where there is, humanly speaking, no earthly hope. What does hope mean when there is no hope? Referring to Paul's phrase about Abraham's "hoping against hope" (Rom 4:18), Bosch noted "a change in Abraham's way of interpreting events, of knowing them." Paul knew that nothing could remain the way it was. For Paul, the ultimate conferred meaning on the penultimate, and in similar ways, he argued, "We may, by the grace of God, be empowered to create pockets of human hope in this world," and then concluded with the quote that "it is these structures that are illusionary, for 'the form of this world is passing away'" (1 Cor 7:31).[7] What seems real, powerful, and sometimes indestructible may be the illusion; what hope imagines may be the true reality. In the days of apartheid South Africa, such talk about human and historical hope was indeed an expression of hoping against hope—speaking of a future not yet seen in present imprisonment by a reality of division and separateness, distrust, oppression, and conflict.

Crying with Sorrow

Under these same circumstances, Denise Ackermann (b. 1935), the leading feminist theologian in South Africa for many years and close friend of the Bosch family, learned to lament like children, for children, and with children as an act of hope.[8] Crying about what is wrong is a form of protest against what should not be, and therefore can be a profound expression of hope for things that could and should be different. Children, from their earliest days, know how to cry. Crying could perhaps be an expression that their world is not right. It could be imagined as their protest against what they experience as wrong, painful, or lacking—as a call for help and for change.

In a letter addressed to her own children in her book *After the Locusts: Letters from a Landscape of Faith*, Ackermann explained this logic of lament as a profound form of hope. The letter "To My Children on the Language of Lament" opens with a moving "litany of suffering" listing several unimaginable horrors she witnessed during her lifetime. Acknowledging this as hardly a way to write to

---

[7] David Bosch, "Paul on Human Hopes," *Journal of Theology for Southern Africa* 67 (1989): 3–16.

[8] For background on Ackermann, see the essays honoring her in *Ragbag Theologies: Essays in Honor of Denise M. Ackermann, a Feminist Theologian of Praxis*, ed. Miranda Pillay, Sarojini Nadar, and Clint le Bruyns (Stellenbosch, South Africa: EFSA, 2009).

your children, she claimed that her own discovery of language to deal with such suffering (although not solving it) had been simply too momentous for her not to share with them. For her, this was the language of lament. She identified her discovery of this language as the most significant shift in her own life of faith.

Suffering, Ackermann argued, is not a theological or philosophical problem in need of a solution, but a practical problem requiring a response from a community of people; a proper response found in employing the language of lament. She could have said "tears," she explained, but somehow more is needed—specific forms of tears and specific forms of crying—and for that the notion and tradition of lament as ritual and public performance are best suited. Lament is close (at least in Afrikaans) to accusation, *klag* to *aanklag*, and close to mourning; it is, in fact, difficult at times to distinguish from mourning.

Lament is more purposeful than mourning, Ackermann claimed, because it signals "that relationships and circumstances have gone terribly wrong," like the crying, the weeping, and the tears of small children. She argued that it is "a coil of suffering and hope . . . a desire for healing . . . that beats against the heart of God." It is "our way of bearing the unbearable" and, therefore, "supremely human." It is "risky speech," calling into question structures of power, demanding justice, and pushing the boundaries of our relationships with one another and with God. "It is a refusal to settle for the way things are. It is reminding God that the human situation is not as it should be and that God must act."

Lament, like the weeping of infants, is "undergirded by the hope that God not only can but will hear the cries of the suffering and the penitent and will act with mercy and compassion." Ackermann knows this because of the traditions of lament in Israel and from other ancient literature, as well as her own experiences of crying out to God. As a biblical example, she turned to Rachel's cry, weeping for her children and refusing to be comforted for them. She also turned to Hagar, speaking the dread of every mother who does not want to face the death of her child and therefore cries to God in affliction. Finally, she turned to the cries of lament of thirty-five thousand mothers who daily wept for their children dying of disease and hunger.

Ackermann pleaded for a church that laments suffering and injustice. Every time she witnessed a baptism and heard the baptismal vows, she was struck by a strange mixture of remorse *and* hope. The unknowing infant, she claimed, was brought in trust into a community of faith, receiving a new identity, family, and a body of people who themselves were fractious and unfaithful, yet were "in some inexplicable way God's hands in the world." Furthermore, such unknowing infants are beautiful in baptism because they receive a calling, promises, and a meaningful future.[9]

---

[9] Denise Ackermann, *After the Locusts: Letters from a Landscape of Faith* (Grand Rapids: Eerdmans, 2003), 98–128.

Ackermann later returned to these thoughts in her spiritual autobiography, *Surprised by the Man on the Borrowed Donkey: Ordinary Blessings*, which she wrote in the form of her own contemporary beatitudes. Again, hope played a key role in her reflections; her children and the language of lament were central. To have faith is to have hope, not in the sense of hope for the end times, Ackermann explained, but as lived reality. During the countless dark moments of apartheid, she always had hope, because while lamenting, weeping, and resisting, she continued to trust that injustice would end and equality would prevail. She hoped because of the story of Jesus of Nazareth, and in this process, she learned the meaning of hope. Hope is, Ackermann explained, "never to surrender our power to imagine a better world." Hope is the conviction—for many based on the story of Jesus—that "present unjust arrangements are provisional and precarious, and do not require acceptance." She learned, therefore, that "to lament injustice is an expression of hope for it calls on God to account and rests on the unshakable belief that God will act."[10]

To her surprise, Ackermann found that there were times when she struggled to hope, yet for the sake of her grandchildren, she knew she must remember the one in whom she hopes and how to live with hope. Referencing her earlier writings, she said that she did not have anything to add: hope is not optimism, it is not about some future victory. It is lived in the present. It is risky, since it is daring to trust. It recognizes tragedy in history. It is learning to wait. It is nurtured by prayer and by community. Hope is ultimately trust in the God of surprises found in the man on the donkey and, therefore, a story of unending grace.[10]

These extremities of human experience, of cries of lament within a story of unending grace, are also characteristic of the experiences of infants and small children. Their cries can turn to laughter within an eyewink, almost without interruption. Perhaps it is because crying and laughing are both expressions of the same fundamental trust—of the same childlike hope—in the goodness of the parent who is able and willing to change the pain into joy and well-being. It should not be surprising, therefore, that Ackermann also described chuckling and laughing as one of her ordinary blessings.[11]

Laughing with Joy

In South Africa, no other public figure offers a better demonstration of how weeping and laughter are intimately related and offer different expressions of the same hope than Ackermann's personal friend and spiritual mentor, the

---

[10] Denise Ackermann, *Surprised by the Man on the Borrowed Donkey: Ordinary Blessings* (Cape Town: Lux Verbi, 2014), 32–36.

[11] Ackermann, *Surprised by the Man on the Borrowed Donkey*, 281–309.

respected former Anglican archbishop and inspiring icon Desmond Tutu.[12] He is known worldwide for his tears and laughter—both his weeping in public and his humor, joy, and delight in life and in human beings. One of the most moving moments of his public career, remembered by all who saw it on television, was when, as chairperson of the Truth and Reconciliation Commission, he broke down during the very first hearings and sobbed while listening to the terrifying witness of a tortured former prisoner, now confined to a wheelchair after a stroke. In his reflections on the commission, Tutu recalled, "I could not hold back the tears, I just broke down and sobbed like a child. I bent over the table and covered my face in my hands." He said afterward that he wondered whether he was the right person to lead the commission, since "I laugh easily and I cry easily. . . . I knew I was so weak and vulnerable."[13] It was not surprising that a collection of his sermons was called *Hope and Suffering*.[14]

At the same time, everyone who has listened to his sermons and public speeches, witnessed his interviews on television, read his published works and sermons, or heard him telling jokes knows and is probably surprised by his deep sense of joy in life, his optimism, and his humorous approach even when talking about God. "Tutu Uses Laughter as a Transformative Force for Good" was rightly a headline in the *Mail & Guardian*.[15] In the foreword of a collection of essays honoring him, the theologian and public intellectual Barney Pityana (b. 1945) said that this "towering figure . . . who has been a stern critic of apartheid as well as a priest of deep spirituality [is] much loved for his ability to tell jokes as easily against himself than against the stupidity of white racial prejudice."[16]

One could perhaps be tempted to describe this attitude as optimism and his spirituality as an optimistic spirituality, but this could easily be misleading depending on how one understands and describes optimism. He is clearly not an optimist in the sense of optimism rejected by English intellectual Terry Eagleton (b. 1943).[17] He was deeply aware of the injustices in our history, not

---

[12] For background on Tutu, see the essays honoring him in Buti Tlhagale and Itumeleng Mosala, eds., *Hammering Swords into Ploughshares* (Braamfontein, South Africa: Skotaville, 1986), and Leonard Hulley, Louise Kretzschmar, and Luke Lungile Pato, eds., *Prophetic Witness in South Africa* (Cape Town: Human and Rousseau, 1996); as well as the studies by John Allen, *Rabble-Rouser for Peace: The Authorized Biography of Desmond Tutu* (New York: Free Press, 2006); and Michael Battle, *Reconciliation: The Ubuntu Theology of Desmond Tutu* (Cleveland: Pilgrim Press, 1997).

[13] Desmond Tutu, *No Future without Forgiveness* (London: Rider, 1999), 110.

[14] Desmond Tutu, *Hope and Suffering* (Johannesburg: Skotaville, 1983).

[15] Chris Chivers, "Tutu Uses Laughter as a Transformative Force for Good," *Mail & Guardian*, October 8, 2011.

[16] Hulley, Kretzschmar, and Lungile Pato, *Prophetic Witness in South Africa*, 7.

[17] Terry Eagleton, *Hope without Optimism* (Charlottesville: University of Virginia Press, 2015).

only during apartheid, but also in the democratic society so painfully affected by corruption, crime, and nepotism. He was well informed about the terrible violations of human dignity reported in the hearings to the Truth and Reconciliation Commission, which were not adequately addressed by attempts to attain restorative justice, even if only symbolic. He was sensitive to the many forms of oppression, marginalization, and exclusion prevalent in South African (and African) society even today. His childlike joy and delight probably stems from his deep spirituality and his characteristic view of God's goodness, mercy, grace, and love—of the God who is, of course, not a Christian, according to Tutu.[18]

Time magazine once depicted him as "the Laughing Bishop" and quoted him as saying, "The texture of our universe is one where there is no question at all that good and laughter and justice will prevail." In the end, Tutu said, "the perpetrators of injustice or oppression . . . will bite the dust." Delighting in this thought, according to *Time*, he roared, "Ha-ha-ha-ha-ha . . . Wonderful! Wonderful! Wonderful!"[19]

Knowing Like Children?

No wonder Bosch described childlike hope as a different way of knowing, a different way of seeing and interpreting, a different perspective on the same realities. After all, this was precisely the claim of Hebrews 11, on seeing the invisible and what others could not yet see, and the claim of Luther that faith is this ability to see the unseen and to reckon with the unseen as real and true.

One dimension of knowing like children, expressed in the life and work of several South African theologians, is the childlike ability to live and imagine without full knowledge and certainties. Three figures who lived out and wrote about this childlike capacity come from the Reformed tradition and were friends: systematic theologian W. D. (Willie) Jonker (1929–2006), ecumenical leader and public icon Beyers Naudé (1915–2004), and systematic theologian and public intellectual Jaap Durand (b. 1934). All three exemplified this childlike knowing powerfully in their lives and work.

Seeing Only Fragments

Jonker was one of the most prominent Reformed theologians of his time. He served for over twenty years as a professor at Stellenbosch University and often accepted invitations to speak at conferences, retreats, and meetings and

---

[18] Desmond Tutu, *God Is Not a Christian and Other Provocations* (New York: HarperCollins, 2011).

[19] Alex Perry, "The Laughing Bishop," *Time*, October 11, 2010.

to preach in student congregations. In September 1974, he addressed student members of the (Afrikaans) Christian Student Movement on "The Bible and God's Will for Our Life."[20] In this popular series of four lectures, he argued that our knowledge of God's will is fragmented and provisional, never complete and final. Searching to walk in wisdom, we should be careful of many temptations in reading the Bible to draw conclusions and make claims. We need sensitivity for what is truly important: spiritual discernment, patience, humility, and the willingness to listen to the voices of others.

In academic publications and in studies and reports for church bodies, he emphasized that human knowledge is fragmented and provisional. Yes, in the biblical message we hear God's living Word. Yes, Christ rules through his Word and Spirit. Yes, the Spirit leads, guides, convinces, and assures believers. Yes, in the confessional tradition and community of the church, we find orientation. Yet we never fully know and understand; we are always in need of Word and Spirit.[21]

Jonker often described this as a "hermeneutical approach," understanding hermeneutics as the ongoing process of sensemaking and finding orientation with the help of community and tradition, without ever being able to claim final insight and knowledge. Often, those deeply conscious of hermeneutics are aware that "we do not know who we are—that is who we are," as American philosopher John D. Caputo (b. 1940) famously stated.[22] Regarding Jonker, this awareness has been described as an ecumenical approach to truth—namely the conviction that we all need one another's insights and contributions—and therefore, we need openness, respect, and the willingness to listen and learn.[23]

Our limited understanding coupled with the assurance of God's grace was a fundamental theme in Jonker's spirituality and theology. We are all like small children and infants: safe and taken care of, surrounded by love and grace, but in some ways ignorant of important realities around us. Our knowledge, like the knowledge of children, is fallible, fragmented, and provisional. We are known,

---

[20] For the original in Afrikaans, see Willie Jonker, *Die Bybel en Gods wil vir ons lewe* (Kaapstad, South Africa: NGKerk, 1975). For background (mostly in Afrikaans) on Jonker, see the essays honoring him in *Koninkryk, Kerk en Kosmos. Huldigingsbundel ter ere van Prof. W. D. Jonker*, ed. P. F. Theron and Johann Kinghorn (Bloemfontein, South Africa: Pro-Christo, 1989); also Christo Lombard, "Willie Jonker's Gentle Reformed Promptings towards Justice," in *Reformed Churches in South Africa and the Struggle for Justice. Remembering 1960–1990*, Mary-Anne Plaatjies–Van Huffel and Robert Vosloo, eds. (Stellenbosch, South Africa: Sun Press, 2013), 280–292.

[21] Jonker, *Die Bybel en Gods wil vir ons lewe*.

[22] John D. Caputo, *More Radical Hermeneutics: On Not Knowing Who We Are* (Bloomington: Indiana University Press, 2000).

[23] See D. J. Smit, "'. . . om saam met al die heiliges Christus te ken.' Persoonlike indrukke van 'n ekumeniese waarheidsoeke," in Theron and Kinghorn, *Koninkryk*, 11–32.

much more than we know. Like children, what we know is that we are known in the biblical sense of intimacy, we are loved, and we are cared for.

In a popular brochure on the meaning of baptism, often given as a gift by church councils to parents bringing their children for baptism, Jonker carefully explains that, although the children do not understand what is happening to them, it is no reason not to bring them to baptism, since God has proclaimed grace to them. Jonker then added that there are, after all, many other things the children do not yet know about themselves that will also determine their lives in the future.[24]

In his regular sermons in many congregations, Jonker proclaimed the same assuredness: we are known, like small children, and this is much more important than what we know and understand ourselves. Furthermore, Jonker, who published for almost two decades in the editorial pages of the nation's two major Afrikaans newspapers, spelled out these convictions in many ways and contexts.[25] In one meditation titled "We Are Limited," Jonker explained that we know far less than we sometimes think, and understanding and appreciating this fact may free us to allow our children more space and freedom to find their own ways in life during new times and challenges. In another meditation, "Possibilities Not Thought Of," Jonker explained that life often offers far more possibilities than we can see or discern, and that we should learn trust and be open to newness and surprise.[26]

In one particularly instructive meditation, titled "This Is Our Comfort,"[27] Jonker wrote about painful experiences in which we see people we know to be able and strong being broken down by old age until they no longer know anyone, including themselves or God. In such moments, it is our comfort, he noted, to remember that our belonging to God does not depend on our knowledge of God. It is comforting that reality does not equal our consciousness of what is real. In that context, he again referred to our time as infants, when we do not consciously understand anything of the relations in which we live and on which we depend. Why, if that is true of us when we are small children, could it not also be true when we grow old and frail and are no longer conscious of ourselves and others? Why would it not be true even when we think that we are young, strong, and full of knowledge? We are known and loved far beyond anything that we know and far beyond the ways in which we love, Jonker

---

[24] Willie Jonker, 'n Brief aan Doopouers (Wellington, South Africa: Lux Verbi, 2001).

[25] Some of the meditations are published in Willie Jonker, *Die Hand wat My Vashou* (Kaapstad, South Africa: Lux Verbi, 1987), and Willie Jonker, *Soms Kom dit Later* (Kaapstad, South Africa: NGKerk, 1982).

[26] Willie Jonker, "Ons is beperk" and "Ongedagte Moontlikhede," both in *Soms Kom dit Later*, 25–26 and 67–78, respectively.

[27] In Afrikaans, "Dit is Ons Troos," *Die Burger* (November 15, 1980).

argued. The hand of God over us when we were born is also over us when our consciousness ebbs. This is our comfort.[28]

Reckoning with Surprise

Naudé, a friend and mentor to Jonker, was a leading figure in the ecumenical movement, including the South African Council of Churches, as well as in public life. He was also highly engaged in the struggles of apartheid, eventually leading to his lengthy house arrest.

In his many activities, Naudé exemplified a childlike knowing by remaining open to what others around him could hardly expect, imagine, or hope, and by embodying a childlike reckoning with surprises. Naudé's childlike openness to the unexpected and willingness to commit himself to the incalculable resonates with the state described by Karl Rahner (1904–1984) in his well-known essay "Ideas for a Theology of Childhood." Here Rahner famously posits "the state [of our human life] in which our original childhood is preserved forever" as "a state in which we are open to expect the unexpected, to commit ourselves to the incalculable, a state which endows us with the power to play, to recognize that the powers presiding over existence are greater than our own designs, and to submit to their control as our deepest good."[29] Although such a description is also applicable to several other South African witnesses of faith (e.g., Desmond Tutu), it is characteristic of Naudé's life and work.

Naudé so deeply embodied the childlike openness to imagine the unimaginable and expect the unexpected that many associated his name with hope. For example, two collections of essays by colleagues and friends honoring him were *Resistance and Hope*[30] and *With the Courage of Hope*.[31] In an earlier collection of essays published in tribute to Naudé, his close collaborator Charles Villa-Vicencio describes Naudé as a "source of hope."[32] During the 1980s and

---

[28] Jonker, "Dit is Ons Troos."

[29] Karl Rahner, "Ideas for a Theology of Childhood," in *Theological Investigations*, vol. 8, ed. Karl Rahner (New York: Herder and Herder, 1971), 33–50, 42.

[30] John de Gruchy and Charles Villa-Vicencio, eds., *Resistance and Hope: South African Essays in Honour of Beyers Naudé* (Grand Rapids: Eerdmans, 1985).

[31] Title here is translated from the Dutch. See Erik van den Bergh et al, eds., *Met de Moed der Hoop. Opstellen aangeboden aan Dr. C.F. Beyers Naudé* (Baarn, The Netherlands: Ten Have, 1985).

[32] Peter Randall, ed., *Not without Honour: Tribute to Beyers Naudé* (Johannesburg: Ravan Press, 1982). See also a study on his public speeches by Louis van der Riet, "Beyers Naudé: Advocate of Hope?" (master's thesis, Stellenbosch University, 2015). There is also a comprehensive collection of interviews with Naudé by Murray Coetzee, Retief Muller, and Len Hansen, eds., *Cultivating Seeds of Hope: Conversations on the Life of Beyers Naudé* (Stellenbosch, South Africa: Sun Media, Beyers Naudé Center for Public Theology, 2015).

the height of the struggle against apartheid, the World Council of Churches published a conversation between Naudé and Dorothee Sölle under the title *Hope for Faith: A Conversation*.[33] It is no surprise that the theme of hope appears in the many works and conversations with those who knew him. In fact, he was the one who continually surprised those who worked with and met him with his openness for a different future, for the unexpected and the unimaginable, and for the newness and the surprise possible through God.

Naudé himself identified with hope, calling his autobiography *My Land of Hope*.[34] For him, hope had to do with imagining the unimaginable and being open to surprise. In contemporary jargon, made popular by Nassim Nicholas Taleb, one could say that hope is the ability not to be overwhelmed by unexpected black swans but rather to develop and practice "anti-fragility," that is, the ability to grow in insight and strength through unexpected events.[35]

Despite events that often disillusioned others around him, he did not submit to cynicism, and he did not lose hope, imagination, or openness to surprise. He saw too many faces who were beautiful to him, because they were full of promise and possibility. Indeed, Naudé demonstrated by his actions and life story what Rahner meant when he said that childlike life knows that the powers of existence are greater than our own designs, that childlike life is not looking toward the outcome of a predetermined design, that childlike life is receptivity, and that childlike life is "hope which is still not disillusioned."[36] Naudé's own hope indeed refused to become disillusioned, even when most others around him lost their trust in newness, the unexpected, and surprise.

Trusting without Control

In the struggle against apartheid, few theologians spoke with more clarity and conviction about hope as distrusting one's own designs than J. J. F. (Jaap) Durand, a personal friend of both Jonker and Naudé.[37] He served the Black

---

[33] Beyers Naudé and Dorothee Sölle, *Hope for Faith: A Conversation* (Grand Rapids: Eerdmans, 1986).

[34] Beyers Naudé, *My Land of Hope: The Life of Beyers Naudé* (Cape Town: Human and Rousseau, 1995).

[35] See, for example, Nassim Nicholas Taleb, *The Black Swan: The Impact of the Highly Improbable* (New York: Random House, 2007), and Nassim Nicholas Taleb, *Anti-Fragile: Things That Gain from Disorder* (New York: Random House, 2012).

[36] Rahner, "Ideas for a Theology of Childhood," 47.

[37] For background on Durand, see the essays honoring him in *Discerning God's Justice in Church, Society, and Academy: Festschrift for Jaap Durand*, ed. Ernst Conradie and Christo Lombard (Stellenbosch, South Africa: Sun Press, 2009); also D. J. Smit, "[T]hose Who Pray and Do Justice and Wait for God's Own Time," in *Reformed Churches in South Africa and*

Reformed churches over many decades and in different capacities and was also a professor and vice rector at the University of the Western Cape. He had extensive interactions with children and young people, was moved by them, and cared about their education. He spoke powerfully about how the hope of faith is radically different from optimism or trusting in our own abilities and plans; for him, hope is built, rather, on the promises of the cross and the resurrection of the living God.

As one of the leading systematic theologians of his day, Durand was known for his groundbreaking role in South African education. In his life and work, his deep concern for children was already obvious in many ways, publishing several volumes directly intended for his own children.[38]

As vice rector of the University of the Western Cape, Durand's passion for the youth and their future and his commitment to the struggle for their education was most evident. Contributions in a collection of essays honoring him on his seventieth birthday, *Discerning God's Justice in Church, Society, and Academy: Festschrift for Jaap Durand,* tell this story in different ways, and a front-page picture in a local newspaper of him courageously challenging the police while they were firing on protesting students at the University of the Western Cape became iconic.[39]

As a systematic theologian and scholar, Durand often wrote on themes of hope and suffering, faith and mystery, and the cross and resurrection.[40] His

---

the Struggle for Justice: Remembering 1960–1990, ed. Mary-Anne Plaatjies–Van Huffel and Robert Vosloo (Stellenbosch, South Africa: Sun Press, 2013), 293–302.

[38] Among these works were *Iemand soos ek en jy* (Stellenbosch, South Africa: Wever, 2003), a simple introduction to Jesus, dedicated to his children; J. J. F. Durand, *Jaap Durand Praat oor Eenheid, Versoening en Geregtigheid,* ed. Danie du Toit (Wellington, South Africa: Bybelkor, 2014), a collection of his sermons and speeches encouraged by his children; and J. J. F. Durand, *Protesstem* (Wellington, South Africa: Bibel Media, 2016), an autobiographical account originally and primarily intended for his children about some of the most crucial and difficult episodes in his career.

[39] As discussed in Plaatjies–Van Huffel and Vosloo, *Reformed Churches in South Africa and the Struggle for Justice.*

[40] As a young minister, he wrote a groundbreaking study titled *Swartman, Stad en Toekoms* (Kaapstad, South Africa: Tafelberg, 1970) on the future of Black South Africans in the cities. In his inaugural lecture at the University of the Western Cape, he reflected on the theology of the cross and the suffering of God, under the title *Kruisteologie en die Lydende God* (Bellville, South Africa: Universiteit van die Wes-Kaapland, 1974). After his wife died, he wrote on hope and resurrection in "Theology and Resurrection: Metaphors and Paradigms," *Journal of Theology for Southern Africa* 82 (1993): 3–20. During this time, he became increasingly aware of the importance of metaphors in theology and even described his own development in terms of this growing insight, in "When Theology Became Metaphor," *Journal of Theology for Southern Africa* 111 (2001): 12–16. After his retirement, he wrote

views on hope became particularly clear in 1986, a year of deep crisis in South African history, when he was invited to speak on the topic of "The Church as the Bearer of Hope."[41] The country was in a state of emergency: there was violence in the streets; security forces were employed in townships; and many leaders, including ministers, were imprisoned or put under house arrest without trial. There was suppression of information, no free press, and no protest or public expression of resistance permitted. In the previous year (1985), education for Black children across large areas came to a complete halt. The so-called lost generation was beginning to face their bleak future.

Durand began his talk with pessimistic, almost apocalyptic scenarios for the future of South Africa taken at the time from *The Economist*, but he then made his central claim, namely that the church can and may never practice futurology or *toekomskunde*—trying to foresee what is going to happen based on what is happening. The church is a bearer of hope, he said, but never such that the church calculates or promises what will happen. Should the church do this, he claimed, it would sacrifice its own message of hope and proclaim a false hope. This, he underlined, is most important.

For Durand, therefore, the church's message of hope is not a form of optimism, conclusion, calculation, prognosis, or even prescription for a better future based on newspaper reports, studies, and statistics. The church's message of hope is not based on what can be seen. It is not the result of viewing the present with rose-tinted glasses or pointing to encouraging political or economic tendencies. It is not optimism based on discerning rays of light within the darkness of the present and promising those who listen that things will soon be better. The hope of the church is something qualitatively different, he argued—namely, the assurance of things hoped for and the conviction of things not seen, according to Hebrews 11.

Durand distinguished two ways of thinking about the future, expressed respectively in the Latin words *futurum* and *adventus*. *Futurum* refers to future events that can perhaps be foreseen and foretold based on the present. The future, in this sense, is in some way already implicitly present within the present, whether as an inevitable outcome or as a potential that could be pursued and achieved. This is the future of futurology, of calculation and strategy, achieve-

---

several monographs on mystery and mysticism, also in science (with Teilhard and Pascal as some key figures), for example, *The Many Faces of God* (Stellenbosch, South Africa: Sun Press, 2007); *Evolusie, Wetenskap en Geloof* (Wellington, South Africa: Bybel-Media, 2013); and *God's Mystery: The Story of Science and Mystical Faith* (Wellington, South Africa: Bybel-Media, 2016).

[41] Published only in Afrikaans, as "Die kerk as draer van die hoop," in *Teks Binne Konteks. Versamelde Opstelle oor Kerk en Politiek* (Bellville, South Africa: UWK, 1986), 179–190.

ment and success, organizing and investing, moral exertion and activism. This is development and progress, and, whether personal or political, it is the future of optimism.

The future of the gospel is the *adventus* of God—the coming of God to us and the promise that God is already and always with us and in us. God is our future, said Durand, and therefore this future cannot be calculated or predicted, because God cannot be calculated or predicted. This future is open, contingent, full of surprise, and filled with what cannot be expected based on what we see. This future may be completely and surprisingly different from what one would have thought.

This trust and hope are based on the message of the resurrection. The resurrection could not have been predicted or calculated. It was the ultimate transformation, the ultimate reversal of everything we know and would have expected and would have been able to predict. What's more, it was the resurrection of the Living One who is with us always, who has all power in heaven and on earth, who is the friend of sinners and outcasts, who compassionately cared for the suffering, who welcomed children into his presence, and who proclaimed justice for the poor and the oppressed. The way to resurrection, Durand insists, is the way of the cross. The church, therefore, becomes the bearer of this hope by sharing in the suffering and need of the downtrodden, marginalized, and oppressed.

According to Durand, our trust in the future is based not on optimism but on the "paradigm of God's grace"—the grace which we have seen in Jesus Christ. It is based on the assurance of God's compassionate care and justice for those in all forms of suffering and need. The church proclaiming this trust through word and deed is indeed a bearer of the hope of the good news of the Coming God who is with us always, even in the darkest times.

Hoping Like Children?

Finally, childlike hope is the ability to imagine radically new tomorrows, which shows itself in the childlike practices of playing and dreaming. During the dark days of the past, when few could see brighter futures and often failed to imagine constructive options for action, several South African theologians, mostly from Black theological persuasion, kept these childlike abilities alive in remarkable and inspiring ways. Again, three particular thinkers can represent many others for their far-reaching inspiration. Former president of both the South African Council of Churches and the Southern African Alliance of Reformed Churches Russel Botman (1953–2014) imagined a new future for the children of South Africa, the continent of Africa as a whole, and the global world, and dedicated his career in church, public life, and education to this hope. South African philosopher Hennie Rossouw (b. 1933), despite personal tragedy, witnessed the joy of being human through childlike playfulness before the face of God. South African clergyman and politician Allan Boesak (b. 1946) was a prophet for a different world of which he dreamed for many years, courageously proclaiming an alternative reality in the face of resistance and oppression.

Looking toward Tomorrow

Very few embody this hope more explicitly and consistently, even during the darkest of times, and proclaim the hope of children and future generations in Africa than one of Durand's former students at the University of the Western Cape, Russel Botman.[42] Throughout his life, Botman held various roles, including student leader, Reformed minister, ecumenical church leader (president of the South African Council of Churches), ethicist and professor of theology, public intellectual, rector and vice chancellor of the University of Stellenbosch, and national and international leader in circles of tertiary education. In his roles, Botman recognized the transformative power of this hope in spite of despair. Like others, he saw that children are beautiful, and therefore he did not fear the realities, darkness, and hopelessness that so many others saw in apartheid South Africa.

Botman was particularly intrigued by the future generations in South Africa, the rest of Africa, and globally. Early in his career, he dedicated his dissertation to "the children who will know apartheid only by hearsay" at a time when people could hardly imagine that such a time would come. Botman's dissertation on Bonhoeffer was titled "Discipleship as Transformation? Towards a Theology of Transformation."[43] A key role was raised by the question from Bonhoeffer's *Letters and Papers from Prison* about what a successful life really means. For Bonhoeffer, the ultimate question that responsible people ask themselves was how the coming generation was going to live. It was only by considering this question that fruitful solutions could arise, even if they were humiliating for the time being. He called this "concrete responsibility" and claimed that rising generations will always instinctively discern whether we were indeed acting upon this question, for it was their future at stake.

---

[42] For background on Botman, see the essays in Albert Grundling, Ruda Landman, and Nico Koopman, eds., *Russel Botman: A Tribute* (Stellenbosch, South Africa: Sun Media, 2016). He often publicly acknowledged his gratitude for Durand's contribution to his life and thought.

[43] Hayman Russel Botman, "Discipleship as Transformation?: Towards a Theology of Transformation" (Bellville, South Africa: University of the Western Cape, unpublished doctoral dissertation, 1994).

For Botman, an ethics of transformation was this concrete responsibility. This concern—how future generations would live—became his passion as pastor, public theologian, and later as rector. And as rector, this question defined his initiative, often described as "the hope project," for which he became widely known and respected. For him, this was the challenge of an ethic of responsibility, transformation, and discipleship. Transformation, he stated, was "making history for the coming generation."[44]

He was intrigued by the scriptural passage, "For the present form of this world is passing away" (1 Cor 7:29–31), and Paul's call to live as "if not." This same passage was also considered by Bosch, as well as many other contemporary writers on writing about hope and political theology. Following words from Bonhoeffer's *Ethics*, Botman argued that all these engagements are penultimate, not ultimate; indeed they are important, but not so important that their present form should claim and dominate us as if they possess us.[45] Pauline ethics is eschatological ethics, explained Botman, since the form of this world is passing away and being transformed. This places the Christian within critical relation to the passing form of the world. When Christians say *no* to the sinful world, he claimed, they simultaneously shout *yes* for the new creation that is becoming a visible reality in our midst.

In Reformed South African church circles at the time, this was a theological logic with explosive potential. Quoting his mentor, Durand, Botman explained that the Christian ethical stance against the status quo is based on the realization that nothing is absolute about the status quo, because in Jesus Christ on Good Friday and Easter Sunday, we have been shown that "the form of this world is passing." For Christians, therefore, "whatever exists is continuously relativized by that which can be and that which must be and that which undoubtedly shall be," he said, in a phrase, as a kind of motto, that he would repeat four times in his meditation on 1 Corinthians 7:29–31.[46]

Botman recognized some of his own ideas in the work *Tomorrow's Child: Imagination, Creativity, and the Rebirth of Culture* by Rubem Alves. Significantly, this title is also a description of Botman himself. He was Alves's "tomorrow's child" in that he lived for tomorrow's children, because he himself

---

[44] Botman, "Discipleship as Transformation?"; also D. J. Smit, "Making History for the Coming Generation: On the Theological Logic of Russel Botman's Commitment to Transformation," *Stellenbosch Journal of Theology* 1, no. 2 (2016): 607–632.

[45] See especially Dietrich Bonhoeffer, "The Last Things and the Things before the Last," in *Ethics* (London: SCM, 1978), 98–160.

[46] H. R. Botman and D. J. Smit, "1 Corinthians 7:29–31: 'To Live . . . As If It Were Not!'" *Journal of Theology of Southern Africa* 65 (1988): 73–79. Botman would often again refer to this meditation and to the lasting influence of these ideas in his own life and thought.

was a child of tomorrow. His imagination fed his creativity and belief in the seemingly impossible possibilities of the rebirth of a whole culture.

Alves had a fascinating chapter on the playful imaginations of children. Adults take their own values for granted, he stated, and no one ever seems to doubt that the adult style of life is superior to that of children. Adults impose an adult reality on children; we want children to play the game of life according to our rules. Yet in the children's world of play and imagination, there is joy, freedom, possibility, and surprise.

Jesus said, "'Unless you change and become like children, you will never enter the kingdom of heaven'" (Matt 18:3). Alves explained that unless we give up the dominant logic of the present order for a different logic and become imaginative and creative, we will not live to see the future. Children's play always ends with the universal resurrection of the dead. At the end of the game, everyone is alive again.[47] In many ways, this could have been a metaphor for Botman's life and work.

Playing with Abandon

Yet another vice rector of the University of Stellenbosch and Reformed systematic theologian, H. W. (Hennie) Rossouw (b. 1933)—a widely respected intellectual and extraordinarily popular preacher for generations of students—would famously describe the life of faith as the playful life of children.[48]

After the tragic accidental death of his own son, colleagues persuaded Rossouw to publish an extended meditation on the meaning of life (in Afrikaans: *Die sin van die lewe*). It received South Africa's major prize for theological literature and became a best seller, widely read and discussed. It is difficult to translate Rossouw's poetic style, but in a key section he argues that life is good and the Gospel (God's Word-play) is the affirmation that we are called to gladly and playfully delight in life. Rossouw develops this argument using his own continued wordplay on living joyfully and playfully like children. His description of this life, before the face of God, serves as one sustained metaphor on being like children, with diverse and rich allusions, comparisons, and wordplays.

---

[47] Rubem Alves, *Tomorrow's Child: Imagination, Creativity, and the Rebirth of Culture* (New York: Harper and Row, 1972), esp. 85–101.

[48] For background (in Afrikaans) on Rossouw, see the essays honoring him in *Intellektueel in Konteks. Opstelle vir Hennie Rossouw*, ed. Anton van Niekerk, Willie Esterhuyse, and Johan Hattingh (Pretoria: Raad vir Geesteswetenskaplike Navorsing, 1993), as well as his own collected essays on the nature of universities and their scientific and cultural roles, with a concluding essay on theology and the future, *Universiteit, Wetenskap en Kultuur* (Kaapstad, South Africa: Tafelberg, 1993), and his groundbreaking early study on hermeneutics, *Klaarheid en Interpretasie* (Amsterdam: Jacob van Campen, 1963).

For Rossouw, the gospel saves us from our old age and invites us to become like children again; the gospel is a rejuvenating cure. Why? Because only children can play, rejoicing and laughing (Afrikaans: *juigend en laggend*), since children do not yet know the yoke and burden of life. Therefore, the gospel wants to save us from the heavy load of our old life so that we may delight in the newness of life. The gospel invites us into the festival hall so that, as playful children, we may delight the heart of our Father. The gospel wants to assure that we do not waste (Afrikaans: *verspeel*, a wordplay on the verb "play," as in gamble away) life with our somber stodginess (Afrikaans: *Somber swaarwigtigheid*).

Rossouw wonders whether we are willing to share in the pleasure and delight of the gospel or if we find it all too childish. Is it a childish syndrome or neurosis that we should outgrow once we mature, become realists, and no longer fool around about life like children? For Rossouw, the proper response to this gospel is saying, "Hurrah to life!," exclaiming "Hallelujah!," and celebrating the goodness of life together with God. Rossouw wonders, Do we share in the fun? Are we glad with God? Do we partake fully in the joy of the festivities that life is?

Faith, as he continues his metaphorical description, can only defend itself—against the criticism that it lacks maturity and realism—by making public work of its child's play before God's face. This public celebration of joy is called "liturgy." In liturgy, faith praises life together with God. This liturgy becomes the focal point of faith's whole festival of life (Afrikaans: *lewensfees*). From there, the hurrah of the liturgy sounds in everyday life. The liturgy serves as an amplifier for the joyful, playful worship of everyday life.

This public celebration and witness are not childish mockeries of those suffering the absurd theater of meaninglessness that being rational and realistic may sometimes make of life. On the contrary, faith does not find such meaninglessness amusing at all. For faith, it is terrible when there is no music left in life. Faith learned this lesson at the cross. Faith knows that its own happiness is the happiness of grace, of being forgiven, of a toast to new life. Faith, therefore, has all reason to rejoice like children—to dance out of pure joy, like small children who can hardly wait for surprises and gifts coming their way.

This gospel message that life is good, he continues, sounds so simple that in our maturity we may perhaps find it anticlimactic. The gospel speaks in such simple terms that we may swear that it wants to play the fool with us, like children. The truth is, however, that God has hidden the wisdom of life from so-called wise people and has revealed it to children. The answer to the "why?" questions about life can only be received by the childlike faith that our Father in heaven knows what is best for us.

Whoever has received these eyes of childlike faith reads the book of life with the excitement of a child—like the text of a (divine) comedy (Afrikaans: *blyspel*, another wordplay on play, literally: happy play); like the composition of a song of praise, resonating with the festive sounds of God's victory over the meaninglessness of sin and death.[49] One may hear in Rossouw's words something similar to Moltmann's thoughts on playfulness in his essays on joy and freedom.[50] Rossouw dedicated the book—this extended metaphor on the childlike life of faith as playfulness and joy and praise—to the memory of his son.

Dreaming with Courage

The internationally known Reformed pastor Allan Boesak has had a lifelong passion for students and young people's hopes, futures, longings, and dreams. He has been described as a theologian and political activist, a powerful preacher and "prophet of the south," a scholar and author; and as an ecumenical speaker and church leader. Throughout the years, his commitment to children and their hopes remained unmistakable.[51]

In his life and work, he emphasizes that "hoping *is* dreaming." In a series of recent speeches, he argues that only those can speak of hope who dare to speak of woundedness, anger, courage, struggle, peace, fragile faith, and dreaming.[52] This passion for dreaming with courage motivated Boesak's life and work from the earliest years. Returning from the Netherlands after his doctoral studies,[53] he became a student pastor at the University of the Western Cape. In weekly sermons to students and a collection of letters addressed to them, he used the language of dreaming, hope, and courage. He often addressed students and young people as "friends" (in Afrikaans: *maats*).[54]

---

[49] H. W. Rossouw, *Die sin van die lewe* (Kaapstad, South Africa: Tafelberg, 1981), esp. 71–85.

[50] See Jürgen Moltmann, *Die erste Freigelassenen der Schöpfung. Versuche über die Freude an der Freiheit und das Wohlgefallen am Spiel* (München: Chr Kaiser, 1971), translated first as *The First Liberated Men in Creation* and later published as *Theology and Joy* (London: SCM, 1973). The first four of the five essays in the collection *Theology of Play* (New York: Harper and Row, 1972) all deal with play. It is impossible to say whether Rossouw read these texts, but Moltmann thanks Arnold A. van Ruler in his preface, and it is not unthinkable that Rossouw's ideas were also developed in conversation with these thinkers.

[51] For background on Boesak, see his autobiographical *Running with Horses: Reflections of an Accidental Politician* (Cape Town: JoHo, 2009), and essays honoring him in *Prophet from the South: Essays in Honour of Allan Aubrey Boesak*, ed. Prince Dibeela, Puleng Lenka-Bula, and Vuyani Vellem (Stellenbosch, South Africa: Sun Press, 2014).

[52] See especially his chapter "Only If We Speak of Dreaming," in A. A. Boesak, *Dare We Speak of Hope?: Searching for a Language of Life in Faith and Politics* (Grand Rapids: Eerdmans, 2014), particularly 146–174.

[53] Allan A. Boesak, *Farewell to Innocence: A Social-Ethical Study of Black Theology and Black Power* (Braamfontein, South Africa: Ravan, 1976).

[54] See his collection of sermons, Allan A. Boesak, *The Finger of God: Sermons on Faith*

It comes as no surprise that the interdisciplinary project he cochaired between German and South African Reformed churches—which studied the implications of the Accra Declaration of the World Alliance of Reformed Churches on global economic injustice and ecological destruction—concluded with a report titled (in English) *Dreaming a Different World*.[55] In many ways, the words "dreaming a different world" represent Boesak's own lifelong passion; they have everything to do with children, youth, and an alternative future that eyes of faith and hope can see, despite seeming realities.

These words of hope also reflect a conviction more widely shared in African theological circles today, seen in the titles of works by other African church leaders. This includes such works by the formal general secretary of the World Council of Churches Samuel Kobia (b. 1947), as well as the ecumenical study document *Journey of Hope: Towards a New Ecumenical Africa* after the Harare Assembly, with its opening chapter titled "Journey of Hope to a New Africa."[56] Imagining a different world could indeed be seen as an expression of faith for the future of the children of Africa today. Seeing a beautiful future for them and acting out this imagination of the unseen are surely expressions of faith and hope.

Conclusion

Perhaps imagination of the unseen is what caused the parents of Moses to see the baby as beautiful and to act courageously, like people of hope. Perhaps that is what so many South African and other African theologians imagined when they looked at the children, students, and young people around them in apartheid South Africa. Perhaps that is also what Black theologians elsewhere imagined when they spoke about the courage to hope in the face of suffering.[57]

---

and Socio-Political Responsibility (Maryknoll, NY: Orbis Books, 1982), and collection of letters, *Met die Oog op Môre. Briewe aan my Maats* (Kasselsvlei, South Africa: VCS, 1980).

[55] Boesak edited several volumes of papers and essays produced during these years, and he colaunched a litany (and press release, together with Desmond Tutu) with the same title: Allan Boesak, Johann Weusmann, and Charles Amjad-Ali, eds., *Dreaming a Different World: Globalisation and Justice for Humanity and the Earth* (Stellenbosch, South Africa: Uniting Reformed Church in Southern Africa, 2010).

[56] Samuel Kobia, *Called to the One Hope. A New Ecumenical Epoch* (Geneva: World Council of Churches, 2006); Samuel Kobia, *The Courage to Hope. The Roots for a New Vision and the Calling of the Church in Africa* (Geneva: World Council of Churches, 2003); Nicholas Otieno with Hugh McCullum, *Journey of Hope: Towards a New Ecumenical Africa* (Geneva: World Council of Churches, 2005).

[57] See, for example, Quinton Dixie and Cornel West, eds., *The Courage to Hope: From Black Suffering to Human Redemption* (Boston: Beacon Press, 1999).

From the perspective of a "future childhood," a "new beginning," and a "world of unlimited possibilities," we construct childhood as a metaphor of hope and bring promises of God into history as an orientation toward the future. As theologian Jürgen Moltmann points out, generations are now aligned toward children as the carriers of hope and as signs of God's promise that the future now takes the place of origin, freedom takes the place of security, and unknown possibility takes the place of known reality.[58] This is what the parents of Moses imagined, what Luther called faith, and what Calvin called future excellency and approaching deliverance. In this way and others, children become metaphors of God's hope for us and represent the beauty of newness, promise, and imagination. Therefore, in acting like children, knowing like children, and hoping like children, we can join the long cloud of witnesses who saw what the eye cannot see, dreamed of different worlds, and acted out these imaginations.[59]

---

[58] Jürgen Moltmann, "Child and Childhood as Metaphors of Hope," *Theology Today* 56, no. 4 (2000): 592–603.

[59] Imagination is not used here in a technical sense. See, for example, the rich and complex ways in which imagination is understood in different disciplines in Eva T. H. Brann, *The World of the Imagination: Sum and Substance* (Lanham, MD: Rowman and Littlefield, 1991). She discusses the histories and uses of imagination in philosophy, psychology, logic, literature, depiction, and the worldly imagination. For an interesting discussion of Kant's views on imagination (implied here in the threefold question of knowing, doing, and hoping), see, for example, David J. Bryant, *Faith and the Play of Imagination: On the Role of Imagination in Religion* (Macon, GA: Mercer University Press, 1989).

List of Contributors

Dr. Marcia J. Bunge is Professor of Religion and the Bernhardson Distinguished Chair of Lutheran Studies at Gustavus Adolphus College (Minnesota, USA) and also serves as an extraordinary research professor at North-West University (South Africa). She earned her PhD in theology from the University of Chicago. She has written widely on religious understandings of children and childhood and has edited and contributed to five volumes on the subject, including: *The Child in Christian Thought* (Eerdmans, 2001); *The Child in the Bible* (Eerdmans, 2008); *Children and Childhood in World Religions: Primary Sources and Texts* (Rutgers University Press, 2009); and *Children, Adults, and Shared Responsibilities: Jewish, Christian, and Muslim Perspectives* (Cambridge University Press, 2012).

Rev. Dr. Wanda Deifelt is Professor of Religion at Luther College (Iowa, USA). She earned her PhD from the Joint Garrett-Evangelical Theological Seminary and Northwestern University Doctoral Program (Evanston, Illinois). She was recognized with an honorary degree in theology from the University of Oslo (Norway). Her primary areas of study are Lutheranism, creation, Christology, and liberation theology, and she has contributed to several volumes on these subjects, including *Voices of Feminist Liberation* (Routledge, 2014); *New Feminist Christianity: Many Voices, Many Views* (SkyLight Paths, 2012); and *Theologies on the Move: Religion, Migration, and Pilgrimage in the World of Neoliberal Capital* (Fortress, 2020).

Rev. Megan Eide is an ordained minister with the Evangelical Lutheran Church in America and a rising scholar in the fields of media and religion, as well as religious understandings of children and childhood. She graduated from the innovative and accelerated MDiv program, MDivX, at Luther Seminary (Minnesota, USA). Eide studies the representation of diverse religious traditions in children's visual media, and her article "Religion in Children's Visual Media: A Qualitative Content Analysis of Preschool Holiday Specials" was published in the *Journal of Media and Religion*.

Dr. Ivone Gebara is an Emerita Professor of Philosophy and Systematic Theology at the Theological Institute of Recife (Brazil), one of Latin America's leading theologians and philosophers, and a Roman Catholic nun. She earned a Doctor of Philosophy from the Pontifical Catholic University (São Paulo City, Brazil) and a second doctorate in religious sciences at the Catholic University of Louvain in Belgium. During her career, she taught at the Universidade Católica de São Paulo and at the Auburn and Union Theological Seminaries in New York City. She has published numerous articles and eleven books, including *Longing for Running Water: Ecofeminism and Liberation* (Fortress, 1999) and *Out of the Depths: Women's Experience of Evil and Salvation* (Fortress, 2002). Her current work focuses on feminist and ecological perspectives.

Rev. Dr. Rohan P. Gideon is Associate Professor of Christian Theology at United Theological College (Bangalore, India) and an ordained deacon in the Church of South India. He earned his PhD from the University of Manchester. His research focuses primarily on postcolonial and liberationist hermeneutics, child-related theologies, and children's rights. He has published several articles and is author of *Child Labour in India: Challenges for Theological Thinking and Christian Ministry in India* (ISPCK, 2011) and *Children-at-Risk: Towards Inclusive Communities* (Board of Theological Education of the Senate of Serampore, 2017). He also conducts workshops on human sexuality and Christian theology.

Rev. Dr. Perry T. Hamalis is the Cecelia Schneller Mueller Professor of Religion at North Central College (Illinois, USA) and an ordained deacon in the Orthodox Church. He earned his PhD from the University of Chicago and was awarded a Fulbright Senior Research Fellowship (2015). He is the co-editor of *Orthodox Christian Perspectives on War* (Notre Dame, 2017) and has published numerous articles and contributed chapters to several books, including *Thinking through Faith: New Perspectives from Orthodox Christian Scholars* (SVS Press, 2008); *The Orthodox Christian World* (Routledge, 2012); *Toward an Ecology of Transfiguration* (Fordham University Press, 2013); and *Christianity, Democracy, and the Shadow of Constantine* (Fordham University Press, 2017).

Dr. D. J. Konz is Associate Dean of the Faculty of Theology and Head of the Theology Department at Alphacrucis College (Australia). He earned a PhD in theology from the University of Aberdeen (Scotland). He served for several years as the Executive Director of Child Advocacy at Compassion Australia, responsible for championing the value, needs, nurture, and potential of children to Australian church and government leaders. He is the author of several theological articles and coeditor of *Theology, Mission, and Child: Global Perspectives* (Regnum, 2014).

LIST OF CONTRIBUTORS

Dr. Valerie Michaelson is an assistant professor in the Department of Health Sciences at Brock University. Before transitioning to health sciences, she worked for over twenty years as an Anglican priest. She earned her DMin from the Toronto School of Theology. Her research is focused on the health and well-being of children and adolescents and the social determinants that impact their health. Her current research projects focus on violence, spirituality, mental health, and decolonization and reconciliation. She recently coedited the volume *Decolonizing Discipline: Children, Corporal Punishment, Christian Theologies, and Reconciliation* (University of Manitoba Press, 2020).

Rev. Dr. Kenneth Mtata is the General Secretary of the Zimbabwe Council of Churches and an ordained pastor of the Evangelical Lutheran Church in Zimbabwe. He earned his PhD in theology from KwaZulu-Natal University (Pietermaritzburg, South Africa). Mtata served as Executive Study Secretary for Lutheran Theology and Practice at the Lutheran World Federation (Geneva, Switzerland), directing projects related to Lutheran hermeneutics, social transformation, and religion and development (2010–2016). He continues to work for the Lutheran World Federation as a project developer and serves as Executive Secretary of the Zimbabwe Heads of the Christian Denominations (ZHOCD). He speaks and publishes widely on religion and development policy, and has organized and directed several national and international public policy projects.

Rev. Dr. Craig L. Nessan is the Academic Dean, the William D. Streng Professor for the Education and Renewal of the Church, and Professor of Contextual Theology and Ethics at Wartburg Theological Seminary (Iowa, USA). He received his MDiv STM from Wartburg Theological Seminary and his ThD from the University of Munich. He is an ordained minister of the Evangelical Lutheran Church in America. He has taught courses on child maltreatment and advocated for child protection policies within the church. He is coeditor of the journal *Currents in Theology and Mission*, and his publications include *Shalom Church: The Body of Christ as Ministering Community* (Fortress, 2010); *Beyond Maintenance to Mission: A Theology of the Congregation* (Fortress, 2010); and *The Vitality of Liberation Theology* (Wipf & Stock, 2012).

Dr. Agbonkhianmeghe E. Orobator, SJ, is a Jesuit priest and the President of the Jesuit Conference of Africa and Madagascar. He earned his PhD in theology and religious studies from the University of Leeds (England). He is the author of several publications, including *Theology Brewed in an African Pot* (Orbis, 2008); *Religion and Faith in Africa: Confessions of an Animist* (Orbis,

2018); and *The Pope and the Pandemic: Lessons in Leadership in a Time of Crisis* (Orbis, 2021).

Rev. Dr. Dirk J. Smit is the Chair of Reformed Theology and Public Life at Princeton Theological Seminary (Princeton, USA). He holds a DTh from Stellenbosch University (South Africa) and honorary degrees from Umeå University (Sweden) and the Protestant Theological University (Groningen, Netherlands). Other current appointments include honorary professor at the Humboldt-Universität (Berlin, Germany); extraordinary professor at Stellenbosch University; fellow of the Institute for Advanced Study (Berlin, Germany); and member of the Academy of Science in South Africa (ASSAF). Smit has written extensively on the legacy of the Reformed tradition and its relevance to contemporary theological, social, and political questions. He was also a prominent and influential voice in the church's repudiation of apartheid and one of the primary authors of the Belhar Confession (Dutch Reformed Mission Church, 1986).

Rev. Dr. Michael Welker is a senior professor of systematic theology at the University of Heidelberg (Germany) and the Executive Director of the Research Center for International and Interdisciplinary Theology (FIIT). He received his PhD in systematic theology from the University of Tübingen and a Doctor of Philosophy from the University of Heidelberg. He is an ordained minister of the Protestant Church in Germany. He has written, edited, and contributed to a vast number of publications on Christology, the doctrine of creation, anthropology, eschatology, biblical theology, and the dialogue between theology and the natural sciences, including *God the Spirit* (Fortress, 1994); *Creation and Reality* (Fortress, 1999); *The Theology and Science Dialogue: What Can Theology Contribute?* (Neukirchener Verlag 2012); and *God the Revealed: Christology* (Eerdmans, 2013). In 2019, he delivered the Gifford Lectures at the University of Edinburgh.

Dr. Amos Yong is Dean of the School of Mission and Theology and Professor of Theology and Mission at Fuller Seminary. He earned his PhD in religious studies and theology from Boston University. He has authored and edited numerous volumes on the Holy Spirit and Pentecostal theology, including *The Spirit Poured Out on All Flesh: Pentecostalism and the Possibility of Global Theology* (Baker Academic, 2005); *The Spirit of Creation: Modern Science and Divine Action in the Pentecostal-Charismatic Imagination* (Eerdmans, 2011); *The Bible, Disability, and the Church: A New Vision of the People of God* (Eerdmans, 2011); *Renewing Christian Theology: Systematics for a Global Christianity* (Baylor University Press, 2014); and *Mission after Pentecost: The Witness of the Spirit from Genesis to Revelation* (Baker Academic, 2019).

Index

abortion, 56, 148
Abraham, Patriarch, 98, 207, 211
Accra Declaration, 228
Achebe, Chinua, 134, 136, 137, 139–40
Ackerman, Denise, 208, 209, 211–13
Adichie, Chimamanda Ngozi, 188
adultism, 3, 37, 38, 46
Adverse Childhood Experiences (ACE) study, 10
The African Child (Laye), 134
African communitarianism, 33–34, 36, 37–41, 44, 46, 51
African Synod of Bishops, 144
African Traditional Religion (Parrinder), 40
After the Locusts (Ackermann), 211–12
Akpan, Uwem, 134, 135
Alice's Adventures in Wonderland (Carroll), 64–65
All Africa Conference of Churches (AACC), 35
Alves, Rubem, 224–25
American Academy of Pediatrics, 9
anabasis (Logo's ascent), 154, 155, 161, 163
Andraos, Michel, 173
Anglican Church of Canada, 178
Anthony the Great, Saint, 164–66
apophaticism (negative theology), 159
Arendt, Hannah, 206
askesis (spiritual struggle), 164

Augustine of Hippo, 116
Azusa Street Revival, 111

Bantu Philosophy (Tempels), 39
Barth, Karl, 83, 191, 204
  child-attentive mission, 202–3
  Christian witness, 199–201
  church, mission of, 197–98
  co-humanity, emphasis on, 195–96
Bathsheba, 75
Battiste, Marie, 189
Bellarmine, Robert, 143
Berkovits, Shira M., 10
Berryman, Jerome W., 14
"The Bible and God's Will for Our Life" (address), 216
Bill C-262 (Canadian legislation), 178
Blyden, Edward, 36
Boesak, Allan, 223, 227–28
Boff, Clodovis, 84
Boff, Leonardo, 79, 84
Bonhoeffer, Dietrich, 19, 223, 224
Bosch, David, 208, 209–11, 215, 224
Botman, Russel, 222–24, 225
boys, 142, 157, 209
  African society, status of boys in, 139–40
  "bad boys" and evil, 55
  boy with five barley loaves, xix, 100
  circumcision concerns, 44–45
  in the messianic era, 97
  physical labor, used for, 59–60
  as socialized to oppress women, 58

Brazil, 55, 58
  lack of childcare options, 79–80
  poverty concerns, 54, 57, 61
  religion as linked to social status in, 62
Brueggemann, Walter, 14
Buffalo Shout, Salmon Cry (Heinrichs), 181
Bultmann, Rudolf, 83
Bunge, Marcia J., 139

Calls to Action for reconciliation, 179
Calvin, John, 207, 229
Canada, 178, 184, 189
  colonization, harms done by, 173, 176–77
  Original Peoples, reconciling with, 174, 179–80
  racism and anti-racism responses, 181–83, 185–86
Canadian Council of Churches, 186
Canadian Decolonial Theology Project, 173, 189
Caputo, John D., 216
Centers for Disease Control and Prevention (CDC), 7–8
Chalcedonian Creed, 73
"Child Abuse and the Church: Prevention, Pastoral Care, and Healing," 18
child hunger, 5–6, 55, 59, 60, 80, 212
child neglect, 18, 127, 156
  freedom from neglect, 7–8, 15
  multiple dimensions of, 3
  social science studies on, 5
child-attentive theology, 23, 34, 127, 130, 202
  advocacy for children, 148–49
  in Eastern Orthodoxy, 171
  humility, child-attentive approach to, 152–53, 156–58, 167
  Jesus on parent-child relations, 120
  mission with children, practice of, 191, 203–4
  the mystery of children, 104–6
  in relational theology of the human person, 46–50
  salvation, including children in, 102, 107
children and community
  African community, value of children in, 136–37, 139
  agency and role of children in communities, 48–49
  child maltreatment, ignoring signs of, 9
  child-attentive anthropology of community, 47
  global community, children recognizing themselves in, 60
  marginalized communities, children of, 25, 59, 102–3
children's rights, 67, 91, 103
  advancement of, 127
  Catholic Church, as a focus of, 144, 148
  Christ Child as the foundation of, 126
  CRC, nations not observing, 55
Circle of Concerned African Women Theologians, 45
circumcision, 44–45
Clement of Rome, 154
clitoris ablation of young girls, 55
Coakley, Sarah, 152
Cobb, John, 73
Collier, John, xvi
Commentary on Hebrews (Calvin), 207
community
  community lament, 212
  community of hope, 210, 213
  community of solidarity, 30, 31

community violence, increasing awareness of, 187
cyber technologies as helping communities thrive, 70
good and evil, community determinations of, 52
human rights, addressing, 12, 90
peaceful communities, investing into, 50
rooted solidarity of the caring community, 92, 102, 104, 107
witness by works in at-risk communities, 203
See also children and community; faith community
Cone, James, 84
Convention on the Rights of the Child (CRC), 12, 55, 148
Cornelius (biblical figure), 117
corporal punishment, 5, 183, 187
  Bible not warranting, 19
  Canadian laws on, 179
  in the Christian community, 16, 18, 127
  harms caused by, 173–74
  liberation of children from, 8–10, 15
Council of Trent, 142
creation, 22, 64, 68, 138, 149
  anabasis of all creation, 161, 163
  biblical creation account, 11, 24–27, 77
  in Christian theology, 21
  creation as "good," 28–30
  Creator's need for creation, 164
  God as rejoicing and suffering with, 74
  God's ultimate love for, 154
  Jesus as the firstborn of all creation, 12
  theologies of creation and childhood, 23, 31–32

Yes! for the new creation, 200, 224
Crossan, John Dominic, 97

Daly, Mary, 84
David, King, 75, 97
Decolonizing Discipline (Michaelson/ Durrant), 179
Deifelt, Wanda, xx
Descartes, René, 37
DiAngelo, Robin, 186
Dickson, Kwesi, 36
Discerning God's Justice in Church, Society, and Academy, 220
discipleship, 82, 85, 98
  of children, 186, 188
  faith formation and, 174–75, 183, 185
  love of neighbor as tenet of, 184
  as an ongoing process, 88
  transformation, as leading to, 223–24
  Western European approaches to, 189
divine intervention, 75, 98, 141
Doctrine of Discovery, 177, 178, 181, 183
Dorotheos of Gaza, Saint, 165–66
Dreaming a Different World (report), 228
Dube, Musa, 45
Dulles, Avery, 143
Durand, J. J. F. (Jaap), 215, 219–22, 224

Eagleton, Terry, 214
Eastern Orthodoxy. *See* Orthodox Christianity
Ebeling, Gerhard, 48
ecclesiology, 36
  children's issues, including in, 106
  rethinking ecclesiology, 142–49
  social crises, paying attention to, 130

Elizabeth, Saint, 119
Enoch, Patriarch, 207
Ethics (Bonhoeffer), 224
Evangelical Lutheran Church in America (ELCA), 17, 18
Evans, Craig, 170–71
evil, 57, 64, 166
  in cyber culture, 63, 66
  evils faced by children, 52–54, 54–55, 67, 68, 70, 71
  good gifts, evil ones providing, 123
  obstacles to empowering children, 60–61
  superheroes as fighting against, 56
Extreme Humility icon, 160, 161, 163, 168

faith community
  children's contributions, recognizing, 3, 25, 126
  children's values as shaped by, 66
  Christian community, danger of objectification in, 204
  church, recognizing diversity in community, 69
  community humility, 151, 152, 155, 158, 167
  community of worship and the girl-child, 149
  community service, Christians called to, 211
  in God's dominion-free order, 81
  growth in community, encouraging, 82
  joining via baptism, 212
  living witness to Christ, 194, 196, 200, 201, 203
  ministering cooperation of the Christian community, 199
  orientation, finding in community of the church, 216
  protection of children in Christian community, 147–48
  worshiping community of Orthodoxy, 166
  Yes! as response of the faith community, 202
feticide, 139
First Nation peoples, 173, 176, 177, 178, 179, 185
First Vatican Council, 142
Freire, Paulo, 81
From Crisis to Kairos (Orobator), 130

Garden of Eden, 97
Gebara, Ivone, 79
Gideon, Rohan P., xxi
girls, 60, 97, 142
  biblical enslavement of daughters, 98–99
  in the Catholic Church, 149
  evil, exposure to, 55
  gender discrimination against, 7
  Mary as a young girl, 74
  in a patriarchal world, 57, 58
  status of girls in African society, 139–40, 148
  teenage girls, 55–56, 59
God-Child paradigm
  adults, including as children of God, 82–88
  childlike attitude of reception, promoting, 89
  divine vulnerability, paradox of, 74–78
  human vulnerabilities and capacities, 78–82
  Jesus as a God-child, 13, 73, 77
Godly Response to Abuse in the Christian Environment (GRACE), 17
Gorodetzky, Nadejda, 169

Greenwood, Margo, 183
Gundry-Volf, Judith M., 14, 97
Gutiérrez, Gustavo, 2, 94
Gyeke, Kwame, 43

Hamalis, Perry, xx
Hannah (biblical figure), 99, 136
healing, 61, 111, 142, 165, 212
Hegel, G. W. F., 21
Heinrichs, Steve, 181
Herdt, Gilbert H., 41
hermeneutics, 102, 113, 125, 141, 216
Higonnet, Anne, 86
Hinson-Hasty, Elizabeth, 152
Holy Spirit, 199
   in Acts 2, 114–17
   baptism of, 109, 111
   believers, guiding and assuring, 216
   conception of Jesus, role in, 75, 76
   history, leading humanity through, 95
   in Luke, 118–22
   in *missio Dei* concept, 197, 198
   in Pentecostal theology, 113–14, 124
   renewed interest in, 108
   Spirit-filled children, 110, 123, 127, 146, 203
hope, 78, 207, 212, 218, 220
   childhood as a metaphor of hope, 206, 229
   childlike hope, 215, 222
   "Church as the Bearer of Hope" speech, 221
   faith and, 167, 220
   Hope for Faith: A Conversation, 219
   "the hope project," 224
   hopes of children, honoring, 92, 103
   hoping against hope, 208–9, 211
   humility, as entwined with, 165
   nurturing of hope, 25, 69, 213

   "Prisoners of History or Prisoners of Hope?" address, 209–10
   societal hope, children as sources of, 48, 49, 97
   South African youth, hopes of, 222–23, 227–28
Hope and Suffering (Tutu), 214
Human Sexuality: Gift and Trust (Lutheran statement), 17
humility, 76, 150, 168, 170, 216
   child-attentive approach to, 156–59, 167
   in early Christian sources, 153–56
   exemplary humility, children modeling, 97, 141
   feminist perceptions of, 151–52
   iconography as depicting, 160–64
   in Orthodox Christian theology, 159, 169
   Saints Anthony and Dorotheos on, 164–66

"Ideas for a Theology of Childhood" (Rahner), 218
Idowu, Bolaji, 36
Ikuenobe, Polycarp, 44
India, 6, 90–91, 109
Indian Residential Schools Settlement Agreement, 178
1876 Indian Act, 176
Indigenous communities, 172, 185, 188, 193
infants/babies, 27, 49, 122, 146, 213
   baby Moses, 206–7, 228
   Herod's murder of infants, 77
   infant baptism, 45, 212
   infant mortality, 5, 7, 136, 139
   infant Samuel in narrative of Hannah, 99
   Jesus as infant, 72, 74, 89, 119, 163, 182

infants/babies *(continued)*
  Jonker, in theology of, 216, 217
  in Orthodox faith, 168
  tales told from the mouths of, 133, 134
  wisdom, infants in receipt of, 100, 121
Inter Caetera papal bull, 177
intergenerationality, 31, 106, 186
  active listening as deepening sense of, 104
  Bible, intergenerational conflicts in, 118
  invitation to build a just society, 69–70
  Jesus, expanding notion of, 101
  theological conversations, 28
  worship services, connections in, 146
Inuit people, 173, 176, 178, 179, 185
I-Thou encounters, 195–96

Jantzen, Grace M., 93–94
Jeremias, Joachim, 83
Jesus Christ, 95, 120, 174, 189, 213, 224
  body of Christ, 4, 12, 89, 100, 130, 131, 146, 149
  Christ Child, 12–13, 16, 126, 169
  crucifixion, 116, 153–54, 160, 161, 168, 171
  discipleship, invitation to, 82–83
  divine incarnation, 72, 73, 82
  as a God-child, 73, 77
  humility of, 150, 153–54, 155, 157
  in iconography, 160–64
  John the Baptist and, 140–41
  living witness to Christ, 194, 196, 202
  the oppressed, identifying with, 90
  resurrection, 79, 82, 93, 94, 154, 163, 198, 220, 222, 225
  self-witness of, 199–200
  Spirit-filled Christ, 122, 123, 124
  as a true human being, 195
  women in genealogy of, 76
  Word and Spirit, ruling through, 204, 216
John the Baptist, 118, 140–41
Jonker, W. D. (Willie), 208, 215–18, 219
Jopling, David A., 44
Joseph, Saint, 74–75, 77, 119, 162, 164
Journey of Hope study document, 228

Kagame, Alexis, 39–40
KAIROS organization, 178–79
Kanyoro, Musimbi, 45
katabasis (Logo's descent), 154, 161, 163
kenosis (self-emptying), 160, 164, 168, 169
Kenya, naming of children in, 44
kerygma (proclamation), 94
kingdom of God, 14, 15, 98, 120, 122
  children as pointing the way to, 105–6
  children as rightful citizens of, 101, 102, 141
  "kingdom of children," comparing to, 97
  receiving the kingdom as a little child, 13, 88, 121
kingdom of heaven, 141, 142, 148, 157, 158, 225
Kobia, Samuel, 228
Konkola, Kari, 150
Konz, D. J., xvii, xx
Krondorfer, Björn, 168
kutenga mwana (birth ritual), 44

LaCugna, Catherine, 48
lament, 208, 211–13

Largen, Kristin Johnston, 73
Laye, Camara, 134
Leeuw, Sarah de, 183
Letters and Papers from Prison (Bonhoeffer), 223
liberation theology, 1, 4, 20, 71, 94
    child liberation theology, 3, 5, 11–12, 14, 15–16
    Latin American expressions of, 2, 5
    oppression and injustice, liberation from, 90
    Paul, reputation in liberation circles, 210
    the suffering, raising up the voices of, 19
Lindsay, Nicole, 183
Lord's Prayer, 85
Luhmann, Niklas, 21
Luther, Martin, 28, 48, 82
    faith, defining, 207, 215, 229
    humility of Mary, highlighting, 76
    Jesus's birth, on the significance of, 73
    parents, as obligated to their children, 16

MacDonald, Mark, 181–82
Magdalen of Essex, Sr., 167, 170
The Magnificat, 74, 76, 119
Mandela, Nelson, 34
Marty, Martin, 104–6
Mary, Mother of God, 75, 164, 182
    devotion to, 57
    God-child paradigm, role in, 77
    humilitas of, 76
    in iconography, 162
    in the Magnificat, 74, 119
Masenya, Madipone, 45
Mbeki, Thabo, 45
Mbiti, John S., 36, 37, 39–40, 41, 46
McFague, Sallie, 85

McGuckin, John A., 163–64
McIntosh, Peggy, 186
Medina, Néstor, 173, 180
Menkiti, Ifeanyi, 43
Mercer, Joyce Ann, 125
Métis peoples, 173, 176, 178, 179, 185
Michaelson, Valerie, xxii
Miller, Robert J., 177, 183
Miller-McLemore, Bonnie, 86
missio Dei theology, 197, 198
missionaries, 35, 38, 42, 118, 140
    Christian mission, defining, 191
    communitarianism and, 37, 40
    harmful missionary practices, 45
    missionary domination, 33, 36
    missionary/anthropologists, 38–39
    Pentecostal missionary ventures, 111
Missionary Oblates of Mary Immaculate, 178
Moltmann, Jürgen, 77, 86, 206, 227, 229
Moses, 116, 141, 206–7, 228–29
Moyo, Fulata, 45
Mtata, Kenneth, xxi
Muzorewa, Gwinyai, 33, 35
My Land of Hope (Naudé), 219
"My Parents' Bedroom" (Akpan), 135

Nadar, Sarojini, 45
Naomi (biblical figure), 75
"Nativity of Christ" icon, 162–63
Naudé, Beyers, 208, 215, 218, 219
Neisser, Ulric, 44
Nessan, Craig L., xxi
Niebuhr, Reinhold, 166
Njoroge, Nyambura, 45
Nkrumah, Kwame, 36
Noah, Patriarch, 207
Norway, Church of, 81
Nyerere, Julius, 36
Nzekwu, Onuora, 134

Oduyoye, Mercy Amba, 45, 46, 137–39
Okure, Teresa, 45
Orobator, Agbonkhianmeghe E., xxii
Orthodox Christianity
   discernment, articulating the role of, 170
   high Christology tradition, 171
   humility in Orthodox praxis, 159, 165, 168
   Orthodox iconography, 153, 160–64, 169
   sacramental practices and teachings, 166–67
Ottino, Arlette, 42

Pachuau, Lalsangkima, xviii
Pais, Janet, 2–3, 11, 12–13
Pakenham, Frank, 153, 157
Papanikolaou, Aristotle, 152
Parrinder, Geoffrey, 40
The Passion of the Christ (film), 168
"Paul on Human Hopes" (Bosch), 210
Pentecostalism, 108
   Book of Acts as central to, 118–22
   children in Pentecostal teachings, 110–12, 114–17, 127
   Day of Pentecost as core, 109, 113, 124
   Spirit of Pentecost, depicting as playful, 125
Philip the deacon, 117
Phiri, Isabel, 45, 46
Pieterson, Hector, 209
pietism, 39
Pityana, Barney, 214
pneumatology
   children, lens on, 109, 123–24, 127–28
   as a classical theological locus, 108
   John the Baptist, role in, 118
   salvation via gift of the Spirit, 116

See also Holy Spirit
Presbyterian Church of Canada, 178, 184
The Primal Vision (Taylor), 41
property paradigm of childhood, 99

Rabens, Volker, 48
Rahab (biblical figure), 75
Rahner, Karl, 94–95, 218, 219
"Reconciliation Activities for Children" report, 184
responsibility, 27, 31, 86, 87, 127
   animals, human responsibility toward, 30
   of child advocates, 103
   of church, to children, 126, 132, 142, 147, 174, 202–3
   concrete responsibility, 223–24
   of decolonialism, 184, 187, 188
   ethical imperatives, 131, 133, 140, 144
   gangs, as absent in, 57
   in God-child paradigm, 85
   of good citizenship, 58
   humanization concept as prompting, 102
   as intergenerational, 70
   of Joseph for protecting Jesus, 75
   to the needs of the group, 43
   of religious education for children, 23
   responsible child-rearing practices, 19
   in rooted solidarity, 104
   shared responsibility for the fate of all children, 13
   of siblings, 80
   vulnerability and, 78, 81
Reudi-Weber, Hans, 97–98
Ricoeur, Paul, 54
Riswold, Caryn, 152

Rossouw, H. W. (Hennie), 223, 225–27
Ruether, Rosemary Radford, 52, 84
Ruth, Matriarch, 75, 137
Rwandan genocide, 135

Saad, Layla, 186, 188
Said, Edward, 39
Sakharov, Nicholas, 160
Samson (biblical figure), 141
Samuel (biblical figure), 99, 141
Sarah (biblical figure), 98
Say You're One of Them (Akpan), 134–35
Sayings of the Desert Fathers, 164
Second Vatican Council, 143–44
Self-Determining Anglican Church in Canada, 181–82
sexual abuse, 5, 7, 15, 18, 98
  in ecclesial settings, 16–17, 130, 147, 176, 192, 193
  freedom from, 10–11
  Indigenous children, sexual violence against, 179
  sex trafficking, 19, 59, 139
  teenage girls' pregnancies from, 55–56
sin, 12, 123, 131, 222, 227
  capacity for sin as developing over time, 87
  children as sinners, 50
  Christians and sinfulness, 82, 86
  forgiveness of sin, 93, 116
  humility as awareness of sin, 152, 155, 156, 157, 165, 171
  Jesus as saving the world from sin, 75, 93
  original sin, 16
  pride as the root of sin, 166
  salvation as deliverance from individual sin, 91
  sinful world, Christians saying no to, 224
  in the story of creation, 31, 68
  structural sin, on the need to address, 60
Sitting Bull, Chief, 20
Smit, Dirk J., xix
Smitherman, Geneva, 42
Sobrino, Jon, 79
Sölle, Dorothee, 72, 86, 219
Solomon, King, 75
soteriology, 90, 122, 202
  biblical text, soteriological reading of, 113–14, 115
  holistic approach to, 101–6
  soteriological work of the Spirit, 116, 117
South Africa, 220, 224
  apartheid South Africa, 33, 37, 40, 211, 223, 228
  "Church as the Bearer of Hope" speech, 221
  Desmond Tutu as role model for, 213–15, 218
  "Prisoners of History or Prisoners of Hope?" address, 209–10
  theological literature of, 225–26
  youth, hopes for the future, 222–23, 227–28
  Zuma as president of, 44–45
South African Council of Churches, 218, 222, 223
Soyinka, Wole, 134
Spirit. *See* Holy Spirit
Spivak, Gayatri Chakravorty, 39
Steinberg, Naomi, 99
Stollar, Ryan, 3, 13
Suffer the Children (Pais), 3
Sundermeier, Theo, 40–41
Surprised by the Man on the Borrowed Donkey (Ackerman), 213

Taleb, Nassim Nicholas, 219
Tamar (biblical figure), 75, 137
Taylor, John, 40, 41
Taylor, Mark Lewis, 104–5
Tchividjian, Basyle, 10, 11
Tempels, Placide, 39–40
Thatcher, Adrian, 126
The Child Safeguarding Policy Guide for Churches and Ministries, 17
Theognostos, Saint, 169–70
theologies of childhood, xv, 24, 110
   child theologies, distinguishing from, xvii, xxiii
   major theological themes, influence on reframing, xvi
   in Pentecostalism, 109, 111
   the vulnerable, giving voice to, xiv
Theology Brewed in an African Pot (Orobator), 132
Things Fall Apart (Achebe), 136, 137
Thiong'o, Ngugi wa, 134
Thomas, M. M., 95
Thurow, Roger, 6, 7
Tillich, Paul, 1, 79
Tracy, David, 1
Trinitarianism, 73, 108, 197
Truth and Reconciliation Commission (South Africa), 214, 215
Truth and Reconciliation Commission of Canada (TRC), 176–77, 178, 179, 180, 187
Tuck, Eve, 184
Turner, Victor W., 76
Turtle Island peoples, 181, 188
Tutu, Desmond, 34, 40, 209, 214, 215, 218

ubuntu, African concept of, 34, 38, 40
uhlanga collective of the Zulu peoples, 41
United Church of Canada, 178

United Nations Declaration on the Rights of Indigenous Peoples (UNDRIP), 178
Universal Declaration of Human Rights (UDHR), 12

Vatican I, 142
Vatican II, 143–44
Veggie Tales (animated series), 168
Vieth, Victor, 9, 10, 14, 18
Villa-Vicencio, Charles, 218
virtue ethics, 151
Vondey, Wolfgang, 125

Wartburg Theological Seminary, 18
Welker, Michael, xix
Westhelle, Vítor, 73
Where Are the Children website, 176
White, Keith, 158
Whitehead, Alfred North, 21
whiteness, 12, 184, 186
   Canada, white settlers of, 187
   in children's Bibles, 182, 185
   white racial prejudice, 156, 214
   white South Africans, 40
Whitla, Becca, 173
Willmer, Haddon, 146
Wink, Walter, 81–82
womanist theology, 2, 33, 45–46, 90
World Alliance of Reformed Churches, 228
The World Bank, 7
World Council of Churches, 219, 228
World Health Organization, 5–6
Wright, N. T., 85

Xhosa peoples, 44–45

Yang, K. Wayne, 184
Yong, Amos, xix

Index

Zechariah, Prophet, 97, 210
Zechariah, Saint, 119
Zulu peoples, 41, 44–45
Zuma, Jacob, 44–45

www.ingramcontent.com/pod-product-compliance
Lightning Source LLC
Chambersburg PA
CBHW052047220426
43663CB00012B/2477